SHEFFIELD UNITED

HEAD *to* HEAD
SHEFFIELD UNITED

Peter Waring

breedon **books**
PUBLISHING

First published in Great Britain in 2004 by
The Breedon Books Publishing Company Limited
Breedon House, 3 The Parker Centre,
Derby, DE21 4SZ.

The publisher would like to thank Andy
Daykin, Andy Pack, Jason Denial and Step
Firth at Sheffield United FC for their
cooperation and support in the production
of this book.

ISBN 1 85983 416 9

Printed and bound by Cromwell Press Ltd,
Trowbridge, Wiltshire.

Introduction

This book contains the results of all matches played by Sheffield United in the following competitions:

Premiership and Football League

FA Cup

League Cup

Football League play-offs and test matches

European Cup, Cup-Winners Cup and UEFA Cup

Some clubs have changed their names over the course of their history. Where this has happened, the results are nonetheless included under the club's current name, unless there have been no matches since the name change. Some of the more significant name changes are as follows:

Arsenal (known as Royal Arsenal until 1893, then Woolwich Arsenal until 1914)

Birmingham (known as Small Heath until 1905)

Gateshead (known as South Shields until 1930)

Leyton Orient (known as Clapton Orient until 1946, and Orient between 1967 and 1987)

Manchester City (known as Ardwick until 1894)

Manchester United (known as Newton Heath until 1902)

Furthermore, some clubs have merged, notably in Burton, Rotherham and Walsall, though these are explained under the relevant entries where applicable.

Notes on cups

FA Cup ties have always been straight knockout affairs, except in 1945-46, when all ties up to and including the quarter-finals were played over two legs. Between 1970 and 1974, the losing semi-finalists participated in third place play-offs. Penalty shoot-outs were introduced in 1991 to replace multiple replays.

League cup ties have been decided over one leg, with the following exceptions (played over two legs):

First round ties (1975-76 to 2000-01)

Second round ties (1979-80 to 2000-01)

Semi-finals (every season)

To give you some idea of exactly what stage of the competition each FA Cup tie was played, the following is a list of each season's round of 16 (ie. the round immediately preceding the quarter-finals):

1873-74 to 1875-76	Round 2
1876-77 to 1878-79	Round 3
1879-80 to 1883-84	Round 4
1884-85 to 1887-88	Round 5
1889-90 to 1904-05	Round 2
1905-06 to 1924-25	Round 3
1925-26 to present	Round 5

In the league cup, Round 4 has been the round of 16 every season.

An asterisk after a cup result denotes extra-time was played.

Two final points

The letters appearing after some final league positions denote the following:

P   club was promoted

R   club was relegated

F   club failed to retain league membership for the following season

In the lists entitled 'Played for both clubs', an entry reading, for example, Liverpool 1980-83 would indicate that the player first appeared in a league match for Liverpool in the 1980-81 season, and last appeared in the 1982-83 season. Only league matches are taken into consideration on these lists.

v. Accrington

Test Matches		Result	Away Blades Accrington	Division Blades Accrington
1892-93 Div 1 v Div 2 22 April	Nottingham	Won	1 0	2ndP(D2) 15thF(D1)

Summary	P	W	D	L	F	A
Blades' cup record:	1	1	0	0	1	0
TOTAL:	**1**	**1**	**0**	**0**	**1**	**0**

FACT FILE

- At the end of their first season of league football, United faced a play-off against first division Accrington for the right to play first division football the following season. A good goal by Jack Drummond sealed victory, and United stayed in the top flight for 41 years. Incidentally, Accrington resigned from the league following this defeat, and are the only club to have played all their league football in the top flight.

v. Aldershot

Season	League	Date	Result	Blades	Aldershot	Date	Result	Blades	Aldershot	Blades	Aldershot
				Home				**Away**		*Final Positions*	
1981-82	Division 4	5 December	Won	**2**	**0**	17 April	Drew	**1**	**1**	1stP	16th
1988-89	Division 3	1 May	Won	**1**	**0**	8 November	Lost	**0**	**1**	2ndP	24thR

FA Cup — *Division*

Season	League	Date	Result	Blades	Aldershot	Date	Result	Blades	Aldershot	Blades	Aldershot
1978-79	Round 3	9 January	Drew	**0**	**0**	15 January	Lost	**0**	**1**	Div 2	Div 4

Summary	P	W	D	L	F	A
Blades' home league record:	2	2	0	0	3	0
Blades' away league record:	2	0	1	1	1	2
Blades' cup record:	2	0	1	1	0	1
TOTAL:	**6**	**2**	**2**	**2**	**4**	**3**

FACT FILE

- **There have been no away victories for either side in this six-match series.**

Played for both clubs

Andy Wilson	Blades 1959-61	Aldershot 1968-69
Dennis Longhorn	Blades 1976-78	Aldershot 1977-80
Francis Joseph	Aldershot 1987-88	Blades 1988-89
Mark Morris	Aldershot 1985-86	Blades 1989-91
David Barnes	Aldershot 1987-89	Blades 1989-94

Dennis Longhorn spent time with the Shots after his spell with the Blades.

v. Altrincham

FA Cup		Date		Home Result	Blades	Altrincham	Date		Away Result	Blades	Altrincham	Division Blades	Altrincham
1981-82	Round 1	21 November	Drew		2	2	23 November		Lost	0	3	Div 4	Non L

Summary	P	W	D	L	F	A
Blades' cup record:	2	0	1	1	2	5
TOTAL:	2	0	1	1	2	5

FACT FILE

● **This was United's last FA Cup exit at the hands of non-league opposition.**

v. Arsenal

		Home					Away			Final Positions	
Season	League	Date	Result	Blades	Arsenal	Date	Result	Blades	Arsenal	Blades	Arsenal
1904-05	Division 1	28 December	Won	4	0	24 December	Lost	0	1	6th	10th
1905-06	Division 1	9 September	Won	3	1	6 January	Lost	1	5	13th	12th
1906-07	Division 1	27 October	Won	4	2	2 March	Won	1	0	4th	7th
1907-08	Division 1	29 February	Drew	2	2	2 November	Lost	1	5	17th	14th=
1908-09	Division 1	31 October	Drew	1	1	1 April	Lost	0	1	12th	6th
1909-10	Division 1	8 January	Won	2	0	4 September	Drew	0	0	6th	18th
1910-11	Division 1	7 January	Won	3	2	10 September	Drew	0	0	9th	10th
1911-12	Division 1	23 September	Won	2	1	27 January	Lost	1	3	14th	10th
1912-13	Division 1	21 September	Lost	1	3	18 January	Won	3	1	15th	20thR
1919-20	Division 1	6 March	Won	2	0	13 March	Lost	0	3	14th	10th
1920-21	Division 1	2 April	Drew	1	1	26 March	Won	6	2	20th	9th
1921-22	Division 1	3 September	Won	4	1	27 August	Won	2	1	11th	17th
1922-23	Division 1	2 October	Won	2	1	28 April	Lost	0	2	10th	11th
1923-24	Division 1	9 February	Won	3	1	25 February	Won	3	1	5th	19th
1924-25	Division 1	24 January	Won	2	1	20 September	Lost	0	2	14th	20th
1925-26	Division 1	24 October	Won	4	0	17 March	Lost	0	4	5th	2nd
1926-27	Division 1	4 September	Won	4	0	22 January	Drew	1	1	8th	11th
1927-28	Division 1	7 January	Won	6	4	3 September	Lost	1	6	13th	10th
1928-29	Division 1	23 March	Drew	2	2	10 November	Lost	0	2	11th	9th
1929-30	Division 1	16 December	Won	4	1	12 April	Lost	1	8	20th	14th
1930-31	Division 1	7 February	Drew	1	1	4 October	Drew	1	1	15th	1st
1931-32	Division 1	25 December	Won	4	1	26 December	Won	2	0	7th	2nd
1932-33	Division 1	6 May	Won	3	1	24 December	Lost	2	9	10th	1st
1933-34	Division 1	23 December	Lost	1	3	5 May	Lost	0	2	22thR	1st
1946-47	Division 1	7 June	Won	2	1	2 November	Won	3	2	6th	13th
1947-48	Division 1	30 August	Lost	1	2	3 January	Lost	2	3	12th	1st
1948-49	Division 1	4 September	Drew	1	1	15 January	Lost	3	5	22ndR	5th
1953-54	Division 1	24 August	Won	1	0	1 September	Drew	1	1	20th	12th
1954-55	Division 1	18 April	Drew	1	1	11 September	Lost	0	4	13th	9th
1955-56	Division 1	24 March	Lost	0	2	12 November	Lost	1	2	22ndR	5th
1961-62	Division 1	9 December	Won	2	1	28 April	Lost	0	2	5th	10th
1962-63	Division 1	13 April	Drew	3	3	10 November	Lost	0	1	10th	7th
1963-64	Division 1	2 November	Drew	2	2	28 March	Won	3	1	12th	8th
1964-65	Division 1	24 October	Won	4	0	6 March	Drew	1	1	19th	13th
1965-66	Division 1	25 April	Won	3	0	6 November	Lost	2	6	9th	14th
1966-67	Division 1	10 December	Drew	1	1	25 March	Lost	0	2	10th	7th
1967-68	Division 1	9 September	Lost	2	4	13 January	Drew	1	1	21stR	9th
1971-72	Division 1	29 January	Lost	0	5	24 August	Won	1	0	10th	5th
1972-73	Division 1	7 October	Won	1	0	3 March	Lost	2	3	14th	2nd
1973-74	Division 1	4 September	Won	5	0	11 September	Lost	0	1	13th	10th
1974-75	Division 1	28 December	Drew	1	1	31 March	Lost	0	1	6th	16th
1975-76	Division 1	19 August	Lost	1	3	31 January	Lost	0	1	22ndR	17th
1990-91	Division 1	6 April	Lost	0	2	29 December	Lost	1	4	13th	1st
1991-92	Division 1	18 April	Drew	1	1	21 September	Lost	2	5	9th	4th

		Home					Away			Final Positions	
Season	League	Date	Result	Blades	Arsenal	Date	Result	Blades	Arsenal	Blades	Arsenal
1992-93	Premiership	19 September	Drew	1	1	9 January	Drew	1	1	14th	10th
1993-94	Premiership	4 April	Drew	1	1	29 December	Lost	0	3	20thR	4th

FA Cup   *Division*

Season	League	Date	Result	Blades	Arsenal	Date	Result	Blades	Arsenal	Blades	Arsenal
1902-03	Round 1					7 February	Won	3	1	Div 1	Div 2
1926-27	Round 3	8 January	Lost	2	3					Div 1	Div 1
1935-36	Final	25 April	Wembley				Lost	0	1	Div 2	Div 1
1958-59	Round 5	18 February	Won	3	0	14 February	Drew	2	2	Div 2	Div 1
1977-78	Round 3	7 January	Lost	0	5					Div 2	Div 1
1995-96	Round 3	17 January	Won	1	0	6 January	Drew	1	1	Div 1	Prem
1998-99	Round 5					23 February	Lost	1	2	Div 1	Prem
2002-03	Semi-Final	13 April	Old Trafford				Lost	0	1	Div 1	Prem

League Cup

Season	League	Date	Result	Blades	Arsenal	Date	Result	Blades	Arsenal	Blades	Arsenal
1971-72	Round 4	8 November	Won	2	0	26 October	Drew	0	0	Div 1	Div 1
1972-73	Round 4	31 October	Lost	1	2					Div 1	Div 1
1981-82	Round 2	6 October	Won	1	0	27 October	Lost*	0	2	Div 4	Div 1

Summary	P	W	D	L	F	A
Blades' home league record:	46	24	14	8	99	62
Blades' away league record:	46	9	8	29	50	110
Blades' cup record:	15	5	3	7	17	20
TOTAL:	**107**	**38**	**25**	**44**	**166**	**192**

FACT FILE

- The FA Cup tie of 1999 was originally played at Highbury on 13 February. Arsenal won 2-1, but their winning goal was highly controversial as United had kicked the ball out of play for a player to receive treatment. Rather than give the ball back, however, recent signing Kanu crossed for Overmars to score. In an unprecedented move, Arsenal offered a rematch which the Blades accepted. Ten days later, the same scoreline ensued.
- The winning goal in the 2003 tie was not without controversy either, but David Seaman's fantastic late save from Paul Peschisolido secured Arsenal's third consecutive FA Cup final appearance.
- Sheffield United were the last lower division team to beat Arsenal, in an FA Cup tie in 1996.
- United have not won in their last 12 away games (13 if you include the first 1999 match), a sequence stretching back to 1971.
- United lost only once in their first 23 home league games.
- Arsenal twice scored eight in a game against United.
- United's last FA Cup Final appearance was in 1936, when Ted Drake's goal was the difference between the sides.

Blades' top scorers vs Arsenal

Harry Johnson 16
Billy Gillespie 9
Jimmy Dunne 8
Len Allchurch, Mick Jones, Joe Kitchen 5
Arthur Brown, Bert Menlove, Bert Oswald,
Albert Partridge, Fred Tunstall 4

Blades hat-tricks vs Arsenal

26 Mar 1921 Harry Johnson
 3 Sep 1921 Harry Johnson
 7 Jan 1928 Harry Johnson (4)
13 Apr 1963 Len Allchurch

Played for both clubs

Ralph Gaudie	Blades 1897-98	Arsenal 1899-1901
Walter Anderson	Blades 1899-1902	Arsenal 1901-03
Alf Common	Blades 1901-04	Arsenal 1910-13
Edward Anderson	Arsenal 1903-04	Blades 1905-06
Joe Fidler	Blades 1903-05	Arsenal 1912-14
Peter Kyle	Arsenal 1906-08	Blades 1908-09
Joe Lievesley	Blades 1904-13	Arsenal 1913-15
Wally Hardinge	Blades 1907-13	Arsenal 1913-20
Bob Benson	Blades 1905-14	Arsenal 1913-15
Jimmy Dunne	Blades 1926-34	Arsenal 1933-36
Alex Forbes	Blades 1946-48	Arsenal 1947-56
Paddy Sloan	Arsenal 1946-48	Blades 1947-48
Jack Wilkinson	Arsenal 1954-55	Blades 1955-57
Colin Addison	Arsenal 1966-68	Blades 1967-71
John Barnwell	Arsenal 1956-64	Blades 1967-71
John Matthews	Arsenal 1974-78	Blades 1978-82
Trevor Ross	Arsenal 1974-78	Blades 1982-84
Wilf Rostron	Arsenal 1974-77	Blades 1989-91
Colin Hill	Arsenal 1982-85	Blades 1989-92
Brian Marwood	Arsenal 1987-90	Blades 1990-92
Scott Marshall	Arsenal 1992-98	Blades 1994-95
Paul Shaw	Arsenal 1994-97	Blades 2003-04

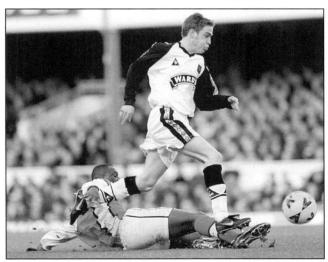

Action from the 1999 FA
Cup Fifth Round game
at Highbury as Blades'
Lee Morris rounds
Patrick Vieira.

v. Aston Villa

Season	League	Date	Result	Home Blades	Villa	Date	Result	Away Blades	Villa	Final Positions Blades	Villa
1893-94	Division 1	2 October	Won	3	0	30 October	Lost	0	4	10th	1st
1894-95	Division 1	22 October	Won	2	1	12 November	Lost	0	5	6th	3rd
1895-96	Division 1	14 September	Won	2	1	16 November	Drew	2	2	12th	1st
1896-97	Division 1	3 October	Drew	0	0	12 September	Drew	2	2	2nd	1st
1897-98	Division 1	8 January	Won	1	0	15 January	Won	2	1	1st	6th
1898-99	Division 1	21 January	Lost	1	3	24 September	Drew	1	1	16th	1st
1899-00	Division 1	8 October	Won	2	1	3 March	Drew	1	1	2nd	1st
1900-01	Division 1	24 November	Drew	2	2	30 March	Drew	0	0	14th	15th
1901-02	Division 1	1 January	Won	6	0	16 September	Won	2	1	10th	8th
1902-03	Division 1	20 December	Lost	2	4	18 April	Lost	2	4	4th	2nd
1903-04	Division 1	31 October	Lost	1	2	27 February	Lost	1	6	7th	5th
1904-05	Division 1	19 November	Lost	0	3	18 March	Lost	0	3	6th	4th
1905-06	Division 1	14 April	Drew	1	1	9 December	Lost	1	4	13th	8th
1906-07	Division 1	20 April	Drew	0	0	15 December	Lost	1	5	4th	5th
1907-08	Division 1	21 December	Drew	1	1	18 April	Lost	0	1	17th	2nd
1908-09	Division 1	6 February	Won	3	1	9 April	Lost	0	3	12th	7th
1909-10	Division 1	25 December	Lost	0	1	27 December	Lost	1	2	6th	1st
1910-11	Division 1	28 December	Won	2	1	14 April	Lost	0	3	9th	2nd
1911-12	Division 1	23 October	Lost	0	1	23 December	Lost	0	1	14th	6th
1912-13	Division 1	14 December	Won	3	2	28 April	Lost	2	4	15th	2nd
1913-14	Division 1	1 January	Won	3	0	26 December	Lost	0	3	10th	2nd
1914-15	Division 1	20 March	Won	3	0	14 November	Lost	0	1	6th	14th
1919-20	Division 1	22 November	Lost	1	2	29 November	Lost	0	4	14th	9th
1920-21	Division 1	30 October	Drew	0	0	23 October	Lost	0	4	20th	10th
1921-22	Division 1	26 December	Lost	2	3	27 December	Lost	3	5	11th	5th
1922-23	Division 1	2 December	Drew	1	1	9 December	Won	1	0	10th	6th
1923-24	Division 1	15 December	Won	2	1	22 December	Drew	2	2	5th	6th
1924-25	Division 1	13 September	Drew	2	2	17 January	Drew	1	1	14th	15th
1925-26	Division 1	7 November	Won	4	1	20 March	Drew	2	2	5th	6th
1926-27	Division 1	27 December	Won	3	1	25 December	Lost	0	4	8th	10th
1927-28	Division 1	1 October	Lost	0	3	11 February	Lost	0	1	13th	8th
1928-29	Division 1	6 October	Lost	1	3	20 February	Lost	2	3	11th	3rd
1929-30	Division 1	19 April	Drew	3	3	14 December	Lost	1	5	20th	4th
1930-31	Division 1	6 December	Lost	3	4	11 April	Lost	0	4	15th	2nd
1931-32	Division 1	12 December	Won	5	4	23 April	Lost	0	5	7th	5th
1932-33	Division 1	24 April	Won	1	0	15 October	Lost	0	3	10th	2nd
1933-34	Division 1	1 January	Drew	3	3	2 April	Lost	0	3	22ndR	13th
1936-37	Division 2	31 October	Won	5	1	6 March	Lost	1	2	7th	9th
1937-38	Division 2	9 April	Drew	0	0	27 November	Lost	0	1	3rd	1stP
1946-47	Division 1	5 April	Lost	1	2	30 November	Won	3	2	6th	8th
1947-48	Division 1	6 March	Won	3	1	18 October	Lost	0	2	12th	6th
1948-49	Division 1	26 February	Lost	0	1	2 October	Lost	3	4	22ndR	10th
1953-54	Division 1	26 April	Won	2	1	26 September	Lost	0	4	20th	13th
1954-55	Division 1	27 November	Lost	1	3	16 April	Lost	1	3	13th	6th

Season	League	Date	Result	Home Blades	Villa	Date	Result	Away Blades	Villa	Final Positions Blades	Villa
1955-56	Division 1	3 December	Drew	2	2	14 April	Lost	2	3	22ndR	20th
1959-60	Division 2	10 October	Drew	1	1	27 February	Won	3	1	4th	1stP
1961-62	Division 1	2 September	Lost	0	2	13 January	Drew	0	0	5th	7th
1962-63	Division 1	1 May	Won	2	1	15 September	Won	2	1	10th	15th
1963-64	Division 1	8 February	Drew	1	1	28 September	Won	1	0	12th	19th
1964-65	Division 1	5 December	Won	4	2	17 April	Lost	1	2	19th	16th
1965-66	Division 1	21 August	Won	1	0	29 January	Won	2	0	9th	16th
1966-67	Division 1	18 March	Drew	3	3	22 October	Drew	0	0	10th	21stR
1968-69	Division 2	10 August	Won	3	1	1 March	Lost	1	3	9th	18th
1969-70	Division 2	22 November	Won	5	0	13 April	Lost	0	1	6th	21stR
1975-76	Division 1	14 February	Won	2	1	8 November	Lost	1	5	22ndR	16th
1987-88	Division 2	26 December	Drew	1	1	26 September	Drew	1	1	21stR	2ndP
1990-91	Division 1	2 March	Won	2	1	1 December	Lost	1	2	13th	17th
1991-92	Division 1	14 December	Won	2	0	31 March	Drew	1	1	9th	7th
1992-93	Premiership	29 August	Lost	0	2	27 January	Lost	1	3	14th	2nd
1993-94	Premiership	16 April	Lost	1	2	20 November	Lost	0	1	20thR	10th

FA Cup

Season	Round	Date	Result	Blades	Villa	Venue/Date	Result	Blades	Villa	Division Blades	Villa
1900-01	Semi-Final	6 April				City Ground, Nottingham	Drew	2	2	Div 1	Div 1
		11 April				Baseball Ground, Derby (replay)	Won	3	0		
1964-65	Round 4	30 January	Lost	0	2					Div 1	Div 1
1974-75	Round 4					25 January	Lost	1	4	Div 1	Div 2
1995-96	Round 4	28 January	Lost	0	1					Div 1	Prem

Summary	P	W	D	L	F	A
Blades' home league record:	60	27	16	17	111	85
Blades' away league record:	60	8	12	40	55	145
Blades' cup record:	5	1	1	3	6	9
TOTAL:	**125**	**36**	**29**	**60**	**172**	**239**

Dean Saunders, who represented both Blades and the Villa.

FACT FILE

- **The Blades suffered 16 straight defeats at Villa Park between 1903 and 1921.**
- **The Blades suffered 10 straight defeats at Villa Park between 1926 and 1937.**
- **United have lost the last five matches.**
- **Between 1963 and 1991, United were unbeaten in 11 league matches at home.**
- **Of teams United have played at least 25 times, their record against Villa is the worst.**

Blades' top scorers vs Villa
Jimmy Dunne, Billy Gillespie, Harry Johnson
Derek Pace 7
Walter Bennett, Fred Priest 6
Fred Tunstall 5
Thomas Boyle, Joe Kitchen 4

Blades hat-tricks vs Villa
14 Dec 1912 Dicky Leafe
27 Feb 1960 Derek Pace

Played for both clubs

Billy Brawn	Blades 1899-1902	Villa 1901-06
Robert Evans	Villa 1906-08	Blades 1908-15
Peter Kyle	Villa 1907-09	Blades 1908-09
Jimmy Harrop	Villa 1912-21	Blades 1920-22
John Roxburgh	Villa 1922-23	Blades 1925-27
William Hamilton	Blades 1956-61	Villa 1965-67
Derek Pace	Villa 1950-58	Blades 1957-65
Trevor Hockey	Blades 1970-73	Villa 1973-74
Simon Stainrod	Blades 1975-79	Villa 1985-88
Chico Hamilton	Villa 1969-76	Blades 1976-78
Bobby Campbell	Villa 1973-75	Blades 1977-78
Bruce Rioch	Villa 1969-74	Blades 1978-79
Dennis Mortimer	Villa 1975-85	Blades 1984-85
John Burridge	Villa 1975-77	Blades 1984-87
Ken McNaught	Villa 1977-83	Blades 1985-86
Peter Withe	Villa 1980-85	Blades 1985-88
Dean Glover	Villa 1984-87	Blades 1986-87
Mervyn Day	Villa 1983-85	Blades 1991-92
Kevin Gage	Villa 1987-91	Blades 1991-96
Franz Carr	Blades 1992-94	Villa 1994-96
Gordon Cowans	Villa 1975-85/88-92/93-94	Blades 1995-96
Adrian Heath	Villa 1989-90	Blades 1995-96
Carl Tiler	Villa 1995-97	Blades 1996-98
Paul McGrath	Villa 1989-96	Blades 1997-98
Dean Saunders	Villa 1992-95	Blades 1997-98
Earl Barrett	Villa 1991-95	Blades 1997-98
Alan Wright	Villa 1994-2003	Blades 2003-04

v. Barnsley

			Home				Away			Final Positions	
Season	League	Date	Result	Blades	Barnsley	Date	Result	Blades	Barnsley	Blades	Barnsley
1934-35	Division 2	26 December	Won	2	1	1 January	Drew	0	0	11th	16th
1935-36	Division 2	4 April	Won	2	0	30 November	Lost	2	3	3rd	20th
1936-37	Division 2	19 September	Won	2	0	23 January	Drew	1	1	7th	14th
1937-38	Division 2	29 January	Won	6	3	18 September	Drew	1	1	3rd	21stR
1949-50	Division 2	31 December	Drew	1	1	3 September	Drew	2	2	3rd	13th
1950-51	Division 2	2 September	Lost	0	2	18 April	Drew	1	1	8th	15th
1951-52	Division 2	29 December	Lost	1	2	1 September	Won	4	3	11th	20th
1952-53	Division 2	24 January	Won	3	0	13 September	Won	3	1	1stP	22ndR
1956-57	Division 2	29 December	Won	5	0	1 September	Won	6	1	7th	19th
1957-58	Division 2	5 October	Drew	0	0	23 April	Won	2	0	6th	14th
1958-59	Division 2	7 February	Won	5	0	20 September	Won	3	1	3rd	22ndR
1979-80	Division 3	15 September	Won	2	0	25 March	Drew	0	0	12th	11th
1980-81	Division 3	31 March	Drew	1	1	30 August	Lost	1	2	21stR	2ndP
1984-85	Division 2	23 February	Won	3	1	13 November	Lost	0	1	18th	11th
1985-86	Division 2	19 October	Won	3	1	8 April	Lost	1	2	7th	12th
1986-87	Division 2	7 March	Won	1	0	25 October	Drew	2	2	9th	11th
1987-88	Division 2	20 February	Won	1	0	29 September	Won	2	1	21stR	14th
1989-90	Division 2	24 March	Lost	1	2	17 October	Won	2	1	2ndP	19th
1994-95	Division 1	16 October	Drew	0	0	29 April	Lost	1	2	8th	6th
1995-96	Division 1	24 February	Won	1	0	17 September	Drew	2	2	9th	10th
1996-97	Division 1	21 December	Lost	0	1	7 March	Lost	0	2	5th	2ndP
1998-99	Division 1	17 October	Drew	1	1	3 April	Lost	1	2	8th	13th
1999-00	Division 1	7 March	Drew	3	3	6 November	Lost	0	2	16th	4th
2000-01	Division 1	7 April	Lost	1	2	9 December	Drew	0	0	10th	16th
2001-02	Division 1	14 December	Drew	1	1	9 March	Drew	1	1	13th	23rdR

FA Cup

										Division	
1989-90	Round 5	18 February	Drew	2	2	21 February	Drew*	0	0	Div 2	Div 2
		(2nd replay)				5 March	Won*	1	0		

League Cup

1982-83	Round 3	9 November	Lost	1	3					Div 3	Div 2

Summary

	P	W	D	L	F	A
Blades' home league record:	25	13	7	5	46	22
Blades' away league record:	25	7	10	8	38	34
Blades' cup record:	4	1	2	1	4	5
TOTAL:	**54**	**21**	**19**	**14**	**88**	**61**

- **The Blades have not won in their last 10 matches with Barnsley.**
- **United had five successive away wins (1951-58).**
- **United's longest unbeaten run in the series is 10 matches (1952-80).**

Blades' top scorers vs Barnsley
Derek Pace 7
Jock Dodds, Colin Grainger, Jack Pickering, Alf Ringstead 4

Blades hat-tricks vs Barnsley
1 Sep 1956 Colin Grainger
7 Feb 1959 Derek Pace

Played for both clubs

Dickie Bourne	Blades 1900-02	Barnsley 1902-03
Johnny Lang	Barnsley 1902-03	Blades 1902-09
James McGuire	Barnsley 1903-05	Blades 1906-13
Billy Batty	Blades 1907-10	Barnsley 1922-23
George Utley	Barnsley 1908-14	Blades 1913-22
Ollie Tummon	Blades 1919-20	Barnsley 1920-21
Percy Beaumont	Blades 1919-21	Barnsley 1921-26
Albert Rawson	Blades 1919-23	Barnsley 1924-25
Wilf Adey	Blades 1931-33	Barnsley 1934-37
Ernie Robinson	Barnsley 1932-33	Blades 1933-34
Tommy Sampy	Blades 1920-34	Barnsley 1934-35
Reg Baines	Blades 1933-34	Barnsley 1938-39
Bill Anderson	Blades 1933-35	Barnsley 1935-36
Teddy Ashton	Barnsley 1927-37	Blades 1936-38
George Jones	Blades 1936-51	Barnsley 1950-52
Julian Broddle	Blades 1981-82	Barnsley 1987-90
Ray McHale	Barnsley 1980-82	Blades 1982-85
Ian Bryson	Blades 1988-93	Barnsley 1993-94
Carl Bradshaw	Barnsley 1986-87	Blades 1989-94
Mitch Ward	Blades 1990-98	Barnsley 2000-03
David Tuttle	Blades 1993-96	Barnsley 1999-2000
Carl Tiler	Barnsley 1987-91	Blades 1996-98
Jan Aage Fjortoft	Blades 1996-98	Barnsley 1997-99
Keith Curle	Blades 2000-02	Barnsley 2002-03
Laurens Ten Heuvel	Barnsley 1995-98	Blades 2002-03
John Curtis	Barnsley 1999-2000	Blades 2002-03
Ashley Ward	Barnsley 1997-99	Blades 2003-04
Chris Morgan	Barnsley 1997-2003	Blades 2003-04
Mick Boulding	Blades 2002-03	Barnsley 2003-04

v. Barrow

FA Cup		Date	Result	Home Blades	Barrow					Division Blades	Barrow
1955-56	Round 3	7 January	Won	**5**	**0**					Div 1	Div 3N

Summary	P	W	D	L	F	A
Blades' cup record:	1	1	0	0	5	0
TOTAL:	1	1	0	0	5	0

Blades' top scorers vs Barrow
Tommy Hoyland 2

Played for both clubs
Norman Wharton	Barrow 1922-25/27-28	Blades 1928-30
Jimmy Shankly	Blades 1926-28	Barrow 1933-35
Wally Webster	Blades 1925-30	Barrow 1934-35
Andy McLaren	Blades 1948-51	Barrow 1950-55
Eric Over	Blades 1954-55	Barrow 1955-58
Keith Eddy	Barrow 1962-66	Blades 1972-76
Tony Field	Barrow 1966-68	Blades 1973-76
Peter Withe	Barrow 1971-72	Blades 1985-88

Tony Field was at Holker Street for a few seasons before arriving at Bramall Lane.

v. Birmingham City

Season	League	Date	Result	Blades	Birm'ham	Date	Result	Blades	Birm'ham	Blades	Birm'ham
				Home				**Away**		*Final Positions*	
1892-93	Division 2	17 September	Won	2	0	3 December	Drew	1	1	2ndP	1st
1894-95	Division 1	13 April	Lost	0	2	1 December	Lost	2	4	6th	12th
1895-96	Division 1	2 September	Won	2	0	7 April	Lost	1	2	12th	15thR
1901-02	Division 1	15 February	Lost	1	4	9 October	Lost	1	5	10th	17thR
1903-04	Division 1	2 January	Drew	1	1	5 September	Won	3	1	7th	11th
1904-05	Division 1	17 September	Won	2	1	14 January	Lost	0	2	6th	7th
1905-06	Division 1	28 December	Won	3	0	30 September	Lost	0	2	13th	7th
1906-07	Division 1	13 October	Won	2	0	16 February	Drew	0	0	4th	9th
1907-08	Division 1	12 October	Won	1	0	8 February	Drew	0	0	17th	20thR
1921-22	Division 1	24 December	Lost	1	2	17 December	Lost	1	2	11th	18th
1922-23	Division 1	17 February	Won	7	1	12 March	Lost	2	4	10th	17th
1923-24	Division 1	12 April	Lost	0	2	19 April	Won	1	0	5th	14th
1924-25	Division 1	21 March	Won	4	3	15 November	Drew	1	1	14th	8th
1925-26	Division 1	3 October	Won	4	1	13 February	Lost	0	2	5th	14th
1926-27	Division 1	18 December	Won	4	3	7 May	Won	3	2	8th	17th
1927-28	Division 1	29 October	Won	3	1	10 March	Lost	1	4	13th	11th
1928-29	Division 1	20 April	Won	3	2	8 December	Drew	2	2	11th	15th
1929-30	Division 1	14 September	Won	4	2	18 January	Lost	1	2	20th	11th
1930-31	Division 1	27 December	Won	3	1	30 August	Lost	1	3	15th	19th
1931-32	Division 1	30 January	Won	1	0	19 September	Won	3	1	7th	9th
1932-33	Division 1	19 November	Won	2	1	1 April	Lost	1	4	10th	13th
1933-34	Division 1	25 December	Won	2	1	26 December	Lost	2	4	22ndR	20th
1948-49	Division 1	26 March	Won	4	0	27 November	Won	2	1	22ndR	17th
1950-51	Division 2	18 November	Won	3	2	7 April	Lost	0	3	8th	4th
1951-52	Division 2	27 October	Won	4	2	15 March	Lost	0	3	11th	3rd
1952-53	Division 2	25 October	Drew	2	2	14 March	Won	2	1	1stP	6th
1955-56	Division 1	27 August	Lost	0	3	24 December	Won	2	0	22ndR	6th
1961-62	Division 1	25 November	Won	3	1	14 April	Lost	0	3	5th	17th
1962-63	Division 1	3 November	Lost	0	2	23 March	Won	1	0	10th	20th
1963-64	Division 1	19 October	Won	3	0	25 April	Lost	0	3	12th	20th
1964-65	Division 1	19 September	Won	3	1	23 January	Drew	1	1	19th	22ndR
1968-69	Division 2	7 December	Won	2	0	4 March	Drew	2	2	9th	7th
1969-70	Division 2	13 December	Won	6	0	13 September	Lost	1	2	6th	18th
1970-71	Division 2	17 April	Won	3	0	10 October	Won	1	0	2ndP	9th
1972-73	Division 1	17 February	Lost	0	1	12 August	Won	2	1	14th	10th
1973-74	Division 1	3 November	Drew	1	1	30 March	Lost	0	1	13th	19th
1974-75	Division 1	26 October	Won	3	2	29 April	Drew	0	0	6th	17th
1975-76	Division 1	4 May	Drew	1	1	4 October	Lost	0	2	22ndR	19th
1984-85	Division 2	1 January	Lost	3	4	8 April	Lost	1	4	18th	2ndP
1986-87	Division 2	6 September	Drew	1	1	19 December	Lost	1	2	9th	19th
1987-88	Division 2	20 October	Lost	0	2	9 April	Lost	0	1	21stR	19th
1995-96	Division 1	26 December	Drew	1	1	2 March	Won	1	0	9th	15th
1996-97	Division 1	24 August	Drew	4	4	22 March	Drew	1	1	5th	10th
1997-98	Division 1	27 September	Drew	0	0	22 February	Lost	0	2	6th	7th

			Home				Away		Final Positions	
Season	League	Date	Result	Blades	Birm'ham	Date	Result	Blades Birm'ham	Blades	Birm'ham
1998-99	Division 1	22 August	Lost	0	2	26 December	Lost	0 1	8th	4th
1999-00	Division 1	25 March	Lost	1	2	26 December	Won	2 0	16th	5th
2000-01	Division 1	10 February	Won	3	1	9 September	Lost	0 1	10th	5th
2001-02	Division 1	17 November	Won	4	0	21 April	Lost	0 2	13th	5thP

FA Cup *Division*

1933-34	Round 3					13 January	Lost	1 2	Div 1	Div 1
1952-53	Round 4	31 January	Drew	1	1	4 February	Lost	1 3	Div 2	Div 2
1983-84	Round 3	6 January	Drew	1	1	10 January	Lost	0 2	Div 3	Div 1

League Cup

1966-67	Q'ter Final	7 December	Lost	2	3				Div 1	Div 2

Summary	P	W	D	L	F	A
Blades' home league record:	48	29	8	11	107	63
Blades' away league record:	48	12	9	27	47	85
Blades' cup record:	6	0	2	4	6	12
TOTAL:	**102**	**41**	**19**	**42**	**160**	**160**

FACT FILE

- Between 1925 and 1951, United had 13 successive home wins.
- United won one of 19 matches from 1975 to 1998.
- United have not been undefeated for more than five matches in a row.

Blues' Martyn O'Connor tackles Blades' Nick Montgomery.

Blades' top scorers vs Birmingham

Harry Johnson 12
Fred Tunstall, Alan Woodward 8
Arthur Brown, Jimmy Hagan 5
Jimmy Dunne, George Green, Tommy Sampy 4

Blades hat-tricks vs Birmingham

17 Feb 1923 Harry Johnson (4)
3 Oct 1925 Bert Menlove
19 Oct 1963 Derek Pace

Played for both clubs

Walter Wigmore	Blades 1895-96	Birmingham 1898-1912
Harry Howard	Blades 1895-1901	Birmingham 1902-06
Oakey Field	Blades 1898-1902	Birmingham 1901-06
Billy Beer	Blades 1898-1902	Birmingham 1901-10
Alonzo Drake	Blades 1903-08	Birmingham 1907-08
Edgar Bluff	Blades 1905-08	Birmingham 1907-08
Jack Peart	Blades 1907-10	Birmingham 1919-20
George Gallimore	Blades 1908-10	Birmingham 1910-11
Fred Hawley	Blades 1912-15	Birmingham 1919-20
Albert Rawson	Blades 1919-23	Birmingham 1922-24
Roy Warhurst	Blades 1946-50	Birmingham 1949-57
Trevor Hockey	Birmingham 1965-71	Blades 1970-73
Bruce Rioch	Birmingham 1978-79	Blades 1978-79
Don Givens	Birmingham 1978-81	Blades 1980-81
Bob Hatton	Birmingham 1971-76	Blades 1980-83
Paul Tomlinson	Blades 1983-87	Birmingham 1986-87
Dennis Mortimer	Blades 1984-85	Birmingham 1986-87
Steve Wigley	Blades 1985-87	Birmingham 1986-89
Peter Withe	Birmingham 1975-77/87-88	Blades 1985-88
Andy Kennedy	Birmingham 1984-88	Blades 1986-87
Martin Kuhl	Birmingham 1982-87	Blades 1986-88
Roger Hansbury	Birmingham 1986-90	Blades 1987-88
Chris Marsden	Blades 1987-88	Birmingham 1997-99
Alan Kelly	Blades 1992-99	Birmingham 2001-02
Phil Starbuck	Birmingham 1987-88	Blades 1994-97
Gary Ablett	Blades 1995-96	Birmingham 1996-99
Carl Tiler	Blades 1996-98	Birmingham 2000-01
David Holdsworth	Blades 1996-99	Birmingham 1998-2002
Marcelo	Blades 1997-2000	Birmingham 1999-2002
Curtis Woodhouse	Blades 1997-2001	Birmingham 2000-03
Paul Devlin	Birmingham 1995-96/2001-04	Blades 1997-2002
Jonathan Hunt	Birmingham 1994-97	Blades 1998-2000
Olivier Tebily	Blades 1998-99	Birmingham 2001-04
Steve Bruce	Birmingham 1996-98	Blades 1998-99
Paul Peschisolido	Birmingham 1992-94/95-96	Blades 2000-04
Peter Ndlovu	Birmingham 1997-2001	Blades 2000-04
Paul Furlong	Birmingham 1996-2002	Blades 2001-02
Richard Edghill	Birmingham 2000-01	Blades 2002-03
Tommy Mooney	Birmingham 2001-03	Blades 2002-03

v. Blackburn Rovers

Season	League	Date	Result	Blades	Blackburn	Date	Result	Blades	Blackburn	Blades	Blackburn
				Home				**Away**		*Final Positions*	
1893-94	Division 1	3 March	Won	3	2	15 January	Lost	1	4	10th	4th
1894-95	Division 1	8 October	Won	3	0	26 December	Lost	2	3	6th	5th
1895-96	Division 1	7 March	Drew	1	1	25 January	Lost	0	1	12th	8th
1896-97	Division 1	9 January	Won	7	0	6 February	Won	3	1	2nd	14th
1897-98	Division 1	4 October	Won	5	2	20 November	Drew	1	1	1st	15th
1898-99	Division 1	3 December	Drew	1	1	1 April	Lost	1	2	16th	6th
1899-00	Division 1	9 September	Won	3	0	13 April	Drew	3	3	2nd	14th
1900-01	Division 1	15 September	Won	2	1	12 January	Lost	0	1	14th	9th
1901-02	Division 1	18 January	Won	4	1	21 September	Lost	1	2	10th	4th
1902-03	Division 1	10 January	Won	2	1	13 September	Lost	0	2	4th	16th
1903-04	Division 1	28 November	Drew	2	2	26 March	Lost	0	3	7th	15th
1904-05	Division 1	25 March	Won	3	1	26 November	Won	4	2	6th	13th
1905-06	Division 1	20 January	Lost	0	2	16 September	Lost	1	2	13th	9th
1906-07	Division 1	29 September	Won	3	0	29 March	Drew	1	1	4th	12th
1907-08	Division 1	28 September	Won	4	2	25 January	Drew	3	3	17th	14th=
1908-09	Division 1	30 January	Drew	0	0	26 September	Won	1	0	12th	4th
1909-10	Division 1	25 September	Won	3	0	23 April	Lost	1	3	6th	3rd
1910-11	Division 1	28 January	Drew	1	1	24 September	Won	2	1	9th	12th
1911-12	Division 1	2 March	Drew	1	1	28 October	Lost	0	1	14th	1st
1912-13	Division 1	2 November	Drew	0	0	7 April	Lost	1	3	15th	5th
1913-14	Division 1	27 September	Drew	1	1	24 January	Lost	2	3	10th	1st
1914-15	Division 1	26 December	Lost	1	2	1 January	Won	2	1	6th	3rd
1919-20	Division 1	20 October	Won	2	0	1 May	Lost	0	4	14th	20th
1920-21	Division 1	12 February	Drew	1	1	19 February	Drew	1	1	20th	11th
1921-22	Division 1	27 February	Lost	0	1	21 January	Won	3	2	11th	15th
1922-23	Division 1	4 September	Drew	1	1	18 September	Lost	0	1	10th	14th
1923-24	Division 1	23 February	Won	4	0	16 February	Drew	1	1	5th	8th
1924-25	Division 1	30 August	Lost	2	3	27 December	Drew	2	2	14th	16th
1925-26	Division 1	19 September	Drew	1	1	1 March	Lost	1	3	5th	12th
1926-27	Division 1	2 April	Won	5	3	13 November	Won	4	3	8th	18th
1927-28	Division 1	28 April	Lost	2	3	17 December	Lost	0	1	13th	12th
1928-29	Division 1	3 November	Won	2	1	16 March	Drew	1	1	11th	7th
1929-30	Division 1	3 March	Lost	5	7	12 October	Won	1	0	20th	6th
1930-31	Division 1	11 October	Drew	1	1	19 February	Lost	1	2	15th	10th
1931-32	Division 1	1 January	Won	3	2	28 March	Won	2	1	7th	16th
1932-33	Division 1	11 March	Won	2	1	29 October	Lost	0	3	10th	15th
1933-34	Division 1	25 November	Won	1	0	7 April	Lost	1	3	22ndR	8th
1936-37	Division 2	31 August	Lost	0	1	21 September	Lost	1	3	7th	12th
1937-38	Division 2	9 October	Drew	1	1	19 February	Won	3	2	3rd	16th
1938-39	Division 2	26 April	Drew	0	0	8 October	Won	2	1	2ndP	1stP
1946-47	Division 1	22 February	Lost	0	1	19 October	Lost	0	2	6th	17th
1947-48	Division 1	6 December	Won	4	1	24 April	Lost	0	4	12th	21stR
1949-50	Division 2	1 April	Won	4	0	26 November	Won	2	0	3rd	16th
1950-51	Division 2	19 August	Lost	0	3	16 December	Won	2	0	8th	6th

		Home				Away				Final Positions	
Season	League	Date	Result	Blades	Blackburn	Date	Result	Blades	Blackburn	Blades	Blackburn
1951-52	Division 2	15 December	Drew	1	1	18 August	Won	5	1	11th	14th
1952-53	Division 2	4 October	Won	3	0	21 February	Won	2	1	1stP	9th
1956-57	Division 2	2 February	Lost	0	2	22 September	Lost	1	3	7th	4th
1957-58	Division 2	26 December	Won	4	2	25 December	Lost	0	1	6th	2ndP
1961-62	Division 1	20 February	Drew	0	0	30 September	Won	2	1	5th	16th
1962-63	Division 1	5 September	Drew	1	1	17 September	Won	2	1	10th	11th
1963-64	Division 1	28 August	Lost	0	1	4 September	Drew	2	2	12th	7th
1964-65	Division 1	27 February	Drew	1	1	17 October	Lost	0	4	19th	10th
1965-66	Division 1	29 March	Won	2	0	2 October	Drew	0	0	9th	22ndR
1968-69	Division 2	12 April	Won	3	0	21 September	Lost	0	1	9th	19th
1969-70	Division 2	1 November	Won	4	0	28 February	Won	2	1	6th	8th
1970-71	Division 2	20 March	Won	5	0	7 November	Won	3	1	2ndP	21stR
1976-77	Division 2	25 September	Drew	1	1	5 March	Lost	0	1	11th	12th
1977-78	Division 2	10 December	Won	2	0	22 April	Drew	1	1	12th	5th
1978-79	Division 2	2 May	Lost	0	1	7 April	Lost	0	2	20thR	22ndR
1979-80	Division 3	1 January	Won	2	1	7 April	Lost	0	1	12th	2ndP
1984-85	Division 2	6 May	Lost	1	3	8 December	Lost	1	3	18th	5th
1985-86	Division 2	16 November	Drew	3	3	19 April	Lost	1	6	7th	19th
1986-87	Division 2	4 April	Won	4	1	8 November	Won	2	0	9th	12th
1987-88	Division 2	29 August	Won	3	1	1 January	Lost	1	4	21stR	5th
1989-90	Division 2	30 December	Lost	1	2	1 May	Drew	0	0	2ndP	5th
1992-93	Premiership	17 April	Lost	1	3	19 December	Lost	0	1	14th	4th
1993-94	Premiership	15 January	Lost	1	2	18 October	Drew	0	0	20thR	2nd
1999-00	Division 1	19 December	Won	2	1	1 April	Lost	0	5	16th	11th
2000-01	Division 1	15 September	Won	2	0	4 April	Drew	1	1	10th	2ndP

FA Cup

										Division	
1896-97	Round 1					30 January	Lost	1	2	Div 1	Div 1
1960-61	Round 5	18 February	Won	2	1					Div 2	Div 1
1992-93	Q'ter Final	16 March	Drew*	2	2	6 March	Drew	0	0	Prem	Prem

(won 5-3 pens)

Marcus Bent in action against Blackburn in December 1997. He scored both goals in a 2-1 win.

Summary	P	W	D	L	F	A
Blades' home league record:	69	33	20	16	138	80
Blades' away league record:	69	20	14	35	84	125
Blades' cup record:	4	1	2	1	5	5
TOTAL:	**142**	**54**	**36**	**52**	**227**	**210** (+one penalty shoot-out victory)

FACT FILE

- No club has played United as many times as Blackburn.
- United's first FA Cup penalty shoot-out came against Blackburn, and victory set up a Sheffield derby in the semi-final.
- On New Year's Day 1932 against Blackburn, Jimmy Dunne scored for a club record 12th consecutive game.
- United were unbeaten in their first 12 home games.

Blades' top scorers vs Blackburn
Harry Johnson 10
Walter Bennett, Fred Priest 9
Arthur Brown, Jimmy Dunne, Fred Tunstall 8
Ernest Needham, Derek Pace 6
Alf Ringstead, Alan Woodward 5

Blades hat-tricks vs Blackburn
9 Jan 1897 George Walls
4 Oct 1897 Ernest Needham
18 Jan 1902 Fred Priest
3 Mar 1930 Jimmy Dunne

Played for both clubs
Neil Logan	Blades 1897-98	Blackburn 1902-03
Walter Brayshaw	Blades 1919-20	Blackburn 1924-26
Albert Nightingale	Blades 1946-48	Blackburn 1951-53
Alan Birchenall	Blades 1964-68	Blackburn 1951-53
Mick Heaton	Blades 1966-71	Blackburn 1971-76
Mick Speight	Blades 1971-80	Blackburn 1980-82
Terry Garbett	Blackburn 1971-74	Blades 1973-76
Tony Field	Blackburn 1971-74	Blades 1973-76
David Bradford	Blackburn 1971-74	Blades 1974-77
Viv Busby	Blades 1979-80	Blackburn 1980-81
Neil Ramsbottom	Blackburn 1978-79	Blades 1979-80
Kevin Arnott	Blackburn 1981-83	Blades 1982-87
Andy Kennedy	Blades 1986-87	Blackburn 1988-90
Alan Kelly	Blades 1992-99	Blackburn 1999-2003
Nathan Blake	Blades 1993-96	Blackburn 1998-2002
Phil Starbuck	Blackburn 1990-91	Blades 1994-97
Gordon Cowans	Blackburn 1991-93	Blades 1995-96
Mark Patterson	Blackburn 1983-88	Blades 1995-98
Nicky Marker	Blackburn 1992-97	Blades 1997-99
Marcus Bent	Blades 1999-2001	Blackburn 2000-02
Andrew Morrison	Blackburn 1993-94	Blades 2000-01
James Thomas	Blades 2000-01	Blackburn 2000-01
John Curtis	Blackburn 2000-03	Blades 2002-03
Alan Wright	Blackburn 1991-95	Blades 2003-04
Alan Fettis	Blackburn 1997-2000	Blades 2003-04
Ashley Ward	Blackburn 1998-2000	Blades 2003-04

v. Blackpool

				Home				Away		Final Positions	
Season	League	Date	Result	Blades	Blackpool	Date	Result	Blades	Blackpool	Blades	Blackpool
1930-31	Division 1	26 December	Won	5	1	25 December	Lost	1	2	15th	20th
1931-32	Division 1	7 May	Lost	1	3	31 August	Lost	0	2	7th	20th
1932-33	Division 1	22 April	Won	1	0	10 December	Won	3	0	10th	22ndR
1934-35	Division 2	24 November	Drew	1	1	6 April	Lost	0	1	11th	4th
1935-36	Division 2	20 February	Won	1	0	12 October	Lost	0	3	3rd	10th
1936-37	Division 2	10 October	Drew	2	2	13 February	Lost	0	1	7th	2ndP
1946-47	Division 1	9 November	Won	4	2	15 March	Lost	2	4	6th	5th
1947-48	Division 1	3 April	Won	2	1	15 November	Lost	1	2	12th	9th
1948-49	Division 1	21 August	Won	3	2	18 December	Won	3	0	22ndR	16th
1953-54	Division 1	29 August	Lost	3	4	2 January	Drew	2	2	20th	6th
1954-55	Division 1	16 October	Won	2	1	30 April	Won	2	1	13th	19th
1955-56	Division 1	22 October	Won	2	1	31 March	Drew	1	1	22ndR	2nd
1961-62	Division 1	26 December	Won	2	1	3 April	Won	4	2	5th	13th
1962-63	Division 1	16 April	Drew	0	0	15 April	Lost	1	3	10th	13th
1963-64	Division 1	14 December	Won	1	0	24 August	Drew	2	2	12th	18th
1964-65	Division 1	10 October	Lost	1	3	20 February	Drew	2	2	19th	17th
1965-66	Division 1	11 April	Lost	0	1	8 April	Lost	1	2	9th	13th
1966-67	Division 1	12 November	Drew	1	1	8 April	Won	1	0	10th	22ndR
1968-69	Division 2	28 September	Won	2	1	5 April	Drew	1	1	9th	8th
1969-70	Division 2	18 October	Lost	2	3	30 March	Lost	0	1	6th	2ndP
1976-77	Division 2	12 April	Lost	1	5	13 November	Lost	0	1	11th	5th
1977-78	Division 2	1 April	Drew	0	0	5 November	Drew	1	1	12th	20thR
1979-80	Division 3	18 September	Won	3	1	2 October	Won	3	2	12th	18th
1980-81	Division 3	16 September	Won	4	2	1 October	Lost	1	2	21stR	23rdR
1981-82	Division 4	31 October	Won	3	1	20 March	Won	1	0	1stP	12th
1988-89	Division 3	25 February	Won	4	1	15 October	Won	2	1	2ndP	19th

FA Cup

										Division	
1891-92	Round 1					16 January	Won	3	0	Non L	Non L
1892-93	Round 1					21 January	Won	3	1	Div 2	Non L
1905-06	Round 2	3 February	Lost	1	2					Div 1	Div 2
1914-15	Round 1					9 January	Won	2	1	Div 1	Div 2
1923-24	Round 1					12 January	Lost	0	1	Div 1	Div 2
1938-39	Round 3					7 January	Won	2	1	Div 2	Div 1
1967-68	Round 4	17 February	Won	2	1					Div 1	Div 2

League Cup

1961-62	Q'ter Final	27 March	Lost	0	2	6 February	Drew	0	0	Div 1	Div 1
1993-94	Round 2	5 October	Won	2	0	21 September	Lost	0	3	Prem	Div 2

Summary	P	W	D	L	F	A
Blades' home league record:	26	15	5	6	51	38
Blades' away league record:	26	8	6	12	35	39
Blades' cup record:	11	6	1	4	15	12
TOTAL:	**63**	**29**	**12**	**22**	**101**	**89**

Blades' top scorers vs Blackpool
Jimmy Hagan 7
Jimmy Dunne, Alan Woodward 4
Bob Hatton, Alf Ringstead, Peter Wragg 3

Played for both clubs

Harry Warren	Blackpool 1924-27	Blades 1929-30
Percy Thorpe	Blackpool 1924-28	Blades 1930-33
Jock Dodds	Blades 1934-39	Blackpool 1938-40
Eddie Shimwell	Blades 1946-47	Blackpool 1946-57
Walter Rickett	Blades 1946-48	Blackpool 1947-50
George Farrow	Blackpool 1936-48	Blades 1947-48
Tom McAlister	Blades 1971-76	Blackpool 1979-80
Gary Jones	Blades 1974-75	Blackpool 1978-80
Neil Ramsbottom	Blackpool 1970-72	Blades 1979-80
Bob Hatton	Blackpool 1976-78	Blades 1980-83
Paul Richardson	Blades 1981-83	Blackpool 1982-83
Colin Morris	Blackpool 1979-82	Blades 1981-88
John Burridge	Blackpool 1970-76	Blades 1984-87
Peter Duffield	Blades 1987-92	Blackpool 1992-93
Paul Beesley	Blades 1990-95	Blackpool 1999-2000
John Reed	Blades 1991-96	Blackpool 1997-98
Carl Muggleton	Blackpool 1987-88	Blades 1995-96
Gary Ablett	Blades 1995-96	Blackpool 1999-2000
Mark Patterson	Blades 1995-98	Blackpool 1998-99
Paul Simpson	Blades 1996-97	Blackpool 2000-02
Jon O'Connor	Blades 1997-99	Blackpool 2000-01
James Thomas	Blackpool 1999-2000	Blades 2000-01
Andrew Morrison	Blackpool 1994-96/2000-01	Blades 2000-01
Gary Kelly	Blackpool 1988-89	Blades 2002-03
Alan Wright	Blackpool 1987-92	Blades 2003-04
Ashley Ward	Blackpool 1992-93	Blades 2003-04

v. Bolton Wanderers

Season	League	Date	Result	Blades	Bolton	Date	Result	Blades	Bolton	Blades	Bolton
		Home						**Away**		*Final Positions*	
1893-94	Division 1	23 September	Won	4	2	14 October	Won	1	0	10th	13th
1894-95	Division 1	15 April	Won	5	0	14 January	Lost	2	6	6th	10th
1895-96	Division 1	30 December	Won	1	0	3 April	Lost	1	4	12th	4th
1896-97	Division 1	29 December	Won	1	0	16 April	Won	2	0	2nd	8th
1897-98	Division 1	7 February	Won	4	0	8 April	Won	1	0	1st	11th
1898-99	Division 1	11 March	Won	3	1	12 November	Lost	0	3	16th	17thR
1900-01	Division 1	27 October	Lost	0	2	2 March	Drew	0	0	14th	10th
1901-02	Division 1	7 April	Won	2	0	28 March	Lost	0	1	10th	12th
1902-03	Division 1	26 December	Won	7	1	28 February	Lost	0	1	4th	18thR
1905-06	Division 1	30 December	Won	5	2	2 September	Won	2	1	13th	6th
1906-07	Division 1	5 January	Won	2	1	8 September	Lost	1	6	4th	6th
1907-08	Division 1	30 December	Won	1	0	5 October	Drew	1	1	17th	19thR
1909-10	Division 1	11 September	Drew	2	2	22 January	Lost	0	1	6th	20thR
1911-12	Division 1	9 September	Lost	0	5	6 January	Won	3	0	14th	4th
1912-13	Division 1	26 December	Lost	0	2	1 January	Lost	2	4	15th	8th
1913-14	Division 1	6 April	Won	2	0	1 November	Lost	1	3	10th	6th
1914-15	Division 1	19 December	Won	3	1	26 April	Won	1	0	6th	17th
1919-20	Division 1	17 April	Won	3	2	24 April	Lost	0	1	14th	6th
1920-21	Division 1	12 March	Drew	2	2	19 March	Drew	2	2	20th	3rd
1921-22	Division 1	11 February	Won	1	0	4 February	Lost	1	3	11th	6th
1922-23	Division 1	27 January	Drew	2	2	20 January	Drew	1	1	10th	13th
1923-24	Division 1	27 August	Drew	0	0	3 September	Lost	2	4	5th	4th
1924-25	Division 1	6 December	Won	2	0	11 April	Lost	1	3	14th	3rd
1925-26	Division 1	5 December	Won	2	0	17 April	Lost	1	2	5th	8th
1926-27	Division 1	18 April	Drew	1	1	15 April	Lost	1	4	8th	4th
1927-28	Division 1	24 December	Won	4	3	5 May	Drew	1	1	13th	7th
1928-29	Division 1	9 March	Drew	1	1	27 October	Lost	1	3	11th	14th
1929-30	Division 1	8 March	Lost	2	3	2 November	Lost	1	2	20th	15th
1930-31	Division 1	8 November	Won	2	0	14 March	Lost	2	6	15th	14th
1931-32	Division 1	14 November	Won	4	0	26 March	Lost	1	3	7th	17th
1932-33	Division 1	17 April	Won	3	2	2 January	Drew	3	3	10th	21stR
1934-35	Division 2	29 September	Won	6	2	9 February	Drew	1	1	11th	2ndP
1946-47	Division 1	7 April	Won	4	2	4 April	Lost	2	3	6th	18th
1947-48	Division 1	25 December	Won	2	1	27 December	Won	3	2	12th	17th
1948-49	Division 1	25 December	Drew	1	1	27 December	Lost	1	6	22ndR	14th
1953-54	Division 1	12 December	Won	3	0	1 January	Lost	1	2	20th	5th
1954-55	Division 1	11 December	Won	2	0	5 March	Lost	0	1	13th	18th
1955-56	Division 1	19 November	Lost	1	3	3 March	Lost	1	2	22ndR	8th
1961-62	Division 1	24 March	Won	3	1	4 November	Lost	0	2	5th	11th
1962-63	Division 1	20 October	Won	4	1	9 March	Lost	2	3	10th	18th
1963-64	Division 1	16 November	Lost	0	1	8 April	Lost	0	3	12th	21stR
1968-69	Division 2	22 March	Won	5	2	31 August	Lost	2	4	9th	17th
1969-70	Division 2	28 March	Lost	0	1	15 November	Drew	0	0	6th	16th
1970-71	Division 2	20 October	Drew	2	2	16 January	Lost	1	2	2ndP	22ndR

				Home				Away		Final Positions	
Season	League	Date	Result	Blades	Bolton	Date	Result	Blades	Bolton	Blades	Bolton
1976-77	Division 2	28 December	Lost	2	3	9 April	Won	2	1	11th	4th
1977-78	Division 2	14 January	Lost	1	5	27 August	Lost	1	2	12th	1stP
1983-84	Division 3	31 December	Won	5	0	7 May	Lost	1	3	3rdP	10th
1988-89	Division 3	4 February	Won	4	0	1 October	Lost	0	2	2ndP	10th
1994-95	Division 1	10 September	Won	3	1	22 March	Drew	1	1	8th	3rdP
1996-97	Division 1	22 November	Drew	1	1	15 February	Drew	2	2	5th	1stP
1998-99	Division 1	16 January	Lost	1	2	29 August	Drew	2	2	8th	6th
1999-00	Division 1	14 November	Lost	1	2	21 March	Lost	0	2	16th	6th
2000-01	Division 1	25 November	Won	1	0	6 May	Drew	1	1	10th	3rdP

FA Cup

				Home				Away		Division	
1889-90	Round 2					1 February	Lost	0	13	Non L	Div 1
1901-02	Round 2	8 February	Won	2	1					Div 1	Div 1
1903-04	Round 3	5 March	Lost	0	2					Div 1	Div 2
1914-15	Semi-Final	27 March		Ewood Park			Won	2	1	Div 1	Div 1
1922-23	Semi-Final	24 March		Old Trafford			Lost	0	1	Div 1	Div 1
1955-56	Round 4					28 January	Won	2	1	Div 1	Div 1
1962-63	Round 3	6 March	Won	3	1					Div 1	Div 1

League Cup

				Home						Division	
1963-64	Round 2	25 September	Lost	1	2					Div 1	Div 1
1994-95	Round 3	25 October	Lost	1	2					Div 1	Div 1

Summary	P	W	D	L	F	A
Blades' home league record:	53	33	9	11	123	66
Blades' away league record:	53	8	12	33	60	116
Blades' cup record:	9	4	0	5	11	24
TOTAL:	115	45	21	49	194	206

FACT FILE

- It was against Bolton, on 4 April 1898, that Ernest Needham scored the goal that secured United's first and only league championship. In beating Celtic the same season, they were declared champions of Great Britain.
- Only eight years earlier, United suffered their first FA Cup defeat at the hands of Bolton, and the 13-0 scoreline, not surprisingly, still stands as United's heaviest ever defeat.
- United have not won in their last eight matches in Bolton, and therefore have yet to win at the Reebok Stadium.
- United won 11 of their first 12 home games in the league.
- The Blades won twice in 29 away matches from 1920 to 1971.

Blades' top scorers vs Bolton

Jimmy Dunne 9
Ernest Needham 7
Harry Johnson, Fred Tunstall 6
Bobby Barclay, Arthur Brown, Billy Gillespie,
Albert Nightingale, Alan Woodward 5

Blades hat-tricks vs Bolton

30 Dec 1905 Arthur Brown
17 Apr 1920 Harry Johnson
 7 Apr 1947 Albert Nightingale
31 Dec 1983 Colin Morris

Played for both clubs

Charlie Henderson	Bolton 1894-95	Blades 1896-97
Harold Gough	Blades 1913-24	Bolton 1927-28
Bruce Longworth	Bolton 1919-24	Blades 1924-26
Vince Matthews	Bolton 1922-25	Blades 1927-31
Malcolm Barrass	Bolton 1946-57	Blades 1956-57
Billy Russell	Blades 1957-63	Bolton 1962-65
Gary Jones	Bolton 1968-79	Blades 1974-75
Terry Poole	Blades 1979-80	Bolton 1980-81
Bob Hatton	Bolton 1966-68	Blades 1980-83
Tony Philliskirk	Blades 1983-88	Bolton 1989-93
Andy Kennedy	Blades 1986-87	Bolton 1991-92
Martin Pike	Blades 1986-90	Bolton 1989-90
Franz Carr	Blades 1992-94	Bolton 1997-98
Nathan Blake	Blades 1993-96	Bolton 1995-99
Andy Walker	Bolton 1991-94	Blades 1995-98
Mark Patterson	Bolton 1990-96	Blades 1995-98
Andy Campbell	Blades 1998-99	Bolton 2000-01
Aidan Davison	Bolton 1993-96	Blades 1999-2000
Mike Whitlow	Bolton 1997-2003	Blades 2003-04

Paul Devlin
shapes up to the
Trotters' Mike
Whitlow.

v. Bootle

				Home				Away		Final Positions	
Season	League	Date	Result	Blades	Bootle	Date	Result	Blades	Bootle	Blades	Bootle
1892-93	Division 2	26 November	Won	8	3	10 September	Lost	0	2	2ndP	8thF

Summary	P	W	D	L	F	A
Blades' home league record:	1	1	0	0	8	3
Blades' away league record:	1	0	0	1	0	2
TOTAL:	2	1	0	1	8	5

FACT FILE

- **Harry Hammond became the first of two Blades players to score five in a league game.**

Blades' top scorers vs Bootle
Harry Hammond 5
Fred Davies 2

Blades hat-tricks vs Bootle
26 Nov 1892 Harry Hammond (5)

v. Boston United

FA Cup		Date	Result	Home Blades	Boston	Date	Result	Away Blades	Boston	Division Blades	Boston
1982-83	Round 2	14 December	Won	5	1	11 December	Drew	1	1	Div 3	Non L

Summary	P	W	D	L	F	A
Blades' cup record:	2	1	1	0	6	2
TOTAL:	2	1	1	0	6	2

Blades' top scorers vs Boston
Alan Young 3
Keith Edwards 2

Blades hat-tricks vs Boston
14 Dec 1982 Alan Young (3) (cup)

Played for both clubs
Peter Duffield	Blades 1987-92	Boston 2002-04
Tony Battersby	Blades 1995-96	Boston 2002-03

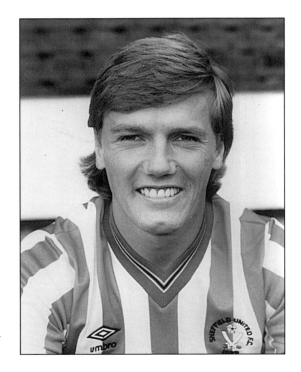

Keith Edwards, scorer of two goals for United against Boston.

v. AFC Bournemouth

Season	League	Date	Result	Home Blades Bournem'th		Date	Result	Away Blades Bournem'th		Final Positions Blades Bournem'th	
1981-82	Division 4	24 April	Drew	0	0	28 November	Drew	0	0	1stP	4th
1982-83	Division 3	29 January	Drew	2	2	11 September	Drew	0	0	11th	14th
1983-84	Division 3	15 October	Won	2	0	24 March	Won	1	0	3rdP	17th
1987-88	Division 2	15 August	Lost	0	1	16 January	Won	2	1	21stR	17th
1989-90	Division 2	28 April	Won	4	2	11 November	Won	1	0	2ndP	22ndR

FA Cup										Division	
1989-90	Round 3	6 January	Won	2	0					Div 2	Div 2

Summary	P	W	D	L	F	A
Blades' home league record:	5	2	2	1	8	5
Blades' away league record:	5	3	2	0	4	1
Blades' cup record:	1	1	0	0	2	0
TOTAL:	**11**	**6**	**4**	**1**	**14**	**6**

FACT FILE

● **United have won their last four matches in the series.**

Blades' top scorers vs Bournemouth
Ian Bryson 3
Tony Agana 2

Played for both clubs

George W.R. Richardson	Blades 1921-23	Bournemouth 1924-25
Clifford Halliwell	Blades 1921-26	Bournemouth 1926-32
Charlie Wilkinson	Blades 1933-38	Bournemouth 1939-40
George Farrow	Bournemouth 1933-36	Blades 1947-48
Alec Blakeman	Blades 1948-49	Bournemouth 1948-50
Jack Cross	Bournemouth 1947-54	Blades 1953-56
Deenis Longhorn	Bournemouth 1967-72	Blades 1976-78
Neil Ramsbottom	Blades 1979-80	Bournemouth 1983-84
Don Givens	Bournemouth 1979-80	Blades 1980-81
Tom Hefferman	Bournemouth 1979-83/85-88	Blades 1983-85
Richard Cadette	Blades 1987-88	Bournemouth 1989-90
Mark Morris	Blades 1989-91	Bournemouth 1991-97
Paul Wood	Blades 1989-92	Bournemouth 1990-94
Phil Kite	Bournemouth 1989-90	Blades 1990-92
Nigel Spackman	Bournemouth 1980-83	Blades 1996-97
Steve Lovell	Bournemouth 1998-99	Blades 2001-02

v. Bradford City

Season	League	Date	Result	Home Blades	Bradf'd C	Date	Result	Away Blades	Bradf'd C	Final Positions Blades	Bradf'd C
1908-09	Division 1	3 October	Won	3	0	27 March	Lost	1	3	12th	18th
1909-10	Division 1	12 March	Lost	1	2	30 October	Lost	0	2	6th	7th
1910-11	Division 1	17 September	Lost	0	1	21 January	Won	1	0	9th	5th
1911-12	Division 1	4 March	Won	7	3	16 September	Lost	0	1	14th	11th
1912-13	Division 1	25 January	Won	3	2	28 September	Lost	1	3	15th	13th
1913-14	Division 1	17 January	Drew	1	1	20 September	Lost	1	2	10th	9th
1914-15	Division 1	3 October	Drew	1	1	6 February	Drew	1	1	6th	11th
1919-20	Division 1	3 April	Drew	0	0	10 April	Won	2	1	14th	15th
1920-21	Division 1	6 September	Won	4	1	30 August	Lost	0	4	20th	15th
1921-22	Division 1	29 October	Won	1	0	22 October	Drew	1	1	11th	21stR
1934-35	Division 2	10 September	Lost	1	2	27 August	Won	5	2	11th	20th
1935-36	Division 2	18 April	Won	3	0	14 December	Lost	1	2	3rd	12th
1936-37	Division 2	27 February	Won	3	1	24 October	Lost	2	3	7th	21stR
1981-82	Division 4	30 March	Drew	1	1	24 October	Won	2	0	1stP	2ndP
1982-83	Division 3	23 April	Won	2	1	8 May	Lost	0	2	11th	12th
1983-84	Division 3	27 September	Won	2	0	7 April	Lost	1	2	3rdP	7th
1985-86	Division 2	11 March	Won	3	1	26 October	Won	4	1	7th	13th
1986-87	Division 2	28 March	Drew	2	2	4 October	Drew	1	1	9th	10th
1987-88	Division 2	4 April	Lost	1	2	14 November	Lost	0	2	21stR	4th
1989-90	Division 2	18 November	Drew	1	1	3 March	Won	4	1	2ndP	23rdR
1996-97	Division 1	10 September	Won	3	0	26 December	Won	2	1	5th	21st
1997-98	Division 1	28 February	Won	2	1	18 November	Drew	1	1	6th	13th
1998-99	Division 1	19 February	Drew	2	2	12 September	Drew	2	2	8th	2ndP
2001-02	Division 1	8 September	Drew	2	2	26 December	Won	2	1	13th	15th
2002-03	Division 1	29 April	Won	3	0	23 November	Won	5	0	3rd	19th
2003-04	Division 1	20 March	Won	2	0	27 September	Won	2	1	8th	23rdR

FA Cup

										Division	
1919-20	Round 2					31 January	Lost	1	2	Div 1	Div 1

League Cup

1983-84	Round 1	13 September	Drew	1	1	29 August	Won	1	0	Div 3	Div 3
1996-97	Round 1	20 August	Won	3	0	3 September	Won	2	1	Div 1	Div 1

Summary	P	W	D	L	F	A
Blades' home league record:	26	14	8	4	54	27
Blades' away league record:	26	10	5	11	42	40
Blades' cup record:	5	3	1	1	8	4
TOTAL:	**57**	**27**	**14**	**16**	**104**	**71**

- **The Blades are unbeaten in their last 16 matches against their Yorkshire rivals.**
- **United have lost two of their last 25 home games.**
- **Only one of the 57 matches between the sides has finished goalless, and that was back in 1920.**

Blades' top scorers vs Bradford

Billy Gillespie 9
Keith Edwards 8
Jock Dodds 5
Carl Asaba, Willie Boyd, Harry Johnson 4

Blades hat-tricks vs Bradford

4 Mar 1912 Billy Gillespie (4)
6 Sep 1920 Harry Johnson
27 Aug 1934 Willie Boyd (4)

Played for both clubs

Sam Bright	Blades 1900-02	Bradford 1903-04
Billy Foulke	Blades 1894-1905	Bradford 1905-07
Pat Cassidy	Blades 1907-08	Bradford 1910-12
Mark Mellors	Blades 1907-08	Bradford 1908-14
Albert Partridge	Blades 1923-29	Bradford 1929-33
Levi Redfern	Bradford 1932-33	Blades 1935-36
Alf Jeffries	Bradford 1935-37	Blades 1939-40
Fred Smith	Blades 1947-52	Bradford 1954-55
Tommy Hoyland	Blades 1949-61	Bradford 1961-63
Derek Hawksworth	Bradford 1948-51/60-62	Blades 1950-58
Peter Wragg	Blades 1952-56	Bradford 1963-65
Max Ashmore	Blades 1957-58	Bradford 1961-62
David Staniforth	Blades 1968-74	Bradford 1979-82
Trevor Hockey	Bradford 1959-62/74-76	Blades 1970-73
Bobby Campbell	Blades 1977-78	Bradford 1979-87
Neil Ramsbottom	Blades 1979-80	Bradford 1980-83
Paul Tomlinson	Blades 1983-87	Bradford 1987-95
Steve Foley	Blades 1985-87	Bradford 1995-96
Peter Beagrie	Blades 1986-88	Bradford 1997-2001
Chris Wilder	Blades 1986-92/97-99	Bradford 1996-98
Chris Kamara	Blades 1992-94	Bradford 1994-95
Carl Muggleton	Blades 1995-96	Bradford 2001-02
Gordon Cowans	Blades 1995-96	Bradford 1996-97
Dean Saunders	Blades 1997-99	Bradford 1999-2001
Des Hamilton	Bradford 1993-97	Blades 1998-99
Aidan Davison	Bradford 1996-97/99-2003	Blades 1999-2000
Gus Uhlenbeek	Blades 2000-02	Bradford 2002-03
Stuart McCall	Bradford 1982-88/98-2002	Blades 2002-04
Laurens Ten Heuvel	Blades 2002-03	Bradford 2002-03
Dean Windass	Bradford 1998-2001/03-04	Blades 2002-03
Ashley Ward	Bradford 2000-03	Blades 2003-04
Simon Francis	Bradford 2002-04	Blades 2003-04
Andy Gray	Bradford 2002-04	Blades 2003-04

v. Bradford Park Avenue

				Home				Away		Final Positions	
Season	League	Date	Result	Blades	Bradf'd PA	Date	Result	Blades	Bradf'd PA	Blades	Bradf'd PA
1914-15	Division 1	3 April	Won	3	2	28 November	Lost	0	2	6th	9th
1919-20	Division 1	25 December	Drew	2	2	26 December	Lost	0	1	14th	11th
1920-21	Division 1	18 September	Won	2	0	11 September	Lost	0	2	20th	22ndR
1934-35	Division 2	2 March	Won	3	1	20 October	Won	3	1	11th	15th
1935-36	Division 2	4 January	Won	2	1	7 September	Drew	3	3	3rd	16th
1936-37	Division 2	9 January	Won	3	0	12 September	Won	3	0	7th	20th
1937-38	Division 2	20 November	Won	3	1	2 April	Lost	1	5	3rd	7th
1938-39	Division 2	10 December	Won	3	1	15 April	Won	3	0	2ndP	17th
1949-50	Division 2	22 October	Won	2	1	11 March	Drew	1	1	3rd	22ndR

FA Cup										Division	
1913-14	Round 2	31 January	Won	3	1					Div 1	Div 2
1914-15	Round 3	20 February	Won*	1	0					Div 1	Div 1

Summary	P	W	D	L	F	A
Blades' home league record:	9	8	1	0	23	9
Blades' away league record:	9	3	2	4	14	15
Blades' cup record:	2	2	0	0	4	1
TOTAL:	**20**	**13**	**3**	**4**	**41**	**25**

FACT FILE

- **United are unbeaten in their 11 home matches against Park Avenue.**
- **United have lost one of their last 13 in the series.**

Blades' top scorers vs Bradford PA

Jock Dodds 8

Jack Pickering 6

Played for both clubs

Harold Gough	Bradford PA 1910-11	Blades 1913-24	
Martin Johnson	Bradford PA 1925-27	Blades 1927-28	
Peter Spooner	Bradford PA 1930-31	Blades 1933-35	
George Henson	Bradford PA 1937-39	Blades 1938-40	
Andy McLaren	Blades 1948-51	Bradford PA 1954-55	
Pat Keating	Blades 1950-51	Bradford PA 1953-54	
Walter Hughes	Blades 1955-56	Bradford PA 1956-58	

v. Brentford

Season	League	Date	Result	Blades	Brentf'd	Date	Result	Blades	Brentf'd	Blades	Brentf'd
				Home				**Away**		*Final Positions*	
1934-35	Division 2	22 December	Lost	1	2	4 May	Lost	1	3	11th	1stP
1946-47	Division 1	25 December	Won	6	1	26 December	Lost	1	2	6th	21stR
1949-50	Division 2	3 December	Drew	1	1	8 April	Lost	0	1	3rd	9th
1950-51	Division 2	26 March	Won	5	1	23 March	Lost	1	3	8th	9th
1951-52	Division 2	5 April	Lost	1	4	17 November	Lost	1	4	11th	10th
1952-53	Division 2	8 September	Won	3	2	17 September	Drew	0	0	1stP	17th
1979-80	Division 3	6 November	Lost	0	2	22 October	Won	2	1	12th	19th
1980-81	Division 3	27 December	Drew	0	0	18 April	Drew	1	1	21stR	9th
1982-83	Division 3	27 November	Lost	1	2	30 April	Lost	1	2	11th	9th
1983-84	Division 3	22 October	Drew	0	0	25 February	Won	3	1	3rdP	20th
1988-89	Division 3	22 April	Drew	2	2	24 September	Won	4	1	2ndP	7th

League Cup

										Division	
1962-63	Round 2					26 September	Won	4	1	Div 1	Div 4

Summary

	P	W	D	L	F	A
Blades' home league record:	11	3	4	4	20	17
Blades' away league record:	11	3	2	6	15	19
Blades' cup record:	1	1	0	0	4	1
TOTAL:	23	7	6	10	39	37

FACT FILE

- **United have not won in their last five home games against Brentford; their last home win was in 1952.**

Jean-Philippe Javary.

Blades' top scorers vs Brentford
Jimmy Hagan 5
Tony Agana 3

Played for both clubs

Bobby Hughes	Blades 1922-23	Brentford 1923-24
Bobby Reid	Brentford 1935-39	Blades 1938-47
Alec Blakeman	Brentford 1946-49	Blades 1948-49
Jack Chisholm	Brentford 1947-49	Blades 1948-50
John Docherty	Brentford 1960-61/65-68/70-74	Blades 1960-66
Ian Benjamin	Blades 1978-80	Brentford 1993-95
Stewart Houston	Brentford 1971-74	Blades 1980-83
Glenn Cockerill	Blades 1983-86	Brentford 1997-98
Richard Cadette	Blades 1987-88	Brentford 1988-92
Graham Benstead	Blades 1987-89	Brentford 1990-94/97-98
Francis Joseph	Brentford 1982-87	Blades 1988-89
Bob Booker	Brentford 1978-80/91-93	Blades 1988-92
Wilf Rostron	Blades 1989-91	Brentford 1990-93
Chris Kamara	Brentford 1981-85	Blades 1992-94
Andy Scott	Blades 1992-98	Brentford 1997-2001
Scott Marshall	Blades 1994-95	Brentford 1999-2003
Scott Fitzgerald	Blades 1995-96	Brentford 2003-04
Marcus Bent	Brentford 1995-98	Blades 1999-2001
Carl Asaba	Brentford 1995-97	Blades 2000-03
Jean-Philippe Javary	Brentford 2000-01	Blades 2001-03

Carl Asaba.

Season	League	Date	Result	Blades	B &HA	Date	Result	Blades	B & HA	Blades	B & HA
			Home				**Away**			*Final Positions*	
1958-59	Division 2	31 March	Won	3	1	30 March	Lost	0	2	3rd	12th
1959-60	Division 2	19 March	Won	4	1	28 November	Won	2	0	4th	14th
1960-61	Division 2	22 October	Won	2	1	11 March	Drew	0	0	2ndP	16th
1977-78	Division 2	4 April	Won	2	0	24 September	Lost	1	2	12th	4th
1978-79	Division 2	4 November	Lost	0	1	17 March	Lost	0	2	20thR	2ndP
1984-85	Division 2	15 December	Drew	1	1	11 May	Lost	0	1	18th	6th
1985-86	Division 2	1 February	Won	3	0	27 August	Drew	0	0	7th	11th
1986-87	Division 2	29 November	Lost	0	1	2 May	Lost	0	2	9th	22ndR
1989-90	Division 2	9 September	Won	5	4	14 March	Drew	2	2	2ndP	18th
2002-03	Division 1	18 March	Won	2	1	19 October	Won	4	2	3rd	23rdR

FA Cup

										Division	
1921-22	Round 1					7 January	Lost	0	1	Div 1	Div 3S
1986-87	Round 3	10 January	Drew	0	0	21 January	Won	2	1	Div 2	Div 2

Summary

	P	W	D	L	F	A
Blades' home league record:	10	7	1	2	22	11
Blades' away league record:	10	2	3	5	9	13
Blades' cup record:	3	1	1	1	2	2
TOTAL:	**23**	**10**	**5**	**8**	**33**	**26**

FACT FILE

- United failed to win in seven away matches from 1961 to 1990.
- The Blades are unbeaten in their last four matches.

Action from a Blades-Seagulls encounter.

Blades' top scorers vs Brighton
Kevin Lewis 4
Carl Asaba 3

Blades hat-tricks vs Brighton
19 Oct 2002 Carl Asaba

Played for both clubs

Fred Hawley	Blades 1912-15	Brighton 1925-26
Fred Brown	Blades 1919-23	Brighton 1923-24
Stan Mace	Blades 1926-27	Brighton 1927-28
Jack Harrison	Blades 1930-31	Brighton 1932-34
Maurice McLafferty	Blades 1951-52	Brighton 1952-53
Wally Gould	Blades 1958-59	Brighton 1963-68
Barry Butlin	Brighton 1975-76	Blades 1979-81
Mike Trusson	Blades 1980-84	Brighton 1987-89
Tony Towner	Brighton 1972-79	Blades 1982-83
Alan Young	Blades 1982-83	Brighton 1983-84
Ray McHale	Brighton 1980-81	Blades 1982-85
Dennis Mortimer	Blades 1984-85	Brighton 1985-86
Andy Kennedy	Blades 1986-87	Brighton 1992-94
Chris Wilder	Blades 1986-92/97-99	Brighton 1999-2000
Darren Carr	Blades 1987-89	Brighton 1999-2001
Mark Morris	Blades 1989-91	Brighton 1996-98
Paul Wood	Brighton 1987-90	Blades 1989-92
Paul Rogers	Blades 1991-96	Brighton 1999-2003
Dean Saunders	Brighton 1985-87	Blades 1997-99

Mike Trusson gave United
good service and later
played for Brighton.

v. Bristol City

				Home				Away		Final Positions	
Season	League	Date	Result	Blades	Bristol C	Date	Result	Blades	Bristol C	Blades	Bristol C
1906-07	Division 1	31 December	Drew	1	1	24 December	Drew	3	3	4th	2nd
1907-08	Division 1	14 March	Won	2	0	16 November	Lost	2	3	17th	10th
1908-09	Division 1	5 April	Won	3	1	21 November	Drew	1	1	12th	8th
1909-10	Division 1	26 March	Won	4	0	13 November	Won	2	0	6th	16th
1910-11	Division 1	29 October	Lost	0	4	4 March	Won	2	0	9th	19thR
1956-57	Division 2	15 September	Drew	1	1	19 January	Lost	1	5	7th	13th
1957-58	Division 2	16 November	Lost	0	3	29 March	Won	4	1	6th	17th
1958-59	Division 2	30 August	Won	4	0	3 January	Lost	1	3	3rd	10th
1959-60	Division 2	19 September	Won	5	2	6 February	Drew	2	2	4th	22ndR
1968-69	Division 2	8 March	Won	2	1	17 August	Drew	1	1	9th	16th
1969-70	Division 2	26 August	Won	2	1	4 April	Won	1	0	6th	14th
1970-71	Division 2	5 September	Drew	3	3	27 March	Won	1	0	2ndP	19th
1988-89	Division 3	26 November	Won	3	0	13 May	Lost	0	2	2ndP	11th
1994-95	Division 1	5 November	Won	3	0	21 January	Lost	1	2	8th	23rdR
1998-99	Division 1	1 May	Won	3	1	5 December	Lost	0	2	8th	24thR

Division 2/3 Play-offs

										Final positions	
1987-88	Semi-Final	18 May	Drew	1	1	15 May	Lost	0	1	22ndR(D2)5th(D3)	

FA Cup

										Division	
1903-04	Round 1					6 February	Won	3	1	Div 1	Div 2
1964-65	Round 3	11 January	Won	3	0	9 January	Drew	1	1	Div 1	Div 3
1974-75	Round 3	4 January	Won	2	0					Div 1	Div 2

League Cup

										Division	
1986-87	Round 2	7 October	Won	3	0	23 September	Drew	2	2	Div 2	Div 3
1992-93	Round 2	7 October	Won	4	1	22 September	Lost	1	2	Prem	Div 1

Summary

	P	W	D	L	F	A
Blades' home league record:	15	10	3	2	36	18
Blades' away league record:	15	5	4	6	22	25
Blades' cup record:	10	5	3	2	20	9
TOTAL:	**40**	**20**	**10**	**10**	**78**	**52**

Blades' top scorers vs Bristol City
Billy Russell 5
Brian Deane 4
Mick Jones, Joe Kitchen, Colin Morris,
Derek Pace, Jimmy Simmons, John Tudor 3

Blades hat-tricks vs Bristol City
29 Mar 1958 Billy Russell

FACT FILE

- The last eight matches between the sides have all resulted in home wins.
- United are unbeaten in their last 13 home matches, winning 11 of these.
- United have won all five cup ties.
- In the first two seasons of play-offs (1986-88), the four participating teams were not, as is currently the case, the four teams who most narrowly missed automatic promotion. The participants were instead the three teams who most narrowly missed automatic promotion, and the team from the higher division who most narrowly avoided automatic relegation. In 1988, Sheffield United thus had to enter the play-offs to retain their place in Division Two, but lost to Bristol City.

Played for both clubs

Harry Thickett	Blades 1893-1904	Bristol C 1904-05
Walter Bennett	Blades 1895-1905	Bristol C 1904-07
Archie Annan	Blades 1903-05	Bristol C 1905-10
Billy Batty	Blades 1907-10	Bristol C 1909-11
Fred Hawley	Blades 1912-15	Bristol C 1922-25
Jack Thompson	Blades 1914-21	Bristol C 1920-22
Arthur Stevenson	Blades 1924-28	Bristol C 1930-31
Arthur Mercer	Blades 1926-28	Bristol C 1930-32
Len Birks	Blades 1924-31	Bristol C 1933-34
Bertie Williams	Bristol C 1927-32	Blades 1931-37
George Hall	Blades 1932-35	Bristol C 1937-39
Jack Dryden	Blades 1935-36	Bristol C 1936-38
Gary Hamson	Blades 1976-79	Bristol C 1986-87
John McPhail	Blades 1978-83	Bristol C 1986-87
Steve Neville	Blades 1980-82	Bristol C 1984-88
Keith Waugh	Blades 1981-85	Bristol C 1984-89
Martin Kuhl	Blades 1986-88	Bristol C 1994-97
Andy Leaning	Blades 1987-88	Bristol C 1988-93
Phil Kite	Blades 1990-92	Bristol C 1994-96
Jamie Hoyland	Blades 1990-95	Bristol C 1993-94
Alan McLeary	Blades 1992-93	Bristol C 1995-97
Billy Mercer	Blades 1994-96	Bristol C 1999-2000
Phil Starbuck	Blades 1994-97	Bristol C 1995-98
Paul Holland	Blades 1995-96	Bristol C 1999-2001
Keith Curle	Bristol C 1983-88	Blades 2000-02
Wayne Allison	Bristol C 1990-95	Blades 2002-04

v. Bristol Rovers

Season	League	Date	Result	Home Blades	Bristol R	Date	Result	Away Blades	Bristol R	Final Positions Blades	Bristol R
1956-57	Division 2	16 February	Drew	0	0	6 October	Lost	1	3	7th	9th
1957-58	Division 2	7 September	Won	2	0	11 January	Drew	2	2	6th	10th
1958-59	Division 2	20 April	Won	5	2	13 December	Drew	1	1	3rd	6th
1959-60	Division 2	2 April	Drew	1	1	14 November	Lost	2	3	4th	9th
1960-61	Division 2	3 December	Lost	2	3	22 April	Lost	1	3	2ndP	17th
1976-77	Division 2	18 December	Lost	2	3	14 May	Lost	1	3	11th	15th
1977-78	Division 2	26 November	Drew	1	1	8 April	Lost	1	4	12th	18th
1978-79	Division 2	31 March	Won	1	0	25 November	Lost	1	2	20thR	16th
1982-83	Division 3	2 May	Won	2	1	29 March	Lost	1	2	11th	7th
1983-84	Division 3	14 April	Won	4	0	3 December	Drew	1	1	3rdP	5th
1988-89	Division 3	3 September	Won	4	1	14 January	Drew	1	1	2ndP	5th

Summary	P	W	D	L	F	A
Blades' home league record:	11	6	3	2	24	12
Blades' away league record:	11	0	4	7	13	25
TOTAL:	**22**	**6**	**7**	**9**	**37**	**37**

FACT FILE

- **United have not won in their 11 away matches.**
- **United failed to win in nine matches (1959-78).**
- **Neither side has failed to score in any of Rovers' 11 home matches.**

Blades' top scorers vs Rovers
Billy Russell 4
Keith Edwards, Bill Hodgson 3

Played for both clubs

Jack Ball	Blades 1919-21	Bristol R 1921-22
Sam Furniss	Blades 1920-21	Bristol R 1921-24
David Staniforth	Blades 1968-74	Bristol R 1973-79
Tom McAlister	Blades 1971-76	Bristol R 1980-81
Alan Warboys	Blades 1972-73	Bristol R 1972-77
Darren Carr	Bristol R 1985-88	Blades 1987-89
Francis Joseph	Bristol R 1987-88	Blades 1988-89
Phil Kite	Bristol R 1980-84	Blades 1990-92
Brian Gayle	Blades 1991-96	Bristol R 1996-98
Mark Foran	Blades 1994-96	Bristol R 2000-02
Gareth Taylor	Bristol R 1991-96	Blades 1995-99
David Lee	Blades 1997-98	Bristol R 1998-99
James Thomas	Blades 2000-01	Bristol R 2001-02
Keith Curle	Bristol R 1981-83	Blades 2000-02
Steve Yates	Bristol R 1986-94	Blades 2002-03

v. Burnley

		Home					Away			Final Positions	
Season	League	Date	Result	Blades	Burnley	Date	Result	Blades	Burnley	Blades	Burnley
1893-94	Division 1	26 March	Won	1	0	25 December	Lost	1	4	10th	5th
1894-95	Division 1	15 September	Drew	2	2	22 December	Won	4	2	6th	9th
1895-96	Division 1	30 March	Drew	1	1	3 February	Lost	0	5	12th	10th
1896-97	Division 1	5 September	Won	1	0	16 January	Drew	1	1	2nd	16thR
1898-99	Division 1	1 October	Drew	1	1	31 March	Lost	0	1	16th	3rd
1899-00	Division 1	11 November	Drew	0	0	23 April	Lost	0	1	2nd	17thR
1913-14	Division 1	4 April	Won	5	0	29 November	Drew	0	0	10th	12th
1914-15	Division 1	13 February	Won	1	0	10 October	Won	2	1	6th	4th
1919-20	Division 1	18 October	Lost	1	3	11 October	Drew	2	2	14th	2nd
1920-21	Division 1	27 December	Drew	1	1	25 December	Lost	0	6	20th	1st
1921-22	Division 1	15 October	Lost	0	1	8 October	Lost	1	2	11th	3rd
1922-23	Division 1	30 December	Won	2	1	6 January	Won	4	1	10th	15th
1923-24	Division 1	20 October	Won	2	1	27 October	Lost	0	2	5th	17th
1924-25	Division 1	6 April	Won	4	0	1 November	Drew	1	1	14th	19th
1925-26	Division 1	19 April	Won	6	1	14 November	Drew	1	1	5th	20th
1926-27	Division 1	2 October	Drew	2	2	29 March	Won	5	2	8th	5th
1927-28	Division 1	10 September	Won	5	2	21 January	Lost	3	5	13th	19th
1928-29	Division 1	19 January	Won	10	0	8 September	Lost	1	2	11th	19th
1929-30	Division 1	22 February	Won	3	1	19 October	Lost	0	5	20th	21stR
1934-35	Division 2	15 September	Drew	0	0	28 January	Won	2	0	11th	12th
1935-36	Division 2	9 November	Won	2	0	14 March	Drew	1	1	3rd	15th
1936-37	Division 2	24 April	Drew	1	1	19 December	Lost	0	1	7th	13th
1937-38	Division 2	20 September	Won	2	1	13 September	Lost	0	2	3rd	6th
1938-39	Division 2	2 January	Drew	1	1	7 April	Won	3	2	2ndP	14th
1947-48	Division 1	4 October	Drew	1	1	21 February	Drew	0	0	12th	3rd
1948-49	Division 1	23 April	Drew	0	0	30 October	Lost	0	2	22ndR	15th
1953-54	Division 1	27 March	Won	2	1	7 November	Lost	1	2	20th	7th
1954-55	Division 1	19 February	Won	1	0	2 October	Lost	1	2	13th	10th
1955-56	Division 1	1 October	Lost	1	2	11 February	Drew	1	1	22ndR	7th
1961-62	Division 1	21 April	Won	2	0	2 December	Lost	2	4	5th	2nd
1962-63	Division 1	2 March	Won	1	0	13 October	Lost	1	5	10th	3rd
1963-64	Division 1	7 March	Won	2	0	26 October	Won	2	1	12th	9th
1964-65	Division 1	29 August	Won	2	0	19 December	Lost	1	3	19th	12th
1965-66	Division 1	15 January	Won	2	1	23 October	Lost	0	2	9th	3rd
1966-67	Division 1	17 December	Drew	1	1	20 August	Lost	0	4	10th	14th
1967-68	Division 1	9 December	Won	1	0	4 May	Won	2	0	21stR	14th
1973-74	Division 1	25 August	Lost	0	2	19 January	Won	2	1	13th	6th
1974-75	Division 1	16 November	Drew	2	2	22 February	Lost	1	2	6th	10th
1975-76	Division 1	23 September	Won	2	1	24 February	Lost	1	3	22ndR	21stR
1976-77	Division 2	2 October	Won	1	0	12 March	Lost	0	1	11th	16th
1977-78	Division 2	15 October	Won	2	1	11 March	Lost	1	4	12th	11th
1978-79	Division 2	16 September	Won	4	0	6 March	Drew	1	1	20thR	13th
1980-81	Division 3	4 November	Drew	0	0	7 October	Lost	2	3	21stR	8th
1983-84	Division 3	21 January	Drew	0	0	8 November	Lost	1	2	3rdP	12th

			Home				Away			Final Positions	
Season	League	Date	Result	Blades	Burnley	Date	Result	Blades	Burnley	Blades	Burnley
1994-95	Division 1	21 February	Won	2	0	20 November	Lost	2	4	8th	22ndR
2000-01	Division 1	28 April	Won	2	0	11 November	Lost	0	2	10th	7th
2001-02	Division 1	23 March	Won	3	0	4 November	Lost	0	2	13th	7th
2002-03	Division 1	12 March	Won	4	2	24 August	Won	1	0	3rd	16th
2003-04	Division 1	8 November	Won	1	0	6 December	Lost	2	3	8th	19th

FA Cup

										Division	
1889-90	Round 1	18 January	Won	2	1					Non L	Div 1
1898-99	Round 1	2 February	Won	2	1	28 January	Drew	2	2	Div 1	Div 1
1913-14	Semi-Final	28 March		Old Trafford			Drew	0	0	Div 1	Div 1
		1 April		Goodison Park			Lost	0	1		
1928-29	Round 3					12 January	Lost	1	2	Div 1	Div 1
1932-33	Round 4					28 January	Lost	1	3	Div 1	Div 2
1935-36	Round 3	16 January	Won	2	1	11 January	Drew	0	0	Div 2	Div 2
1961-62	Q'ter Final	10 March	Lost	0	1					Div 1	Div 1
1992-93	Round 3	2 January	Drew	2	2	12 January	Won	4	2	Prem	Div 2

League Cup

1966-67	Round 3	5 October	Won	2	0					Div 1	Div 1

Summary

	P	W	D	L	F	A
Blades' home league record:	49	30	15	4	93	34
Blades' away league record:	49	10	9	30	57	104
Blades' cup record:	13	5	4	4	18	16
TOTAL:	**111**	**45**	**28**	**38**	**168**	**154**

Peter Ndlovu tussles for possession with Burnley's Mohammed Camara.

FACT FILE

- **The match in January 1929 was the last in which the Blades reached double figures.**
- **United are unbeaten in their last 13 home games.**
- **From 1922 to 1967, United lost once in 25 home league games.**
- **United lost 10 and drew one of their away league games between 1975 and 2001.**
- **United have kept seven clean sheets in their last eight home games.**

Blades' top scorers vs Burnley

Harry Johnson 15
Billy Gillsepie, Fred Tunstall 9
Stan Fazackerley 6
Alan Woodward 4
Bobby Barclay, Brian Deane, Jock Dodds,
Harry Hammond, Mick Jones, Joe Kitchen,
Peter Ndlovu, Jimmy Shankly, Ron Simpson 3

Blades hat-tricks vs Burnley

6 Jan 1923 Harry Johnson
29 Mar 1927 Jimmy Shankly
10 Sep 1927 Harry Johnson
19 Jan 1929 Harry Johnson (4)
12 Jan 1993 Brian Deane (cup)

Played for both clubs

William Egan	Burnley 1893-95	Blades 1895-96
Jack Dryden	Blades 1935-36	Burnley 1938-40
Andy McLaren	Burnley 1948-49	Blades 1948-51
Des Thompson	Burnley 1952-55	Blades 1955-64
Colin Morris	Burnley 1974-76	Blades 1981-88
Tony Philliskirk	Blades 1983-88	Burnley 1993-96
Roger Hansbury	Burnley 1983-85	Blades 1987-88
John Francis	Blades 1988-90	Burnley 1989-96
Jamie Hoyland	Blades 1990-95	Burnley 1994-98
Nathan Peel	Blades 1991-92	Burnley 1993-95
Tom Cowan	Blades 1991-94	Burnley 1998-2000
Doug Hodgson	Blades 1994-97	Burnley 1996-97
Adrian Heath	Burnley 1992-97	Blades 1995-96
Gordon Cowans	Blades 1995-96	Burnley 1997-98
Gareth Taylor	Blades 1995-99	Burnley 2000-03
Paul Shaw	Burnley 1994-95	Blades 2003-04

v. Burscough

FA Cup		Date	Result	Home Blades Burscough						Division Blades Burscough
1979-80	Round 1	24 November	Won	**3**	**0**					Div 3 Non L

Summary	P	W	D	L	F	A
Blades' cup record:	1	1	0	0	3	0
TOTAL:	**1**	**1**	**0**	**0**	**3**	**0**

v. Burton Swifts

			Home					Away		Final Positions	
Season	League	Date	Result	Blades	Burton S	Date	Result	Blades	Burton S	Blades	Burton S
1892-93	Division 2	6 February	Won	3	1	1 April	Won	3	0	2ndP	6th

Summary	P	W	D	L	F	A
Blades' home league record:	1	1	0	0	3	1
Blades' away league record:	1	1	0	0	3	0
TOTAL:	2	2	0	0	6	1

FACT FILE

- On 25 October 1890, the sides met in the second qualifying round of the FA Cup. Swifts won 2-1, but it was discovered that they had used an unregistered player, and they were disqualified. United took their place in the next round.

Blades' top scorers vs Swifts

Hugh Gallacher, Robert Hill 2

v. Burton Wanderers

		Home						**Away**		*Division*	
FA Cup	*Date*	*Result*	Blades	Buron W	*Date*	*Result*	Blades	Burton W	Blades	Burton W
1895-96 Round 1	6 February	Won	**1**	**0**	1 February	Drew	**1**	**1**	Div 1	Div 2

Summary	P	W	D	L	F	A
Blades' cup record:	2	1	1	0	2	1
TOTAL:	2	1	1	0	2	1

Blades' top scorers vs Wanderers
Ernest Needham 2

Ernest Needham.

v. Bury

Season	League	Date	Result	Blades	Bury	Date	Result	Blades	Bury	Blades	Bury
				Home				**Away**		*Final Positions*	
1895-96	Division 1	6 April	Won	**8**	**0**	21 September	Lost	0	1	12th	11th
1896-97	Division 1	21 November	Drew	**2**	**2**	20 March	Won	1	0	2nd	9th
1897-98	Division 1	25 September	Drew	**1**	**1**	9 October	Won	5	2	1st	14th
1898-99	Division 1	4 February	Won	**4**	**1**	8 October	Won	3	1	16th	10th
1899-00	Division 1	23 September	Won	**4**	**0**	20 January	Lost	1	2	2nd	12th
1900-01	Division 1	1 September	Lost	**0**	**3**	29 December	Drew	1	1	14th	5th
1901-02	Division 1	14 September	Won	**3**	**1**	11 January	Won	2	1	10th	7th
1902-03	Division 1	6 September	Won	**1**	**0**	3 January	Lost	1	3	4th	8th
1903-04	Division 1	19 March	Drew	**0**	**0**	21 November	Won	1	0	7th	12th
1904-05	Division 1	11 March	Won	**4**	**0**	12 November	Lost	1	7	6th	17th
1905-06	Division 1	17 March	Drew	**1**	**1**	11 November	Won	5	2	13th	17th
1906-07	Division 1	10 November	Won	**3**	**0**	16 March	Lost	1	2	4th	16th
1907-08	Division 1	11 April	Lost	**0**	**2**	14 December	Lost	2	3	17th	7th
1908-09	Division 1	1 March	Drew	**2**	**2**	1 September	Won	2	1	12th	17th
1909-10	Division 1	20 November	Won	**2**	**0**	2 April	Lost	0	2	6th	13th
1910-11	Division 1	24 December	Won	**3**	**0**	29 April	Drew	1	1	9th	18th
1911-12	Division 1	16 March	Won	**4**	**0**	20 February	Lost	1	3	14th	20thR
1924-25	Division 1	7 February	Lost	**0**	**1**	4 October	Lost	0	1	14th	5th
1925-26	Division 1	6 February	Won	**3**	**1**	26 September	Lost	4	7	5th	4th
1926-27	Division 1	5 May	Won	**2**	**0**	11 December	Drew	4	4	8th	19th
1927-28	Division 1	12 March	Won	**3**	**1**	17 September	Lost	0	1	13th	5th
1928-29	Division 1	9 February	Won	**6**	**1**	29 September	Lost	0	4	11th	21stR
1934-35	Division 2	13 April	Won	**5**	**3**	1 December	Lost	1	3	11th	10th
1935-36	Division 2	2 September	Won	**3**	**0**	9 September	Lost	2	3	3rd	14th
1936-37	Division 2	25 December	Won	**1**	**0**	28 December	Lost	0	2	7th	3rd
1937-38	Division 2	6 September	Won	**2**	**1**	30 August	Lost	0	1	3rd	10th
1938-39	Division 2	8 April	Drew	**1**	**1**	3 December	Drew	2	2	2ndP	16th
1949-50	Division 2	5 November	Drew	**4**	**4**	25 March	Won	5	1	3rd	18th

Blades' 'keeper Paddy Kenny, who arrived at United from Gigg Lane.

				Home				Away		Final Positions	
Season	League	Date	Result	Blades	Bury	Date	Result	Blades	Bury	Blades	Bury
1950-51	Division 2	21 October	Won	3	0	10 March	Drew	1	1	8th	20th
1951-52	Division 2	10 September	Won	1	0	1 January	Lost	0	1	11th	17th
1952-53	Division 2	21 March	Won	3	1	1 November	Won	4	0	1stP	20th
1956-57	Division 2	10 November	Drew	1	1	23 March	Won	1	0	7th	21stR
1968-69	Division 2	1 February	Won	5	0	16 November	Won	2	0	9th	21stR
1979-80	Division 3	1 March	Drew	0	0	20 October	Won	2	1	12th	21stR
1981-82	Division 4	10 April	Drew	1	1	27 April	Drew	1	1	1stP	9th
1988-89	Division 3	29 October	Won	2	1	14 March	Won	2	1	2ndP	13th
1997-98	Division 1	18 April	Won	3	0	20 December	Drew	1	1	6th	17th
1998-99	Division 1	14 November	Won	3	1	11 December	Drew	3	3	8th	22ndR

FA Cup

				Home				Away		Division	
1899-00	Q'ter Final	24 February	Drew	2	2	1 March	Lost	0	2	Div 1	Div 1
1902-03	Round 2	21 February	Lost	0	1					Div 1	Div 1
1903-04	Round 2					20 February	Won	2	1	Div 1	Div 1
1931-32	Round 4					23 January	Lost	1	3	Div 1	Div 2
1961-62	Round 3	10 January	Drew*	2	2	6 January	Drew	0	0	Div 1	Div 2
		15 January		Hillsborough (replay)			Won	2	0		
1997-98	Round 3	3 January	Drew	1	1	13 January	Won	2	1	Div 1	Div 1

League Cup

				Home				Away		Division	
1960-61	Round 2					11 October	Lost	1	3	Div 2	Div 3
1962-63	Round 3					23 October	Lost	1	3	Div 1	Div 2
1987-88	Round 2	7 October	Drew	1	1	22 September	Lost	1	2	Div 2	Div 3
1995-96	Round 2	20 September	Won	2	1	3 October	Lost	2	4	Div 1	Div 3

Summary	P	W	D	L	F	A
Blades' home league record:	38	25	10	3	94	31
Blades' away league record:	38	13	8	17	63	70
Blades' cup record:	16	4	5	7	20	27
TOTAL:	**92**	**42**	**23**	**27**	**177**	**128**

FACT FILE

- On 20 January 1900, defeat at Bury was United's first of the season, and came in their 23rd game. Despite losing only three more league games, United were beaten to the title by Aston Villa, while Bury also knocked them out of the FA Cup.
- United's first-ever league cup match ended in defeat to Bury in 1960.
- The Blades are unbeaten in their last 24 home games; their last defeat was in 1925.
- The Blades are unbeaten in their last 16 league matches since defeat in 1952, but they have lost four League Cup matches since.
- From 1927 to 1937, 14 consecutive games ended in home wins.

Blades' top scorers vs Bury

Arthur Brown 9
George Hedley 8
Harry Johnson 7
Walter Bennett 6
Jock Dodds, Harry Hammond, Ernest Needham
Fred Priest, John Tudor 5

Blades hat-tricks vs Bury

6 Apr 1896 William Egan
6 Apr 1896 Harry Hammond (4)
10 Nov 1906 Arthur Brown
24 Dec 1910 Jimmy Simmons
9 Feb 1929 Harry Johnson (4)
25 Mar 1950 Fred Smith
1 Feb 1969 John Tudor
14 Nov 1998 Petr Katchouro

Played for both clubs

William Fleming	Blades 1893-94	Bury 1895-96
Billy Hendry	Blades 1892-95	Bury 1896-97
John Docherty	Blades 1894-96	Bury 1895-96
Billy Peake	Blades 1909-12	Bury 1912-22
Edward Connor	Blades 1911-12	Bury 1912-15
Jack Ball	Blades 1919-21	Bury 1923-29
Arthur Mercer	Bury 1925-26	Blades 1926-28
Arthur Eggleston	Bury 1930-35	Blades 1937-39
Bobby Reid	Blades 1938-47	Bury 1946-47
Harry Hitchen	Blades 1948-53	Bury 1953-54
Eddie Colquhoun	Bury 1963-67	Blades 1968-78
Neil Ramsbottom	Bury 1965-71	Blades 1979-80
Terry Curran	Bury 1977-78	Blades 1982-83
Trevor Ross	Blades 1982-84	Bury 1984-87
Ray McHale	Bury 1982-83	Blades 1982-85
Jamie Hoyland	Bury 1986-90	Blades 1990-95
Adrian Littlejohn	Blades 1991-95/2001-02	Bury 1998-2001
Andy Scott	Blades 1992-98	Bury 1996-97
Tony Battersby	Blades 1995-96	Bury 1996-98
Mark Patterson	Bury 1989-91/97-99	Blades 1995-98
Andy Woodward	Bury 1994-2000	Blades 1999-2000
Paul Hall	Bury 1998-99	Blades 1999-2000
Laurent D'Jaffo	Bury 1998-99	Blades 1999-2002
John Newby	Blades 2000-01	Bury 2000-03
Darren Bullock	Bury 1998-2002	Blades 2000-01
Paddy Kenny	Bury 1999-2002	Blades 2002-04
Gary Kelly	Bury 1989-96	Blades 2002-03
Andy Gray	Bury 1997-98	Blades 2003-04
Chris Armstrong	Bury 2000-02	Blades 2003-04

v. Cambridge United

				Home				Away		Final Positions	
Season	League	Date	Result	Blades	Cambridge	Date	Result	Blades	Cambridge	Blades	Cambridge
1978-79	Division 2	30 December	Drew	3	3	5 May	Lost	0	1	20thR	12th

Summary	P	W	D	L	F	A
Blades' home league record:	1	0	1	0	3	3
Blades' away league record:	1	0	0	1	0	1
TOTAL:	2	0	1	1	3	4

Blades' top scorers vs Cambridge
Imre Varadi 2

Played for both clubs
Ian Benjamin	Blades 1978-80	Cambridge 1987-88
John Ryan	Blades 1980-82	Cambridge 1984-85
Gary Brazil	Blades 1980-85	Cambridge 1996-97
Keith Waugh	Blades 1981-85	Cambridge 1984-85
Tony Towner	Blades 1982-83	Cambridge 1985-87
Roger Hansbury	Cambridge 1977-78/85-86	Blades 1987-88
John Francis	Blades 1988-90	Cambridge 1992-93
Andy Sayer	Cambridge 1987-88	Blades 1990-91
Tom Cowan	Blades 1991-94	Cambridge 1999-2002
Ian Hamilton	Cambridge 1987-89	Blades 1997-2000
Jonathan Hunt	Blades 1998-2000	Cambridge 1999-2000
Jody Craddock	Cambridge 1993-97	Blades 1999-2000
Stuart Wilson	Blades 1999-2000	Cambridge 2000-01

Jody Craddock, who played for
Cambridge in the mid-1990s.

v. Cardiff City

		Home				Away		Final Positions	
Season	League	Date	Result (Blades / Cardiff)	Date	Result (Blades / Cardiff)	Blades	Cardiff
1921-22	Division 1	11 March	Lost 0 2	26 April	Drew 1 1	11th	4th
1922-23	Division 1	21 April	Drew 0 0	14 April	Lost 0 1	10th	9th
1923-24	Division 1	25 December	Drew 1 1	26 December	Lost 1 3	5th	2nd
1924-25	Division 1	8 September	Won 1 0	1 September	Drew 1 1	14th	11th
1925-26	Division 1	1 January	Won 11 2	5 April	Won 1 0	5th	16th
1926-27	Division 1	26 February	Won 3 1	9 October	Lost 0 3	8th	14th
1927-28	Division 1	26 November	Lost 3 4	7 April	Drew 2 2	13th	6th
1928-29	Division 1	15 September	Won 3 1	26 January	Drew 0 0	11th	22ndR
1949-50	Division 2	19 November	Won 2 0	22 April	Won 2 1	3rd	10th
1950-51	Division 2	14 April	Lost 1 2	25 November	Lost 0 2	8th	3rd
1951-52	Division 2	12 March	Won 6 1	17 September	Drew 1 1	11th	2ndP
1953-54	Division 1	7 September	Lost 0 1	16 September	Lost 0 2	20th	10th
1954-55	Division 1	13 September	Lost 1 3	8 September	Drew 1 1	13th	20th
1955-56	Division 1	21 January	Won 2 1	17 September	Lost 2 3	22ndR	17th
1957-58	Division 2	22 February	Won 3 0	23 November	Drew 0 0	6th	15th
1958-59	Division 2	27 April	Drew 1 1	6 September	Lost 1 3	3rd	9th
1959-60	Division 2	28 December	Won 2 1	26 December	Lost 0 2	4th	2ndP
1961-62	Division 1	28 August	Won 1 0	23 August	Drew 1 1	5th	21stR
1968-69	Division 2	11 March	Drew 2 2	30 November	Lost 1 4	9th	5th
1969-70	Division 2	20 September	Won 1 0	10 January	Lost 0 3	6th	7th
1970-71	Division 2	27 April	Won 5 1	2 September	Drew 1 1	2ndP	3rd
1976-77	Division 2	8 March	Won 3 0	30 October	Won 2 0	11th	18th
1977-78	Division 2	29 April	Lost 0 1	3 December	Won 6 1	12th	19th
1978-79	Division 2	16 December	Won 2 1	21 April	Lost 0 4	20thR	9th
1982-83	Division 3	5 February	Won 2 0	25 September	Lost 0 2	11th	2ndP
1984-85	Division 2	1 September	Won 2 1	22 December	Won 3 1	18th	21stR
1988-89	Division 3	11 April	Lost 0 1	11 February	Drew 0 0	2ndP	16th
2003-04	Division 1	20 September	Won 5 3	27 March	Lost 1 2	8th	13th

FA Cup

							Division	
1924-25	Final	25 April	Wembley	Won 1 0	Div 1	Div 1
1971-72	Round 3	15 January	Lost 1 3		Div 1	Div 2
1998-99	Round 4	27 January	Won 4 1		Div 1	Div 3
2003-04	Round 1		3 January	Won 1 0	Div 1	Div 1

Summary

	P	W	D	L	F	A
Blades' home league record:	28	17	4	7	63	31
Blades' away league record:	28	5	10	13	28	45
Blades' cup record:	4	3	0	1	7	4
TOTAL:	**60**	**25**	**14**	**21**	**98**	**80**

- On New Year's Day 1926, United scored 11 in a match for the only time.
- United's last major trophy was the 1925 FA Cup, won against Cardiff with Fred Tunstall's goal.
- Neither side won away in the league between 1954 and 1976.

Blades' top scorers vs Cardiff

Harry Johnson 8

Fred Tunstall 5

Thomas Boyle, Keith Edwards, Peter Ndlovu, Gil Reece 4

Blades hat-tricks vs Cardiff

1 Jan 1926 Harry Johnson

1 Jan 1926 David Mercer

12 Mar 1952 Len Browning

20 Sep 2003 Peter Ndlovu

Played for both clubs

Don Bird	Cardiff 1929-31	Blades 1935-37
Ernie Marshall	Blades 1936-38	Cardiff 1939-47
William Ross	Cardiff 1946-48	Blades 1948-49
Gil Reece	Blades 1965-73	Cardiff 1972-76
Willie Carlin	Blades 1967-69	Cardiff 1973-74
David Powell	Blades 1968-71	Cardiff 1972-75
Alan Warboys	Cardiff 1970-73	Blades 1972-73
Jim Brown	Blades 1973-78	Cardiff 1982-83
Steve Finnieston	Cardiff 1974-75	Blades 1978-79
Bob Hatton	Blades 1980-83	Cardiff 1982-83
Mick Henderson	Cardiff 1981-82	Blades 1982-85
Tony Philliskirk	Blades 1983-88	Cardiff 1995-97
Jeff Eckhardt	Blades 1984-88	Cardiff 1996-2001
Roger Hansbury	Blades 1987-88	Cardiff 1989-92
Cliff Powell	Blades 1987-89	Cardiff 1989-90
Phil Kite	Blades 1990-92	Cardiff 1993-94
Mel Rees	Cardiff 1984-87	Blades 1991-92
Nathan Blake	Cardiff 1989-94	Blades 1993-96
Carl Muggleton	Blades 1995-96	Cardiff 2000-01
Dean Saunders	Cardiff 1984-87	Blades 1997-99
Andy Campbell	Blades 1998-99	Cardiff 2001-04
Des Hamilton	Blades 1998-99	Cardiff 2001-03
Paul Shaw	Cardiff 1995-96	Blades 2003-04

v. Carlisle United

Season	League	Date	Result	Blades	Carlisle	Date	Result	Blades	Carlisle	Blades	Carlisle
				Home				**Away**		*Final Positions*	
1968-69	Division 2	9 November	Lost	**0**	**1**	18 January	Won	**1**	**0**	9th	12th
1969-70	Division 2	13 March	Won	**1**	**0**	29 November	Won	**1**	**0**	6th	12th
1970-71	Division 2	31 October	Drew	**2**	**2**	27 February	Lost	**0**	**1**	2ndP	4th
1974-75	Division 1	2 November	Won	**2**	**1**	8 February	Won	**1**	**0**	6th	22ndR
1976-77	Division 2	11 September	Won	**3**	**0**	19 February	Lost	**1**	**4**	11th	20thR
1979-80	Division 3	29 March	Lost	**0**	**2**	17 November	Lost	**0**	**1**	12th	6th
1980-81	Division 3	15 November	Drew	**2**	**2**	16 August	Won	**3**	**0**	21stR	19th
1984-85	Division 2	13 April	Drew	**0**	**0**	22 September	Drew	**1**	**1**	18th	16th
1985-86	Division 2	1 January	Won	**1**	**0**	29 March	Lost	**0**	**1**	7th	20thR

FA Cup

Season	Round	Date	Result	Blades	Carlisle	Date	Result	Blades	Carlisle	*Division*	
1946-47	Round 3	11 January	Won	**3**	**0**					Div 1	Div 3N
1972-73	Round 4					3 February	Lost	**1**	**2**	Div 1	Div 2

Summary	P	W	D	L	F	A
Blades' home league record:	9	4	3	2	11	8
Blades' away league record:	9	4	1	4	8	8
Blades' cup record:	2	1	0	1	4	2
TOTAL:	**20**	**9**	**4**	**7**	**23**	**18**

FACT FILE

● Neither side has won more than three in a row.

Jonathan Cullen.

Blades' top scorers vs Carlisle
Alan Woodward 3

Played for both clubs

Jimmy Shankly	Blades 1926-28	Carlisle 1935-36
Wilf Adey	Blades 1931-33	Carlisle 1936-38
Ernie Robinson	Blades 1933-34	Carlisle 1934-35
Benjamin Clarke	Blades 1934-37	Carlisle 1939-40
Teddy Ashton	Blades 1936-38	Carlisle 1938-39
Ron Simpson	Blades 1958-65	Carlisle 1964-66
Barry Hartle	Blades 1960-66	Carlisle 1966-68
Willie Carlin	Carlisle 1964-68	Blades 1967-69
Steve Ludlam	Blades 1975-77	Carlisle 1977-80
Bob Hatton	Carlisle 1969-72	Blades 1980-83
Tony Philliskirk	Blades 1983-88	Carlisle 1995-96
Andy Barnsley	Blades 1986-89	Carlisle 1991-93
Darren Carr	Blades 1987-89	Carlisle 2000-01
Peter Duffield	Blades 1987-92	Carlisle 2003-04
Jamie Hoyland	Blades 1990-95	Carlisle 1997-98
Mervyn Day	Blades 1991-92	Carlisle 1993-94
Tom Cowan	Blades 1991-94	Carlisle 2003-04
Rob Scott	Blades 1994-96	Carlisle 1998-99
Graham Anthony	Blades 1994-97	Carlisle 1997-99
Paul Simpson	Blades 1994-97	Carlisle 2003-04
Andy Walker	Blades 1995-98	Carlisle 1999-2000
Jonathan Cullen	Blades 1997-99	Carlisle 2000-01

Willie Carlin, who joined
Sheffield United from
Carlisle in 1967.

v. Charlton Athletic

Season	League	Date	Result	Blades	Charlton	Date	Result	Blades	Charlton	Blades	Charlton
				Home				**Away**		*Final Positions*	
1935-36	Division 2	7 March	Drew	2	2	16 November	Drew	1	1	3rd	2ndP
1946-47	Division 1	31 May	Lost	1	3	21 September	Won	2	1	6th	19th
1947-48	Division 1	20 December	Drew	1	1	23 August	Lost	0	4	12th	13th
1948-49	Division 1	12 March	Won	2	0	16 October	Lost	1	2	22ndR	9th
1953-54	Division 1	14 November	Drew	1	1	3 April	Lost	0	3	20th	9th
1954-55	Division 1	9 April	Won	5	0	4 December	Lost	1	3	13th	15th
1955-56	Division 1	22 August	Drew	0	0	1 September	Lost	2	3	22ndR	14th
1957-58	Division 2	2 September	Lost	0	3	29 August	Lost	1	3	6th	3rd
1958-59	Division 2	20 December	Won	5	0	23 August	Drew	1	1	3rd	8th
1959-60	Division 2	23 January	Won	2	0	12 September	Drew	1	1	4th	7th
1960-61	Division 2	27 August	Won	1	0	31 December	Won	3	2	2ndP	10th
1968-69	Division 2	26 October	Won	2	0	25 March	Lost	1	2	9th	3rd
1969-70	Division 2	12 August	Won	2	0	19 August	Lost	2	3	6th	20th
1970-71	Division 2	12 December	Won	3	0	13 February	Won	2	0	2ndP	20th
1976-77	Division 2	2 April	Won	3	0	23 October	Lost	2	3	11th	7th
1977-78	Division 2	15 April	Won	1	0	19 November	Lost	0	3	12th	17th
1978-79	Division 2	28 April	Won	2	1	9 December	Lost	1	3	20thR	19th
1980-81	Division 3	14 March	Won	3	2	11 October	Lost	0	2	21stR	3rdP
1984-85	Division 2	10 November	Drew	1	1	16 April	Drew	0	0	18th	17th
1985-86	Division 2	1 October	Drew	1	1	7 December	Lost	0	2	7th	2ndP
1994-95	Division 1	18 March	Won	2	1	30 August	Drew	1	1	8th	15th
1995-96	Division 1	12 September	Won	2	0	17 February	Drew	1	1	9th	6th
1996-97	Division 1	15 October	Won	3	0	4 May	Drew	0	0	5th	15th
1997-98	Division 1	28 December	Won	4	1	9 December	Lost	1	2	6th	4thP
1999-00	Division 1	18 September	Lost	1	2	26 February	Lost	0	1	16th	1stP

Roger Nilsen battles it out with
Charlton's Mark Kinsella.

FA Cup		Date	Result	Home		Date	Result	Away		Division	
				Blades	Charlton			Blades	Charlton	Blades	Charlton
1966-67	Round 3					28 January	Won	1	0	Div 1	Div 2
1991-92	Round 4	5 February	Won	3	1	26 January	Drew	0	0	Div 1	Div 2

League Cup

		Date	Result			Date	Result				
1972-73	Round 3	3 October	Drew	0	0	10 October	Drew*	2	2	Div 1	Div 3
		23 October	Won*	1	0	(2nd replay)					

Summary	P	W	D	L	F	A
Blades' home league record:	25	16	6	3	50	19
Blades' away league record:	25	3	7	15	24	47
Blades' cup record:	6	3	3	0	7	3
TOTAL:	**56**	**22**	**16**	**18**	**81**	**69**

FACT FILE

- **The Blades have not won in their last 13 away games.**
- **The Blades were unbeaten in 19 home games (winning 16) between 1957 and 1999.**
- **There were 13 home wins in 14 league games from 1968 to 1981.**
- **Between 1958 and 1978, United went an astonishing 10 home games without conceding a goal.**

Blades' top scorers vs Charlton
Derek Pace 10
Alan Woodward 4
Keith Edwards, Jimmy Hagan, Petr Katchouro 3

Blades hat-tricks vs Charlton
20 Dec 1958 Derek Pace (4)

Played for both clubs

Nicky Johns	Blades 1978-79	Charlton 1978-88
Tony Towner	Blades 1982-83	Charlton 1984-86
Clive Mendonca	Blades 1986-88/91-92	Charlton 1997-2000
Chris Wilder	Blades 1986-92/97-99	Charlton 1990-92
Simon Webster	Blades 1987-90	Charlton 1990-93
Steve Thompson	Charlton 1985-88	Blades 1988-89
Alan McLeary	Blades 1992-93	Charlton 1993-95
Carl Tiler	Blades 1996-98	Charlton 1998-2001
Graham Stuart	Blades 1997-99	Charlton 1998-2004

v. Chelsea

Season	League	Date	Result	Home Blades	Aldershot	Date	Result	Away Blades	Aldershot	Final Positions Blades	Aldershot
1907-08	Division 1	4 January	Lost	0	3	7 September	Won	4	2	17th	13th
1908-09	Division 1	19 September	Lost	1	3	23 January	Drew	1	1	12th	11th
1909-10	Division 1	7 March	Drew	0	0	18 September	Drew	2	2	6th	19thR
1912-13	Division 1	4 January	Drew	3	3	14 September	Lost	2	4	15th	18th
1913-14	Division 1	8 November	Won	3	2	14 March	Lost	0	2	10th	8th
1914-15	Division 1	8 March	Drew	1	1	26 September	Drew	1	1	6th	19th
1919-20	Division 1	20 December	Won	3	1	27 December	Lost	0	1	14th	3rd
1920-21	Division 1	27 November	Lost	0	1	20 November	Lost	1	2	20th	18th
1921-22	Division 1	12 November	Lost	1	2	5 November	Won	2	0	11th	9th
1922-23	Division 1	14 October	Lost	0	2	7 October	Drew	0	0	10th	19th
1923-24	Division 1	29 September	Won	1	0	22 September	Drew	1	1	5th	21stR
1930-31	Division 1	21 February	Won	4	0	18 October	Lost	0	1	15th	12th
1931-32	Division 1	28 November	Won	4	2	9 April	Drew	1	1	7th	12th
1932-33	Division 1	21 January	Won	4	1	10 September	Lost	0	3	10th	18th
1933-34	Division 1	9 September	Won	4	1	20 January	Lost	0	5	22ndR	19th
1946-47	Division 1	9 September	Drew	2	2	3 May	Won	4	1	6th	15th
1947-48	Division 1	22 November	Won	3	1	10 April	Lost	0	1	12th	18th
1948-49	Division 1	20 November	Won	2	1	19 March	Lost	0	1	22ndR	13th
1953-54	Division 1	16 January	Lost	1	3	5 September	Won	2	1	20th	8th
1954-55	Division 1	20 September	Lost	1	2	8 April	Drew	1	1	13th	1st
1955-56	Division 1	7 April	Won	2	1	26 November	Lost	0	1	22ndR	16th
1961-62	Division 1	20 January	Won	3	1	9 September	Lost	1	6	5th	22ndR
1963-64	Division 1	31 August	Drew	1	1	21 December	Lost	2	3	12th	5th
1964-65	Division 1	7 November	Lost	0	2	22 March	Lost	0	3	19th	3rd
1965-66	Division 1	30 October	Lost	1	2	7 May	Lost	0	2	9th	5th
1966-67	Division 1	17 April	Won	3	0	19 November	Drew	1	1	10th	9th
1967-68	Division 1	11 May	Lost	1	2	6 September	Lost	2	4	21stR	6th
1971-72	Division 1	25 September	Won	1	0	29 March	Lost	0	2	10th	7th
1972-73	Division 1	16 September	Won	2	1	10 February	Lost	2	4	14th	12th
1973-74	Division 1	1 January	Lost	1	2	1 September	Won	2	1	13th	17th
1974-75	Division 1	15 February	Won	2	1	23 April	Drew	1	1	6th	21stR
1976-77	Division 2	3 December	Won	1	0	30 April	Lost	0	4	11th	2ndP
1990-91	Division 1	16 March	Won	1	0	29 September	Drew	2	2	13th	11th
1991-92	Division 1	3 September	Lost	0	1	21 March	Won	2	1	9th	14th
1992-93	Premiership	8 May	Won	4	2	31 October	Won	2	1	14th	11th
1993-94	Premiership	27 November	Won	1	0	7 May	Lost	2	3	20thR	14th

FA Cup

Season		Date	Result	Home Blades	Aldershot	Date	Result	Away Blades	Aldershot	Division	
1911-12	Round 1					13 January	Lost	0	1	Div 1	Div 2
1914-15	Final	24 April		Old Trafford			Won	3	0	Div 1	Div 1
1951-52	Q'ter Final	8 March	Lost	0	1					Div 2	Div 1
1966-67	Round 5					11 March	Lost	0	2	Div 1	Div 1
1991-92	Round 5					15 February	Lost	0	1	Div 1	Div 1

						Away		Division	

<table>
<tr><td>League Cup</td><td></td><td></td><td></td><td></td><td>Date</td><td>Result</td><td>Blades Aldershot</td><td>Blades Aldershot</td></tr>
<tr><td>1976-77 Round 2</td><td></td><td></td><td></td><td></td><td>1 September</td><td>Lost</td><td>1 3</td><td>Div 2 Div 2</td></tr>
</table>

Summary	P	W	D	L	F	A
Blades' home league record:	36	19	5	12	62	47
Blades' away league record:	36	7	10	19	41	70
Blades' cup record:	6	1	0	5	4	8
TOTAL:	**78**	**27**	**15**	**36**	**107**	**125**

FACT FILE

- On the final day of the season in 1994, United were relegated from the Premiership in heartbreaking circumstances. Midway through the second half, things looked fine as they led 2-1 at Stamford Bridge, and other results were going their way. However, Everton came from 2-0 down to beat Wimbledon (rumours still circulate as to whether the match was fixed), and a last-minute Chelsea goal sent United down, giving Ipswich a reprieve.
- United were unbeaten in eight home games from 1923 to 1948.
- Between 1955 and 1973, United failed to win in 11 away games.

Blades' top scorers vs Chelsea
Jimmy Dunne 7
Joe Kitchen 6
Jimmy Hagan 5
Bobby Barclay, Stan Fazackerley, Billy Gillespie,
Dane Whitehouse, Alan Woodward 4

Blades hat-tricks vs Chelsea
9 Sep 1933 Jimmy Dunne

Played for both clubs

Martin Moran	Blades 1899-1900	Chelsea 1905-08
Billy Brawn	Blades 1899-1902	Chelsea 1907-11
Billy Foulke	Blades 1894-1905	Chelsea 1905-06
Alan Birchenall	Blades 1964-68	Chelsea 1967-70
Chico Hamilton	Chelsea 1966-67	Blades 1976-78
Steve Finnieston	Chelsea 1974-78	Blades 1978-79
Stewart Houston	Chelsea 1967-70	Blades 1980-83
Ray Lewington	Chelsea 1975-79	Blades 1985-86
Vinnie Jones	Blades 1990-92	Chelsea 1991-93
Nigel Spackman	Chelsea 1983-87/92-96	Blades 1996-97
Paul Parker	Chelsea 1996-97	Blades 1996-97
David Lee	Chelsea 1988-98	Blades 1997-98
Graham Stuart	Chelsea 1989-93	Blades 1997-99
Paul Furlong	Chelsea 1994-96	Blades 2001-02
Terry Phelan	Chelsea 1995-97	Blades 2001-02
Jon Harley	Chelsea 1997-2001	Blades 2002-04

v. Cheltenham Town

		Home						Division
FA Cup	*Date*	*Result*	Blades Chelt'ham					Blades Chelt'ham
2002-03 Round 3	4 January	Won	**4**	**0**				Div 1 Div 2

Summary	*P*	*W*	*D*	*L*	*F*	*A*
Blades' cup record:	1	1	0	0	4	0
TOTAL:	1	1	0	0	4	0

Blades' top scorers vs Cheltenham
Steve Kabba 2

Played for both clubs
Carl Muggleton   Blades 1995-96   Cheltenham 2001-02

United against Cheltenham: Robbie Kozluk is the Blades man.

v. Chester City

Season	League	Date	Result	Home Blades	Chester	Date	Result	Away Blades	Chester	Final Positions Blades	Chester
1979-80	Division 3	26 February	Drew	1	1	25 August	Drew	1	1	12th	9th
1980-81	Division 3	7 April	Won	2	0	8 November	Lost	2	3	21stR	18th
1988-89	Division 3	17 September	Won	6	1	19 April	Won	1	0	2ndP	8th

Summary	P	W	D	L	F	A
Blades' home league record:	3	2	1	0	9	2
Blades' away league record:	3	1	1	1	4	4
TOTAL:	6	3	2	1	13	6

FACT FILE

- **In September 1988, two United players scored hat-tricks in the same game for the only time since the war.**

Blades' top scorers vs Chester
Tony Agana 4
Brian Deane 3

Blades hat-tricks vs Chester
17 Sep 1988 Brian Deane
17 Sep 1988 Tony Agana

Played for both clubs

Arthur Mercer	Blades 1926-28	Chester 1931-34
Doug Cole	Blades 1937-38	Chester 1945-48
Ralph Morement	Blades 1949-50	Chester 1950-53
Reg Matthewson	Blades 1961-68	Chester 1972-76
Billy Dearden	Chester 1968-70/75-77	Blades 1970-76
Mick Speight	Blades 1971-80	Chester 1984-86
Steve Ludlam	Blades 1975-77	Chester 1980-83
Ian Benjamin	Blades 1978-80	Chester 1988-89
John Ryan	Blades 1980-82	Chester 1983-84
Paul Richardson	Chester 1976-77	Blades 1981-83
Ross Davidson	Blades 1994-96	Chester 1995-2000
Ian Rush	Chester 1978-80	Blades 1997-98
Earl Barrett	Chester 1985-86	Blades 1997-98

v. Chesterfield

Season	League	Date	Result	Blades	Chesterf'd	Date	Result	Blades	Chesterf'd	Blades	Chesterf'd
				Home				**Away**		*Final Positions*	
1936-37	Division 2	13 March	Won	**5**	**0**	7 November	Drew	**2**	**2**	7th	15th
1937-38	Division 2	6 November	Lost	**0**	**2**	19 March	Lost	**0**	**1**	3rd	11th
1938-39	Division 2	12 November	Drew	**1**	**1**	18 March	Lost	**0**	**1**	2ndP	6th
1949-50	Division 2	4 March	Won	**1**	**0**	15 October	Won	**1**	**0**	3rd	14th
1950-51	Division 2	4 November	Won	**4**	**1**	24 March	Won	**2**	**0**	8th	21stR
1979-80	Division 3	29 April	Lost	**0**	**2**	5 January	Lost	**1**	**2**	12th	4th
1980-81	Division 3	19 August	Won	**2**	**0**	11 November	Lost	**0**	**1**	21stR	5th
1982-83	Division 3	2 April	Won	**3**	**1**	28 December	Lost	**1**	**3**	11th	24thR
1988-89	Division 3	2 January	Lost	**1**	**3**	25 March	Lost	**1**	**2**	2ndP	22ndR

FA Cup

										Division	
1980-81	Round 2	13 December	Drew	**1**	**1**	16 December	Lost	**0**	**1**	Div 3	Div 3

League Cup

1974-75	Round 2	10 September	Won	**3**	**1**					Div 1	Div 3

Summary	P	W	D	L	F	A
Blades' home league record:	9	5	1	3	17	10
Blades' away league record:	9	2	1	6	8	12
Blades' cup record:	3	1	1	1	4	3
TOTAL:	**21**	**8**	**3**	**10**	**29**	**25**

FACT FILE

- **United have lost on their last five trips to Chesterfield.**
- **United won four in a row from 1949 to 1951.**

Shane Nicholson, who
saw action with both
Chesterfield and
Sheffield United.

Blades' top scorers vs Chesterfield
Harold Brook 3
Harold Barton, Jock Dodds, Mike Trusson 2

Played for both clubs

James Pilgrim	Blades 1898-99	Chesterfield 1899-1901
Frank Thacker	Blades 1898-99	Chesterfield 1899-1906
George Simpson	Blades 1897-1900	Chesterfield 1903-04
Edward Connor	Blades 1911-12	Chesterfield 1921-22
Joseph Mitchell	Blades 1909-13	Chesterfield 1921-22
Bernard Oxley	Chesterfield 1925-28	Blades 1928-34
Jim Holmes	Chesterfield 1930-31	Blades 1931-36
Chick Reed	Blades 1931-32	Chesterfield 1935-37
Stan Machent	Blades 1946-48	Chesterfield 1947-49
Herbert Parkin	Blades 1947-51	Chesterfield 1951-53
Arthur Bottom	Blades 1948-54	Chesterfield 1958-60
Pat Keating	Blades 1950-51	Chesterfield 1953-57
Jock Smith	Blades 1950-53	Chesterfield 1956-57
Cliff Mason	Blades 1955-62	Chesterfield 1964-65
Max Ashmore	Blades 1957-58	Chesterfield 1962-63
Andy Wilson	Blades 1959-61	Chesterfield 1966-68
Denis Finnigan	Blades 1959-67	Chesterfield 1968-70
Keith Kettleborough	Blades 1960-66	Chesterfield 1967-69
Len Badger	Blades 1962-76	Chesterfield 1975-78
Tom Fenoughty	Blades 1963-69	Chesterfield 1969-72
Frank Barlow	Blades 1965-72	Chesterfield 1972-76
Charlie Bell	Blades 1966-67	Chesterfield 1968-73
Phil Cliff	Blades 1966-70	Chesterfield 1970-73
Geoff Salmons	Blades 1967-74/77-78	Chesterfield 1978-82
Billy Dearden	Blades 1970-76	Chesterfield 1977-79
Steve Cammack	Blades 1971-76	Chesterfield 1975-79
Jim Brown	Chesterfield 1972-74/83-89	Blades 1973-78
John Matthews	Blades 1978-82	Chesterfield 1984-85
Jeff King	Blades 1981-83	Chesterfield 1983-84
Terry Curran	Blades 1982-83	Chesterfield 1987-88
Ray McHale	Chesterfield 1971-75	Blades 1982-85
Mick Henderson	Blades 1982-85	Chesterfield 1984-89
Kevin Arnott	Blades 1982-87	Chesterfield 1987-90
Paddy McGeeney	Blades 1984-86	Chesterfield 1987-89
Andy Leaning	Blades 1987-88	Chesterfield 1996-2000
Darren Carr	Blades 1987-89	Chesterfield 1993-98
Andy Scott	Blades 1992-98	Chesterfield 1996-97
Billy Mercer	Blades 1994-96	Chesterfield 1995-99
Carl Muggleton	Chesterfield 1987-88/ 99-2000/02-04	Blades 1995-96
Paul Holland	Blades 1995-96	Chesterfield 1995-2000
Christopher Bettney	Blades 1996-97	Chesterfield 1999-2000
Shane Nicholson	Chesterfield 1998-99	Blades 2001-02
Gus Uhlenbeek	Blades 2000-02	Chesterfield 2003-04

v. Colchester United

Season	League	Date	Result	Home Blades	Colchester	Date	Result	Away Blades	Colchester	Final Positions Blades	Colchester
1979-80	Division 3	9 October	Lost	1	2	21 August	Lost	0	1	12th	5th
1980-81	Division 3	1 November	Won	3	0	4 April	Drew	1	1	21stR	22ndR
1981-82	Division 4	12 September	Won	1	0	6 February	Lost	2	5	1stP	6th

FA Cup

										Division	
1988-89	Round 4	28 January	Drew	3	3	31 January	Won	2	0	Div 3	Div 4
2003-04	Round 5	15 February	Won	1	0					Div 1	Div 2

League Cup

2000-01	Round 2	19 September	Won	3	0	27 September	Won	1	0	Div 1	Div 2

Summary	P	W	D	L	F	A
Blades' home league record:	3	2	0	1	5	2
Blades' away league record:	3	0	1	2	3	7
Blades' cup record:	5	4	1	0	10	3
TOTAL:	**11**	**6**	**2**	**3**	**18**	**12**

FACT FILE

- **The Blades are undefeated in their last five matches.**

Blades' top scorers vs Colchester
Brian Deane 3
Paul Devlin, Tony Kenworthy 2

Played for both clubs

Tom McAlister	Blades 1971-76	Colchester 1988-89
Dennis Longhorn	Blades 1976-78	Colchester 1980-83
Stewart Houston	Blades 1980-83	Colchester 1983-86
Roger Hansbury	Blades 1987-88	Colchester 1989-90
Graham Benstead	Colchester 1987-88	Blades 1987-89
Colin Hill	Colchester 1987-89	Blades 1989-92
David Barnes	Blades 1989-94	Colchester 1996-97
Scott Fitzgerald	Blades 1995-96	Colchester 2000-04
Brian Launders	Colchester 1998-2000	Blades 1999-2000
Carl Asaba	Colchester 1994-95	Blades 2000-03

v. Corinthians

FA Cup		Date	Result	Home Blades	Corinthians					Division Blades	Corinthians
1924-25	Round 1	10 January	Won	5	0					Div 1	Non L
1931-32	Round 3	9 January	Won	2	1					Div 1	Non L

Summary	P	W	D	L	F	A
Blades' cup record:	2	2	0	0	7	1
TOTAL:	2	2	0	0	7	1

FACT FILE

● The Corinthians were a unique team. They were an amateur team who for many years played no competitive football, and on occasions they could boast the entire England team. By the time of the two matches against United, however, their glory days had gone.

Blades' top scorers vs Corinthians
Harry Johnson 4
Jimmy Dunne 2

Blades hat-tricks vs Corinthians
10 Jan 1925 Harry Johnson (4) (cup)

Jimmy Dunne, who netted twice against the amateurs.

v. Coventry City

Season	League	Home Date	Result	Blades	Coventry	Away Date	Result	Blades	Coventry	Final Positions Blades	Coventry
1936-37	Division 2	28 November	Drew	2	2	3 April	Lost	0	2	7th	8th
1937-38	Division 2	25 December	Won	3	2	27 December	Drew	2	2	3rd	4th
1938-39	Division 2	29 August	Drew	0	0	29 April	Won	3	0	2ndP	4th
1949-50	Division 2	17 December	Drew	1	1	20 August	Won	4	2	3rd	12th
1950-51	Division 2	2 December	Won	2	0	21 April	Won	3	2	8th	7th
1951-52	Division 2	26 January	Lost	1	2	22 September	Drew	1	1	11th	21stR
1967-68	Division 1	23 December	Won	2	0	26 August	Drew	2	2	21stR	20th
1971-72	Division 1	13 November	Won	2	0	18 April	Lost	2	3	10th	18th
1972-73	Division 1	21 April	Won	3	1	18 November	Lost	0	3	14th	19th
1973-74	Division 1	6 April	Lost	0	1	24 November	Lost	1	3	13th	16th
1974-75	Division 1	20 December	Won	1	0	28 March	Drew	2	2	6th	14th
1975-76	Division 1	13 September	Lost	0	1	10 January	Lost	0	1	22ndR	14th
1990-91	Division 1	27 October	Lost	0	1	4 May	Drew	0	0	13th	16th
1991-92	Division 1	26 December	Lost	0	3	28 August	Lost	1	3	9th	19th
1992-93	Premiership	28 November	Drew	1	1	24 March	Won	3	1	14th	15th
1993-94	Premiership	12 February	Drew	0	0	31 October	Drew	0	0	20thR	11th
2001-02	Division 1	15 September	Lost	0	1	6 March	Lost	0	1	13th	11th
2002-03	Division 1	28 December	Drew	0	0	10 August	Lost	1	2	3rd	20th
2003-04	Division 1	30 August	Won	2	1	26 December	Won	1	0	8th	12th

FA Cup

										Division	
1997-98	Q'ter Final	17 March	Drew*	1	1	7 March	Drew	1	1	Div 1	Prem
			(won 3-1 pens)								

A scramble for the ball between United's Michael Brown and Coventry's Graham Barrett.

Summary	P	W	D	L	F	A
Blades' home league record:	19	7	6	6	20	17
Blades' away league record:	19	5	6	8	26	30
Blades' cup record:	2	0	2	0	2	2
TOTAL:	**40**	**12**	**14**	**14**	**48**	**49** (+one penalty shoot-out victory)

FACT FILE

- **United have won one of their last 15 away matches.**
- **United lost one of their first nine home matches.**

Blades' top scorers vs Coventry
Alan Woodward 5
Jimmy Hagan, Jack Pickering 3

Played for both clubs

Joseph Mitchell	Blades 1909-13	Coventry 1919-21
Fred Hawley	Blades 1912-15	Coventry 1919-20
Jack Ball	Blades 1919-21	Coventry 1930-31
Jimmy Shankly	Coventry 1925-26	Blades 1926-28
Jesse Bennett	Blades 1929-30	Coventry 1932-33
Colin Collindridge	Blades 1946-50	Coventry 1954-56
Ronnie Waldock	Coventry 1952-54	Blades 1954-57
John Tudor	Coventry 1966-69	Blades 1968-71
David Bradford	Blades 1974-77	Coventry 1981-82
Neil Ramsbottom	Coventry 1972-75	Blades 1979-80
Keith Waugh	Blades 1981-85	Coventry 1989-90
Dennis Mortimer	Coventry 1969-76	Blades 1984-85
Chris Marsden	Blades 1987-88	Coventry 1993-94
Paul Williams	Blades 1987-89	Coventry 1992-93
David Barnes	Coventry 1979-82	Blades 1989-94
Andy Goram	Blades 1998-99	Coventry 2001-02
Paul Hill	Coventry 1998-2000	Blades 1999-2000
Peter Ndlovu	Coventry 1991-97	Blades 2000-04
Paul Furlong	Coventry 1991-92	Blades 2001-02

v. Crewe Alexandra

			Home				Away		Final Positions	
Season	League	Date	Result	Blades	Crewe	Date	Result	Blades	Crewe	Blades	Crewe
1892-93	Division 2	18 March	Won	4	0	12 April	Won	4	0	2ndP	10th
1981-82	Division 4	29 September	Won	4	0	1 May	Won	3	2	1stP	24th
1997-98	Division 1	29 November	Won	1	0	30 April	Lost	1	2	6th	11th
1998-99	Division 1	31 August	Won	3	1	30 January	Won	2	1	8th	18th
1999-00	Division 1	24 April	Drew	1	1	9 October	Lost	0	1	16th	19th
2000-01	Division 1	14 October	Won	1	0	6 March	Lost	0	1	10th	14th
2001-02	Division 1	27 October	Won	1	0	30 March	Drew	2	2	13th	22ndR
2003-04	Division 1	4 November	Won	2	0	24 February	Won	1	0	8th	18th

FA Cup										Division	
1947-48	Round 3					10 January	Lost	1	3	Div 1 Div 3N	

Summary	P	W	D	L	F	A
Blades' home league record:	8	7	1	0	17	2
Blades' away league record:	8	4	1	3	13	9
Blades' cup record:	1	0	0	1	1	3
TOTAL:	**17**	**11**	**2**	**4**	**31**	**14**

FACT FILE

● **United won their first three matches 4-0.**

United's Paul Devlin in action against Crewe.

Michael Tonge fights for the ball against Crewe.

Blades' top scorers vs Crewe
Arthur Watson 4
Keith Edwards 3

Played for both clubs

Percy Oldacre	Blades 1921-23	Crewe 1924-25
Roy Warhurst	Blades 1946-50	Crewe 1958-60
Billy Dearden	Crewe 1966-68	Blades 1970-76
Terry Nicholl	Crewe 1971-73	Blades 1973-75
Mike Guy	Blades 1977-79	Crewe 1979-81
Neil Ramsbottom	Crewe 1971-72	Blades 1979-80
Tony Moore	Blades 1979-82	Crewe 1982-83
Darren Carr	Blades 1987-89	Crewe 1990-93
Peter Duffield	Blades 1987-92	Crewe 1992-93
Chris Downes	Blades 1988-89	Crewe 1991-92
Francis Joseph	Blades 1988-89	Crewe 1989-90
John Moore	Blades 1988-89	Crewe 1990-91
John Gannon	Crewe 1986-87	Blades 1988-96
Billy Whitehurst	Blades 1989-91	Crewe 1991-92
Phil Kite	Blades 1990-92	Crewe 1992-93
John Pemberton	Crewe 1984-88/97-98	Blades 1990-94
Mitch Ward	Crewe 1990-91	Blades 1990-98
Mel Rees	Crewe 1989-90	Blades 1991-92
Mark Foran	Blades 1994-96	Crewe 1997-2000
Andy Woodward	Crewe 1992-95	Blades 1999-2000
Brian Launders	Crewe 1996-97	Blades 1999-2000
John Newby	Crewe 1999-2000	Blades 2000-01
Ashley Ward	Crewe 1992-95	Blades 2003-04

Season	League	Date	Result	Home Blades	Home Palace	Date	Result	Away Blades	Away Palace	Final Positions Blades	Final Positions Palace
1968-69	Division 2	26 December	Drew	1	1	5 October	Drew	1	1	9th	2ndP
1971-72	Division 1	22 April	Won	1	0	4 December	Lost	1	5	10th	20th
1972-73	Division 1	7 April	Won	2	0	13 March	Won	1	0	14th	21stR
1977-78	Division 2	17 September	Lost	0	2	11 February	Lost	0	1	12th	9th
1978-79	Division 2	2 September	Lost	0	2	21 November	Lost	1	3	20thR	1stP
1984-85	Division 2	18 September	Lost	1	2	30 March	Won	3	1	18th	15th
1985-86	Division 2	30 November	Drew	0	0	3 May	Drew	1	1	7th	5th
1986-87	Division 2	17 March	Won	1	0	13 September	Won	2	1	9th	6th
1987-88	Division 2	15 September	Drew	1	1	13 December	Lost	1	2	21stR	6th
1990-91	Division 1	12 January	Lost	0	1	1 September	Lost	0	1	13th	3rd
1991-92	Division 1	28 December	Drew	1	1	31 August	Lost	1	2	9th	10th
1992-93	Premiership	20 March	Lost	0	1	5 December	Lost	0	2	14th	20thR
1995-96	Division 1	29 August	Lost	2	3	10 February	Drew	0	0	9th	3rd
1996-97	Division 1	12 April	Won	3	0	17 December	Won	1	0	5th	6thP
1998-99	Division 1	2 March	Drew	1	1	27 September	Lost	0	1	8th	14th
1999-00	Division 1	4 September	Won	3	1	12 February	Drew	1	1	16th	15th
2000-01	Division 1	24 February	Won	1	0	23 September	Won	1	0	10th	21st
2001-02	Division 1	25 September	Lost	1	3	23 February	Won	1	0	13th	10th
2002-03	Division 1	30 November	Won	2	1	5 April	Drew	2	2	3rd	14th
2003-04	Division 1	7 February	Lost	0	3	26 August	Won	2	1	8th	6thP

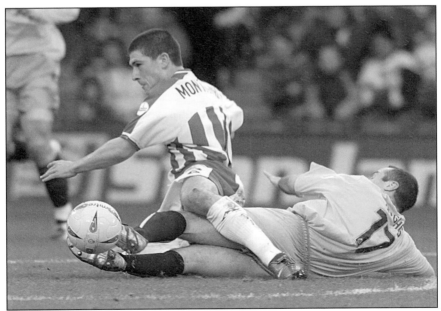

A ground level struggle at Bramall Lane between Nick Montgomery and the Eagles' Hughes.

Division 1 Play-offs	Date	Result	Home Blades	Palace	Date		Result	Away Blades	Palace	Final Positions Blades	Palace
1996-97 Final	26 May		Wembley				Lost	0	1	5th	6thP

FA Cup

									Division	
1958-59 Round 3	10 January	Won	2	0					Div 2	Div 4

League Cup

									Division	
2002-03 Q'ter Final	17 December	Won	3	1					Div 1	Div 1

Summary

	P	W	D	L	F	A
Blades' home league record:	20	7	5	8	21	23
Blades' away league record:	20	7	5	8	20	25
Blades' cup record:	3	2	0	1	5	2
TOTAL:	43	16	10	17	46	50

FACT FILE

- **Palace beat United to promotion in 1997 with David Hopkin's agonising last-minute winner.**
- **United have lost two of their last 11 matches with Palace.**
- **United went 10 matches without a win from 1987 to 1996.**

Blades' top scorers vs Palace

Billy Dearden 3

Wayne Allison, Marcus Bent, Keith Edwards, Marcelo,
Colin Morris, Paul Peschisolido, Billy Russell 2

Played for both clubs

Bert Menlove	Palace 1920-22	Blades 1921-26
Jack Alderson	Palace 1920-24	Blades 1925-29
Alan Birchenall	Blades 1964-68	Palace 1970-72
Mick Hill	Blades 1966-70	Palace 1973-76
Jeff Bourne	Palace 1976-78	Blades 1979-80
John Burridge	Palace 1977-80	Blades 1984-87
John Pemberton	Palace 1987-90	Blades 1990-94
Glyn Hodges	Palace 1990-91	Blades 1990-96
David Tuttle	Blades 1993-96	Palace 1995-2000
Carl Veart	Blades 1994-96	Palace 1995-98
Gareth Taylor	Palace 1995-96	Blades 1995-99
Shaun Derry	Blades 1997-2000	Palace 2002-04
Brian Launders	Palace 1994-96/99-2000	Blades 1999-2000
Marcus Bent	Palace 1997-99	Blades 1999-2001
Shaun Murphy	Blades 1999-2003	Palace 2001-02
Andrew Morrison	Blades 2000-01	Palace 2000-01
Terry Phelan	Palace 1999-2000	Blades 2001-02
Steve Kabba	Palace 1999-2003	Blades 2002-04

v. Darlington

				Home			Away		Final Positions	
Season	League	Date	Result	Blades	Darl'ton	Date	Result	Blades	Darl'ton	Blades	Darl'ton
1981-82	Division 4	26 January	Drew	0	0	15 May	Won	2	0	1stP	13th

FA Cup

										Division
1910-11	Round 1	14 January	Lost	0	1					Div 1 Non L

League Cup

										Division	
1998-99	Round 1	11 August	Won	3	1	18 August	Drew*	2	2	Div 1	Div 3
2001-02	Round 1					20 August	Won	1	0	Div 1	Div 3

Summary	P	W	D	L	F	A
Blades' home league record:	1	0	1	0	0	0
Blades' away league record:	1	1	0	0	2	0
Blades' cup record:	4	2	1	1	6	4
TOTAL:	**6**	**3**	**2**	**1**	**8**	**4**

FACT FILE

● **Darlington have not beaten United since 1911.**

Blades' top scorers vs Darlington
Dean Saunders 3

Played for both clubs

Bob Bolam	Blades 1919-22	Darlington 1922-23
Jimmy Waugh	Blades 1921-27	Darlington 1926-33
Gordon Williams	Blades 1949-50	Darlington 1950-51
Cliff Mason	Darlington 1952-55	Blades 1955-62
John Hope	Darlington 1964-69	Blades 1970-74
John Burridge	Blades 1984-87	Darlington 1995-96
Peter Duffield	Blades 1987-92	Darlington 1998-2000
John Moore	Darlington 1986-87	Blades 1988-89
Alan Roberts	Darlington 1985-88	Blades 1988-90
John Reed	Blades 1991-96	Darlington 1992-93
Jonathan Cullen	Blades 1997-99	Darlington 2002-03

v. Darwen

Season	League	Date	Result	Home Blades	Darwen	Date	Result	Away Blades	Darwen	Final Positions Blades	Darwen
1892-93	Division 2	15 October	Won	2	0	19 November	Lost	1	3	2ndP	3rdP
1893-94	Division 1	9 September	Won	2	1	6 January	Drew	3	3	10th	15thR

Summary	P	W	D	L	F	A
Blades' home league record:	2	2	0	0	4	1
Blades' away league record:	2	0	1	1	4	6
TOTAL:	4	2	1	1	8	7

Blades' top scorers vs Darwen
William Fleming 2

v. Derby County

Season	League	Home Date	Result	Blades	Derby	Away Date	Result	Blades	Derby	Final Positions Blades	Derby
1893-94	Division 1	4 September	Lost	1	2	4 November	Lost	1	2	10th	3rd
1894-95	Division 1	25 December	Lost	1	4	15 December	Lost	1	4	6th	15th
1895-96	Division 1	21 December	Drew	1	1	14 March	Won	2	0	12th	2nd
1896-97	Division 1	31 October	Drew	2	2	10 October	Won	3	1	2nd	3rd
1897-98	Division 1	1 September	Won	2	1	13 November	Drew	1	1	1st	10th
1898-99	Division 1	19 November	Won	2	1	22 April	Lost	0	1	16th	9th
1899-00	Division 1	13 January	Drew	1	1	16 September	Won	1	0	2nd	6th
1900-01	Division 1	11 March	Won	2	1	20 October	Lost	0	4	14th	12th
1901-02	Division 1	26 October	Won	3	0	28 April	Lost	1	3	10th	6th
1902-03	Division 1	30 March	Won	3	2	6 December	Lost	0	1	4th	9th
1903-04	Division 1	26 September	Won	3	2	23 January	Won	5	3	7th	14th
1904-05	Division 1	3 September	Won	3	1	31 December	Won	3	2	6th	11th
1905-06	Division 1	17 February	Won	1	0	14 October	Lost	0	1	13th	15th
1906-07	Division 1	1 September	Won	2	0	29 December	Lost	0	3	4th	19thR
1912-13	Division 1	15 March	Won	4	1	9 November	Lost	1	5	15th	7th
1913-14	Division 1	27 December	Drew	2	2	6 September	Won	5	3	10th	20thR
1919-20	Division 1	9 February	Drew	0	0	24 January	Lost	1	5	14th	18th
1920-21	Division 1	26 February	Lost	0	1	5 March	Drew	1	1	20th	21stR
1926-27	Division 1	13 September	Won	1	0	27 September	Lost	0	1	8th	12th
1927-28	Division 1	15 October	Won	1	0	25 February	Lost	1	2	13th	4th
1928-29	Division 1	20 October	Won	2	1	2 March	Drew	2	2	11th	6th
1929-30	Division 1	22 March	Won	2	0	16 November	Lost	1	2	20th	2nd
1930-31	Division 1	13 September	Drew	3	3	17 January	Lost	3	4	15th	6th
1931-32	Division 1	16 January	Won	3	1	5 September	Won	3	1	7th	15th
1932-33	Division 1	3 December	Won	4	3	15 April	Lost	0	3	10th	7th

Airborne action in the Blades 1-1 draw with the Rams on 23 March 2004. United's Chris Morgan goes up with Paul Boertin, Ian Taylor and Youl Mawene of Derby.

		Home					**Away**			*Final Positions*	
Season	*League*	*Date*	*Result*	Blades	Derby	*Date*	*Result*	Blades	Derby	Blades	Derby
1933-34	Division 1	28 August	Won	2	0	16 December	Lost	1	5	22ndR	4th
1946-47	Division 1	26 October	Won	3	2	17 May	Won	2	1	6th	14th
1947-48	Division 1	8 November	Lost	1	2	27 March	Drew	1	1	12th	4th
1948-49	Division 1	1 January	Won	3	1	28 August	Lost	1	2	22ndR	3rd
1957-58	Division 2	18 January	Lost	0	1	14 September	Lost	0	2	6th	16th
1958-59	Division 2	25 October	Lost	1	2	14 March	Lost	1	2	3rd	7th
1959-60	Division 2	22 August	Won	2	1	19 December	Drew	1	1	4th	18th
1960-61	Division 2	19 April	Won	3	1	10 December	Lost	0	2	2ndP	12th
1968-69	Division 2	20 August	Won	2	0	7 April	Lost	0	1	9th	1stP
1971-72	Division 1	8 April	Lost	0	4	20 November	Lost	0	3	10th	1st
1972-73	Division 1	24 March	Won	3	1	28 October	Lost	1	2	14th	7th
1973-74	Division 1	17 November	Won	3	0	13 April	Lost	1	4	13th	3rd
1974-75	Division 1	15 October	Lost	1	2	24 August	Lost	0	2	6th	1st
1975-76	Division 1	16 August	Drew	1	1	20 December	Lost	2	3	22ndR	4th
1986-87	Division 2	25 April	Lost	0	1	22 November	Lost	0	2	9th	1stP
1990-91	Division 1	26 January	Won	1	0	29 August	Drew	1	1	13th	20thR
1994-95	Division 1	12 November	Won	2	1	4 February	Won	3	2	8th	9th
1995-96	Division 1	7 October	Lost	0	2	2 December	Lost	2	4	9th	2ndP
2002-03	Division 1	22 March	Won	2	0	30 October	Lost	1	2	3rd	18th
2003-04	Division 1	23 March	Drew	1	1	28 January	Lost	0	2	8th	20th

FA Cup

										Division	
1898-99	Final	15 April		Crystal Palace			Won	4	1	Div 1	Div 1
1901-02	Semi-Final	15 March		The Hawthorns			Drew	1	1	Div 1	Div 1
		20 March		Molineux (replay)			Drew*	1	1		
		27 March		City Ground, Nottingham (2nd replay)			Won	1	0		
1969-70	Round 4					24 January	Lost	0	3	Div 2	Div 1
1985-86	Round 4	25 January	Lost	0	1					Div 2	Div 3

Summary

	P	W	D	L	F	A
Blades' home league record:	45	27	8	10	80	53
Blades' away league record:	45	9	6	30	54	99
Blades' cup record:	6	2	2	2	7	7
TOTAL:	**96**	**38**	**16**	**42**	**141**	**159**

FACT FILE

- Derby were the last team to knock United out of the FA Cup while in a lower division, back in 1986.
- United have won one out of 19 away matches since 1947.
- United lost once in 25 home matches between 1895 and 1946.
- Victory over Derby in 1899 gave United the first of their four FA Cups, with Bennett, Beer, Almond and Priest all scoring after Derby had taken the lead.

Blades' top scorers vs Derby
Jimmy Dunne 8
Arthur Brown 7
Billy Gillespie, Joe Kitchen 5
Jack Almond, Syd Gibson, Jack Pickering,
Fred Priest, Fred Tunstall, Alan Woodward 4

Played for both clubs

Thomas Paton	Derby 1904-06	Blades 1905-07
George Thompson	Blades 1906-09	Derby 1908-11
Jack Peart	Blades 1907-10	Derby 1919-20
Joe Smith	Blades 1909-13	Derby 1914-15
Duncan Ritchie	Blades 1912-13	Derby 1913-14
Stan Fazackerley	Blades 1912-21	Derby 1925-26
Bert Chandler	Derby 1919-25	Blades 1926-29
Bobby Barclay	Derby 1928-31	Blades 1931-37
Harry Wilkes	Derby 1927-33	Blades 1933-35
Don Bird	Derby 1934-36	Blades 1935-37
Freddie Jessop	Derby 1930-38	Blades 1937-39
Jimmy Hagan	Derby 1935-39	Blades 1938-58
Alf Jeffries	Derby 1936-39	Blades 1939-40
Fred Smith	Derby 1947-48	Blades 1947-52
Bill Hodgson	Blades 1957-64	Derby 1965-68
Willie Carlin	Blades 1967-69	Derby 1968-71
Bobby Campbell	Blades 1977-78	Derby 1983-84
Bruce Rioch	Derby 1973-80	Blades 1978-79
Jeff Bourne	Derby 1970-77	Blades 1979-80
Barry Butlin	Derby 1967-73	Blades 1979-81
John McAlle	Blades 1981-82	Derby 1981-84
Jeff King	Derby 1975-78	Blades 1981-83
Terry Curran	Derby 1977-78	Blades 1982-83
John Burridge	Derby 1984-85	Blades 1984-87
Martin Kuhl	Blades 1986-88	Derby 1992-95
Simon Webster	Blades 1987-90	Derby 1995-96
Glyn Hodges	Blades 1990-96	Derby 1995-96
Bobby Davison	Derby 1982-88/91-92	Blades 1991-92/93-95
Gary Ablett	Derby 1984-85	Blades 1995-96
Gordon Cowans	Derby 1993-95	Blades 1995-96
Paul Simpson	Derby 1991-98	Blades 1996-97
Paul Parker	Blades 1996-97	Derby 1996-97
Lee Morris	Blades 1997-2000	Derby 1999-2004
Paul McGrath	Derby 1996-97	Blades 1997-98
Vassilios Borbokis	Blades 1997-99	Derby 1998-2000
Dean Saunders	Derby 1988-91	Blades 1997-99
Jonathan Hunt	Derby 1997-99	Blades 1998-2000
Rob Kozluk	Derby 1997-99	Blades 1998-2004
Brian Launders	Derby 1998-99	Blades 1999-2000
Paul Peschisolido	Blades 2000-04	Derby 2003-04
Shane Nicholson	Derby 1992-96	Blades 2001-02
Tommy Mooney	Blades 2002-03	Derby 2002-03
Dean Sturridge	Derby 1991-2001	Blades 2003-04
Ashley Ward	Derby 1995-98	Blades 2003-04
Izale McLeod	Derby 2002-04	Blades 2003-04

v. Derby Junction

FA Cup						Date	Result	Away Blades	Derby J	Division Blades	Derby J
1890-91 1st Qual Rd						4 October	Won	**1**	**0**	Non L	Non L

Summary	P	W	D	L	F	A
Blades' cup record:	1	1	0	0	1	0
TOTAL:	**1**	**1**	**0**	**0**	**1**	**0**

FACT FILE

● **T.B.A. Clarke scored the goal.**

v. Doncaster Rovers

Season	League	Date	Result	Home Blades	Doncaster	Date	Result	Away Blades	Doncaster	Final Positions Blades	Doncaster
1935-36	Division 2	1 January	Won	3	0	10 April	Drew	0	0	3rd	18th
1936-37	Division 2	10 April	Won	3	1	5 December	Drew	1	1	7th	22ndR
1950-51	Division 2	11 September	Drew	0	0	5 May	Drew	1	1	8th	11th
1951-52	Division 2	24 November	Won	2	1	12 April	Lost	1	2	11th	16th
1952-53	Division 2	25 December	Drew	2	2	26 December	Won	2	0	1stP	13th
1956-57	Division 2	24 November	Won	4	0	6 April	Lost	0	1	7th	14th
1957-58	Division 2	5 April	Won	3	0	12 October	Drew	2	2	6th	22ndR
1982-83	Division 3	27 December	Won	3	1	5 April	Lost	0	2	11th	23rdR

FA Cup

Season	Round					Date	Result	Blades	Doncaster	Division	
1937-38	Round 3					8 January	Won	2	0	Div 2	Div 3N
1988-89	Round 2					11 December	Won	3	1	Div 3	Div 4

League Cup

Season	Round	Date	Result	Blades	Doncaster	Date	Result	Blades	Doncaster	Division	
1979-80	Round 1	11 August	Drew	1	1	14 August	Lost	1	3	Div 3	Div 4

Summary

	P	W	D	L	F	A
Blades' home league record:	8	6	2	0	20	5
Blades' away league record:	8	1	4	3	7	9
Blades' cup record:	4	2	1	1	7	5
TOTAL:	**20**	**9**	**7**	**4**	**34**	**19**

Mark Rankine, who joined United a decade after he left his home-town club, Doncaster.

FACT FILE

- United have not lost in nine home games.
- Away from home, United have won one of eight in the league, but two of three in the cups.

Blades' top scorers vs Doncaster
Jock Dodds 5
Harold Brook, Derek Hawksworth 4

Blades hat-tricks vs Doncaster
24 Nov 1956 Derek Hawksworth

Played for both clubs

George Simpson	Blades 1897-1900	Doncaster 1901-03
Alonzo Drake	Doncaster 1901-03	Blades 1903-08
Norman Wharton	Blades 1928-30	Doncaster 1935-36
Reg Baines	Blades 1933-34	Doncaster 1934-37
Mick Killourhy	Blades 1931-36	Doncaster 1936-39
Charlie Leyfield	Blades 1937-39	Doncaster 1938-40
Ted Burgin	Blades 1949-57	Doncaster 1957-58
Graham Shaw	Blades 1951-67	Doncaster 1967-68
Colin Grainger	Blades 1953-57	Doncaster 1964-66
Bobby Rooney	Blades 1958-60	Doncaster 1962-63
John Nibloe	Blades 1958-61	Doncaster 1962-64
Andy Wilson	Blades 1959-61	Doncaster 1965-66
Keith Kettleborough	Blades 1960-66	Doncaster 1966-68
Ted Hemsley	Blades 1968-77	Doncaster 1977-79
Alan Warboys	Doncaster 1966-68/79-82	Blades 1972-73
Terry Curran	Doncaster 1973-76	Blades 1982-83
Don Peattie	Blades 1984-85	Doncaster 1985-86
Clive Mendonca	Blades 1986-88/91-92	Doncaster 1987-88
Cliff Powell	Blades 1987-89	Doncaster 1988-89
Paul Williams	Blades 1987-89	Doncaster 1995-96
Brian Deane	Doncaster 1985-88	Blades 1988-93/97-98
Billy Whitehurst	Blades 1989-91	Doncaster 1990-92
Nathan Peel	Blades 1991-92	Doncaster 1995-96
Steve Hawes	Blades 1995-97	Doncaster 1997-98
Jonathan Cullen	Doncaster 1990-92	Blades 1997-99
Mark Rankine	Doncaster 1987-92	Blades 2002-04
Jack Lester	Doncaster 1996-97	Blades 2003-04

v. Everton

		Home				Away				Final Positions	
Season	League	Date	Result	Blades	Everton	Date	Result	Blades	Everton	Blades	Everton
1893-94	Division 1	9 December	Lost	0	3	2 September	Won	3	2	10th	6th
1894-95	Division 1	26 February	Won	4	2	26 January	Drew	1	1	6th	2nd
1895-96	Division 1	9 November	Lost	1	2	5 October	Lost	0	5	12th	3rd
1896-97	Division 1	1 January	Lost	1	2	17 October	Won	2	1	2nd	7th
1897-98	Division 1	22 February	Drew	0	0	30 October	Won	4	1	1st	4th
1898-99	Division 1	3 September	Drew	1	1	31 December	Lost	0	1	16th	4th
1899-00	Division 1	30 December	Won	5	0	2 September	Won	2	1	2nd	11th
1900-01	Division 1	25 December	Won	2	1	6 October	Lost	1	3	14th	7th
1901-02	Division 1	1 February	Drew	0	0	5 October	Lost	1	2	10th	2nd
1902-03	Division 1	4 October	Lost	0	2	31 January	Lost	0	1	4th	12th
1903-04	Division 1	12 September	Won	2	1	9 January	Lost	0	2	7th	3rd
1904-05	Division 1	7 January	Won	1	0	10 September	Lost	0	2	6th	2nd
1905-06	Division 1	7 October	Won	3	2	10 February	Lost	2	3	13th	11th
1906-07	Division 1	4 March	Won	4	1	20 October	Lost	2	4	4th	3rd
1907-08	Division 1	15 February	Won	2	0	19 October	Lost	1	2	17th	11th
1908-09	Division 1	17 October	Lost	1	5	20 February	Lost	1	5	12th	2nd
1909-10	Division 1	26 February	Won	3	0	16 October	Won	2	1	6th	10th
1910-11	Division 1	15 October	Lost	0	1	18 February	Lost	0	1	9th	4th
1911-12	Division 1	7 October	Won	2	1	10 February	Lost	2	3	14th	2nd
1912-13	Division 1	19 October	Won	4	1	12 March	Won	1	0	15th	11th
1913-14	Division 1	11 October	Won	4	1	14 February	Lost	0	5	10th	15th
1914-15	Division 1	19 September	Won	1	0	23 January	Drew	0	0	6th	1st
1919-20	Division 1	20 March	Drew	1	1	27 March	Lost	0	3	14th	16th
1920-21	Division 1	4 October	Won	2	0	22 September	Lost	0	3	20th	7th
1921-22	Division 1	15 April	Won	1	0	22 April	Drew	1	1	11th	20th
1922-23	Division 1	16 April	Lost	0	1	17 March	Lost	1	5	10th	5th
1923-24	Division 1	3 November	Won	4	0	10 November	Lost	0	2	5th	7th
1924-25	Division 1	20 December	Drew	1	1	27 April	Drew	1	1	14th	17th
1925-26	Division 1	2 January	Drew	1	1	29 August	Drew	2	2	5th	11th
1926-27	Division 1	6 November	Drew	3	3	26 March	Lost	0	2	8th	20th
1927-28	Division 1	14 April	Lost	1	3	3 December	Drew	0	0	13th	1st
1928-29	Division 1	17 November	Won	2	1	30 March	Won	3	1	11th	18th
1929-30	Division 1	21 December	Won	2	0	26 April	Lost	2	3	20th	22ndR
1931-32	Division 1	10 October	Lost	1	5	20 February	Lost	1	5	7th	1st
1932-33	Division 1	17 December	Won	3	2	3 May	Lost	0	1	10th	11th
1933-34	Division 1	11 November	Drew	1	1	24 March	Lost	0	4	22ndR	14th
1946-47	Division 1	19 April	Won	2	0	14 December	Won	3	2	6th	10th
1947-48	Division 1	20 March	Won	2	1	1 November	Lost	0	2	12th	14th
1948-49	Division 1	9 April	Drew	1	1	13 November	Lost	1	2	22ndR	18th
1951-52	Division 2	19 April	Lost	1	2	1 December	Lost	0	1	11th	7th
1952-53	Division 2	25 August	Won	1	0	3 September	Drew	0	0	1stP	16th
1954-55	Division 1	21 August	Lost	2	5	18 December	Won	3	2	13th	11th
1955-56	Division 1	2 April	Drew	1	1	30 March	Won	4	1	22ndR	15th
1961-62	Division 1	14 March	Drew	1	1	21 October	Lost	0	1	5th	4th

Season	League	Date	Result	Blades	Everton	Date	Result	Blades	Everton	Blades	Everton
		Home						**Away**		*Final Positions*	
1962-63	Division 1	30 March	Won	2	1	24 November	Lost	0	3	10th	1st
1963-64	Division 1	22 February	Drew	0	0	15 October	Lost	1	4	12th	3rd
1964-65	Division 1	16 January	Drew	0	0	12 September	Drew	1	1	19th	4th
1965-66	Division 1	13 November	Won	2	0	9 April	Won	3	1	9th	11th
1966-67	Division 1	10 September	Drew	0	0	14 January	Lost	1	4	10th	6th
1967-68	Division 1	13 April	Lost	0	1	18 November	Lost	0	1	21stR	5th
1971-72	Division 1	18 March	Drew	1	1	21 August	Won	1	0	10th	15th
1972-73	Division 1	21 October	Lost	0	1	17 March	Lost	1	2	14th	17th
1973-74	Division 1	2 February	Drew	1	1	15 December	Drew	1	1	13th	7th
1974-75	Division 1	12 October	Drew	2	2	19 April	Won	3	2	6th	4th
1975-76	Division 1	7 February	Drew	0	0	26 August	Lost	0	3	22ndR	11th
1990-91	Division 1	10 November	Drew	0	0	23 February	Won	2	1	13th	9th
1991-92	Division 1	14 September	Won	2	1	11 April	Won	2	0	9th	12th
1992-93	Premiership	12 December	Won	1	0	4 May	Won	2	0	14th	13th
1993-94	Premiership	11 December	Drew	0	0	21 August	Lost	2	4	20thR	17th

FA Cup

Season	League	Date	Result	Blades	Everton	Date	Result	Blades	Everton	Division Blades	Everton
1895-96	Round 2					15 February	Lost	0	3	Div 1	Div 1
1900-01	Round 2	23 February	Won	2	0					Div 1	Div 1
1906-07	Round 1					12 January	Lost	0	1	Div 1	Div 1
1924-25	Round 3	21 February	Won	1	0					Div 1	Div 1
1960-61	Round 3					7 January	Won	1	0	Div 2	Div 1
1969-70	Round 3	3 January	Won	2	1					Div 2	Div 1

League Cup

Season	League	Date	Result	Blades	Everton	Date	Result	Blades	Everton	Division Blades	Everton
1977-78	Round 2	30 August	Lost	0	3					Div 2	Div 1
1984-85	Round 2	26 September	Drew	2	2	10 October	Lost	0	4	Div 2	Div 1
1990-91	Round 3	30 October	Won	2	1					Div 1	Div 1

Summary	P	W	D	L	F	A
Blades' home league record:	59	26	20	13	86	64
Blades' away league record:	59	16	9	34	67	117
Blades' cup record:	10	5	1	4	10	15
TOTAL:	**129**	**47**	**30**	**51**	**163**	**196**

FACT FILE

- **The Blades' first top-flight fixture was against Everton in September 1893.**
- **United lost 10 in a row at Goodison Park between 1900 and 1909.**
- **United are unbeaten in their last seven home league fixtures.**
- **United won five in a row from 1991 to 1993.**
- **The sides drew five times in succession during the 1920s.**

Blades' top scorers vs Everton
Harry Johnson 10
Arthur Brown 7
Walter Bennett 6
Billy Gillespie, Mick Jones, Joe Kitchen 5
Jack Almond, Colin Collindridge, Jimmy Hagan,
Harry Hammond, Walter Hardinge, Fred Priest,
Fred Tunstall 4

Blades hat-tricks vs Everton
26 Feb 1895 Harry Hammond
 4 Mar 1907 Arthur Brown
 3 Nov 1923 Harry Johnson (4)
30 Mar 1956 Jack Wilkinson

Played for both clubs

Joe Davies	Everton 1888-89	Blades 1894-96
Harry Hammond	Everton 1889-90	Blades 1892-97
Bob Cain	Everton 1889-90	Blades 1892-98
Stan Fazackerley	Blades 1912-21	Everton 1920-23
Jack Kendall	Everton 1923-26	Blades 1929-34
Charlie Leyfield	Everton 1934-37	Blades 1937-39
Jock Dodds	Blades 1934-39	Everton 1946-49
David Irving	Everton 1973-76	Blades 1975-76
Imre Varadi	Blades 1978-79	Everton 1979-81
Bruce Rioch	Everton 1976-78	Blades 1978-79
Terry Curran	Blades 1982-83	Everton 1982-85
Trevor Ross	Everton 1977-83	Blades 1982-84
Ken McNaught	Everton 1974-77	Blades 1985-86
Peter Beagrie	Blades 1986-88	Everton 1989-94/97-98
Mitch Ward	Blades 1990-98	Everton 1997-2000
Adrian Heath	Everton 1981-89	Blades 1995-96
Brett Angell	Everton 1993-95	Blades 1995-96
Gary Ablett	Everton 1991-96	Blades 1995-96
Don Hutchison	Blades 1995-98	Everton 1997-2000
John Ebbrell	Everton 1988-97	Blades 1996-97
Carl Tiler	Blades 1996-98	Everton 1997-99
Jon O'Connor	Everton 1995-98	Blades 1997-99
Graham Stuart	Everton 1993-98	Blades 1997-99
Earl Barrett	Everton 1994-98	Blades 1997-98
Terry Phelan	Everton 1996-98	Blades 2001-02
Stuart McCall	Everton 1988-91	Blades 2002-04
Paul Gerrard	Everton 1996-2003	Blades 2003-04

v. Exeter City

Season	League	Date	Result	Home Blades	Exeter	Date	Result	Away Blades	Exeter	Final Positions Blades	Exeter
1979-80	Division 3	1 September	Won	3	1	12 January	Lost	1	3	12th	8th
1980-81	Division 3	18 October	Won	3	1	21 March	Drew	1	1	21stR	11th
1982-83	Division 3	5 March	Won	3	0	23 October	Won	3	0	11th	19th
1983-84	Division 3	12 November	Drew	2	2	10 March	Won	2	1	3rdP	24thR

Summary	P	W	D	L	F	A
Blades' home league record:	4	3	1	0	11	4
Blades' away league record:	4	2	1	1	7	5
TOTAL:	8	5	2	1	18	9

FACT FILE

● **United are unbeaten in their last six fixtures in the series.**

Blades' top scorers vs Exeter
Colin Morris 4
Keith Edwards 3

Blades hat-tricks vs Exeter
23 Oct 1982 Colin Morris

Played for both clubs

Walter Brayshaw	Blades 1919-20	Exeter 1920-21
Harry Warren	Exeter 1927-28	Blades 1929-30
Jack Alderson	Blades 1925-29	Exeter 1929-30
Jack Dryden	Exeter 1934-35	Blades 1935-36
Benjamin Clarke	Blades 1934-37	Exeter 1937-39
Jack Wilkinson	Blades 1955-57	Exeter 1959-61
David Munks	Blades 1965-69	Exeter 1974-76
Ian Benjamin	Blades 1978-80	Exeter 1988-90
Steve Neville	Exeter 1978-81/82-85/88-91	Blades 1980-82
Richard Cooper	Blades 1982-85	Exeter 1987-89
Steve Wigley	Blades 1985-87	Exeter 1993-94
Simon Webster	Exeter 1983-84	Blades 1987-90
Brian Gayle	Blades 1991-96	Exeter 1996-97
David Lee	Blades 1997-98	Exeter 1999-2000
Nicky Marker	Exeter 1981-88	Blades 1997-99
Steve Lovell	Exeter 1999-2000	Blades 2001-02

v. Fulham

Season	League	Date	Result	Blades	Fulham	Date	Result	Blades	Fulham	Blades	Fulham
			Home				**Away**			*Final Positions*	
1934-35	Division 2	22 April	Lost	1	2	19 April	Lost	2	7	11th	7th
1935-36	Division 2	26 March	Lost	0	1	2 November	Lost	1	3	3rd	9th
1936-37	Division 2	12 December	Won	2	0	17 April	Lost	0	4	7th	11th
1937-38	Division 2	23 October	Won	2	1	5 March	Drew	1	1	3rd	8th
1938-39	Division 2	22 April	Won	2	0	17 December	Won	2	1	2ndP	12th
1952-53	Division 2	6 December	Won	2	1	25 April	Won	2	1	1stP	8th
1956-57	Division 2	20 August	Won	5	2	29 August	Won	2	1	7th	11th
1957-58	Division 2	28 April	Drew	1	1	28 September	Lost	3	6	6th	5th
1958-59	Division 2	21 March	Won	2	0	1 November	Lost	2	4	3rd	2ndP
1961-62	Division 1	28 October	Drew	2	2	17 March	Lost	2	5	5th	20th
1962-63	Division 1	22 August	Won	2	0	29 August	Drew	2	2	10th	16th
1963-64	Division 1	4 April	Won	1	0	23 November	Lost	1	3	12th	15th
1964-65	Division 1	9 September	Drew	1	1	16 September	Won	2	1	19th	20th
1965-66	Division 1	15 September	Won	2	0	8 September	Drew	0	0	9th	20th
1966-67	Division 1	7 January	Won	4	0	3 September	Won	1	0	10th	18th
1967-68	Division 1	23 April	Lost	2	3	13 March	Won	1	0	21stR	22ndR
1968-69	Division 2	27 August	Won	1	0	9 October	Drew	2	2	9th	22ndR
1976-77	Division 2	16 October	Drew	1	1	26 March	Lost	2	3	11th	17th
1977-78	Division 2	29 October	Won	2	1	24 March	Lost	0	2	12th	10th
1978-79	Division 2	6 February	Drew	1	1	9 September	Lost	0	2	20thR	10th
1980-81	Division 3	21 April	Lost	1	2	26 December	Lost	1	2	21stR	13th
1984-85	Division 2	6 April	Lost	0	1	26 December	Lost	0	1	18th	9th
1985-86	Division 2	28 December	Won	2	1	17 September	Won	3	2	7th	22ndR
1988-89	Division 3	12 November	Won	1	0	29 April	Drew	2	2	2ndP	4th
1999-00	Division 1	28 December	Won	2	0	15 April	Lost	0	4	16th	9th
2000-01	Division 1	21 November	Drew	1	1	4 February	Drew	1	1	10th	1stP

FA Cup

Season	Round	Date	Result	Blades	Fulham	Date	Result	Blades	Fulham	Division	
1935-36	Semi-Final	21 March		Molineux			Won	2	1	Div 2	Div 2
1965-66	Round 3	22 January	Won	3	1					Div 1	Div 1
1966-67	Round 4	1 March	Won	3	1	18 February	Drew	1	1	Div 1	Div 1
1985-86	Round 3	13 January	Won	2	0					Div 2	Div 2

League Cup

Season	Round	Date	Result	Blades	Fulham	Date	Result	Blades	Fulham	Division	
1961-62	Round 1	25 September	Won	4	0	13 September	Drew	1	1	Div 1	Div 1
1971-72	Round 2	7 September	Won	3	0					Div 1	Div 2

Summary

	P	W	D	L	F	A
Blades' home league record:	26	15	6	5	43	22
Blades' away league record:	26	7	6	13	35	60
Blades' cup record:	8	6	2	0	19	5
TOTAL:	**60**	**28**	**14**	**18**	**97**	**87**

FACT FILE

- **United's first League Cup win came against Fulham in 1961.**
- **United won six in a row from 1938 to 1956.**
- **United lost four in a row from 1980 to 1985.**
- **Between 1936 and 1967, United were undefeated in 16 games at home.**

Blades' top scorers vs Fulham

Alan Woodward 8

Alan Birchenall, Mick Jones 6

Jock Dodds, Bill Hodgson 5

Derek Hawksworth 4

Played for both clubs

Bert Lipsham	Blades 1899-1908	Fulham 1907-10
Arthur Brown	Blades 1902-08	Fulham 1910-12
Tommy Simons	Blades 1910-12	Fulham 1914-15
Walter Hoyland	Blades 1921-27	Fulham 1926-28
Alex Forbes	Blades 1946-48	Fulham 1957-58
Reg Matthewson	Blades 1961-68	Fulham 1967-73
Alan Warboys	Blades 1972-73	Fulham 1976-78
Chris Guthrie	Blades 1975-77	Fulham 1978-80
John Cutbush	Fulham 1972-77	Blades 1976-81
Viv Busby	Fulham 1973-77	Blades 1979-80
John Ryan	Fulham 1965-69	Blades 1980-82
Gary Brazil	Blades 1980-85	Fulham 1990-96
Glenn Cockerill	Blades 1983-86	Fulham 1996-98
Jeff Eckhardt	Blades 1984-88	Fulham 1987-94
Ray Lewington	Fulham 1979-85/86-90	Blades 1985-86
Steve Foley	Fulham 1983-84	Blades 1985-87
Martin Pike	Blades 1986-90	Fulham 1989-94
Francis Joseph	Blades 1988-89	Fulham 1990-91
Andy Sayer	Fulham 1988-90	Blades 1990-91
Alan Cork	Blades 1991-94	Fulham 1994-95
Charlie Hartfield	Blades 1991-97	Fulham 1996-97
Rob Scott	Blades 1994-96	Fulham 1995-99
Paul Parker	Fulham 1980-87/96-97	Blades 1996-97
Gus Uhlenbeek	Fulham 1998-2000	Blades 2000-02
Paul Peschisolido	Fulham 1997-2000	Blades 2000-04
Terry Phelan	Fulham 1999-2001	Blades 2001-02
Jon Harley	Fulham 2001-04	Blades 2002-04

v. Gainsborough Trinity

				Date	Result	Away		Division	
						Blades	Gainsb'gh	Blades	Gainsb'gh
FA Cup									
1891-92 4th Qual Rd				5 December	Won	**1**	**0**	Non L	Non L

Summary	P	W	D	L	F	A
Blades' cup record:	1	1	0	0	1	0
TOTAL:	1	1	0	0	1	0

FACT FILE

● **Sammy Dobson scored the goal.**

Played for both clubs

Walter Wigmore	Blades 1895-96	Gainsborough 1896-99
Edwin Greensill	Blades 1901-02	Gainsborough 1902-04
Arthur Brown	Gainsborough 1901-02	Blades 1902-08
Billy Bromage	Gainsborough 1902-03	Blades 1905-09
John Pattinson	Gainsborough 1903-05/08-11	Blades 1905-07
Joe Kitchen	Gainsborough 1906-08	Blades 1907-21
George Brown	Gainsborough 1907-08	Blades 1908-09
Wally Masterman	Gainsborough 1910-12	Blades 1914-20
Ollie Tummon	Gainsborough 1910-12	Blades 1919-20

v. Gateshead

FA Cup		Date	Result	Home Blades Gateshead						Division Blades Gateshead
1950-51	Round 3	6 January	Won	**1**	**0**					Div 2 Div 3N

Summary	P	W	D	L	F	A
Blades' cup record:	1	1	0	0	1	0
TOTAL:	**1**	**1**	**0**	**0**	**1**	**0**

FACT FILE

- Jimmy Hagan scored the goal.
- The South Shields club relocated to Gateshead in the 1930s, hence the inclusion of the South Shields name in the list below.

Played for both clubs

Charles Johnson	Blades 1905-10	South Shields 1919-20
Joseph Mitchell	Blades 1909-13	South Shields 1919-20
Bob Bolam	Blades 1919-22	South Shields 1923-24
Peter Spooner	Blades 1933-35	Gateshead 1939-40
Sam Kemp	Blades 1956-58	Gateshead 1958-59

v. Gillingham

				Home				Away		Final Positions	
Season	League	Date	Result	Blades	Gillingham	Date	Result	Blades	Gillingham	Blades	Gillingham
1979-80	Division 3	10 November	Won	4	0	22 March	Lost	0	3	12th	16th
1980-81	Division 3	17 January	Lost	0	1	28 October	Drew	2	2	21stR	15th
1982-83	Division 3	2 October	Lost	0	2	15 March	Won	2	0	11th	13th
1983-84	Division 3	27 August	Won	4	0	14 January	Lost	2	4	3rdP	8th
1988-89	Division 3	21 January	Won	4	2	10 September	Lost	1	2	2ndP	23rdR
2000-01	Division 1	4 November	Lost	1	2	14 April	Lost	1	4	10th	13th
2001-02	Division 1	18 August	Drew	0	0	12 January	Won	1	0	13th	12th
2002-03	Division 1	25 March	Drew	2	2	21 September	Drew	1	1	3rd	11th
2003-04	Division 1	9 August	Drew	0	0	10 January	Won	3	0	8th	21st

Summary	P	W	D	L	F	A
Blades' home league record:	9	3	3	3	15	9
Blades' away league record:	9	3	2	4	13	16
TOTAL:	**18**	**6**	**5**	**7**	**28**	**25**

FACT FILE

- **United are unbeaten in their last six games in the series.**

Blades' top scorers vs Gillingham
Keith Edwards 6
Paul Peschisolido 4
Barry Butlin 2

Blades hat-tricks vs Gillingham
27 Aug 1983 Keith Edwards (4)
10 Jan 2003 Paul Peschisolido

Played for both clubs
Fred Brown	Blades 1919-23	Gillingham 1924-27
Fred Cheesemur	Gillingham 1929-31	Blades 1930-34
Ronnie Waldock	Blades 1954-57	Gillingham 1961-64
Terry Nicholl	Blades 1973-75	Gillingham 1976-81
Paul Garner	Blades 1975-84	Gillingham 1983-84
Mike Trusson	Blades 1980-84	Gillingham 1989-92
Gary West	Blades 1982-85	Gillingham 1987-89/90-91
Mel Eves	Blades 1984-86	Gillingham 1986-88
Andy Kennedy	Blades 1986-87	Gillingham 1994-95
Darren Carr	Blades 1987-89	Gillingham 1998-99
Francis Joseph	Blades 1988-89	Gillingham 1988-90
Mark Morris	Blades 1989-91	Gillingham 1996-97
Phil Kite	Gillingham 1986-89	Blades 1990-92
Steve Bruce	Gillingham 1979-84	Blades 1998-99
Carl Asaba	Gillingham 1998-2001	Blades 2000-03
Iffy Onoura	Gillingham 1996-98/99-2002	Blades 2002-03
Paul Shaw	Gillingham 2000-04	Blades 2003-04

v. Glossop

Season	League	Date	Result			Date	Result			Final Positions	
				Home				**Away**			
				Blades	Glossop			Blades	Glossop	Blades	Glossop
1899-00	Division 1	7 April	Won	**4**	**0**	2 December	Drew	**2**	**2**	2nd	18thR

Summary	P	W	D	L	F	A
Blades' home league record:	1	1	0	0	4	0
Blades' away league record:	1	0	1	0	2	2
TOTAL:	2	1	1	0	6	2

Blades' top scorers vs Glossop
Walter Bennett, Billy Brawn 2

Played for both clubs
William Ross	Blades 1895-97	Glossop 1905-08
William Kent	Blades 1899-1900	Glossop 1900-01
Joe Brooks	Glossop 1900-01	Blades 1907-12
Archie Needham	Blades 1902-04	Glossop 1909-10
James Raine	Blades 1904-05	Glossop 1908-11

v. Grimsby Town

			Home				Away		Final Positions	
Season	League	Date	Result	Blades	Grimsby	Date	Result	Blades Grimsby	Blades	Grimsby
1892-93	Division 2	27 September	Won	2	0	31 March	Won	1 0	2ndP	4th
1901-02	Division 1	11 February	Drew	2	2	28 December	Won	1 0	10th	15th
1902-03	Division 1	11 April	Won	3	0	13 December	Won	2 1	4th	17thR
1929-30	Division 1	31 August	Lost	2	3	28 December	Lost	1 4	20th	18th
1930-31	Division 1	18 April	Won	2	1	13 December	Lost	1 2	15th	13th
1931-32	Division 1	5 March	Won	2	1	24 October	Won	2 0	7th	21stR
1946-47	Division 1	14 September	Drew	1	1	18 January	Lost	1 2	6th	16th
1947-48	Division 1	17 January	Won	4	0	6 September	Won	3 0	12th	22ndR
1949-50	Division 2	4 February	Won	3	1	24 September	Lost	0 4	3rd	11th
1950-51	Division 2	3 March	Won	4	2	14 October	Drew	2 2	8th	22ndR
1956-57	Division 2	30 March	Won	2	0	17 November	Won	2 1	7th	16th
1957-58	Division 2	2 November	Won	3	1	15 March	Won	3 1	6th	13th
1958-59	Division 2	27 December	Won	2	1	25 December	Won	2 1	3rd	21stR
1979-80	Division 3	29 December	Drew	1	1	3 May	Lost	0 4	12th	1stP
1984-85	Division 2	29 September	Lost	2	3	2 February	Won	2 0	18th	10th
1985-86	Division 2	15 March	Drew	1	1	12 October	Won	1 0	7th	15th
1986-87	Division 2	20 September	Lost	1	2	28 February	Lost	0 1	9th	21stR
1994-95	Division 1	6 May	Won	3	1	8 October	Drew	0 0	8th	10th
1995-96	Division 1	21 November	Lost	1	2	20 April	Won	2 0	9th	17th
1996-97	Division 1	22 February	Won	3	1	3 November	Won	4 2	5th	22ndR
1998-99	Division 1	8 September	Won	3	2	20 April	Won	2 1	8th	11th
1999-00	Division 1	8 April	Drew	0	0	3 January	Drew	2 2	16th	20th
2000-01	Division 1	18 November	Won	3	2	21 April	Won	1 0	10th	18th
2001-02	Division 1	13 October	Won	3	1	16 February	Lost	0 1	13th	19th
2002-03	Division 1	17 September	Won	2	1	4 March	Won	4 1	3rd	24thR

FA Cup

									Division	
1891-92	3rd Qual Rd					14 November	Won	2 1	Non L	Non L
1938-39	Round 5	11 February	Drew	0	0	14 February	Lost	0 1	Div 2	Div 1
1957-58	Round 3	4 January	Won	5	1				Div 2	Div 2
1979-80	Round 2					15 December	Lost	0 2	Div 3	Div 3

League Cup

									Division	
1982-83	Round 2	26 October	Won	5	1	12 October	Drew	3 3	Div 3	Div 2
1998-99	Round 2	15 September	Won	2	1	22 September	Lost*	0 2	Div 1	Div 1
2001-02	Round 2					11 September	Drew*	3 3	Div 1	Div 1
						(lost 2-4 pens)				

Summary

	P	W	D	L	F	A
Blades' home league record:	25	16	5	4	55	30
Blades' away league record:	25	15	3	7	39	30
Blades' cup record:	10	4	3	3	20	15
TOTAL:	**60**	**35**	**11**	**14**	**114**	**75** (+one penalty shoot-out defeat)

- **United have lost one of the last 13 league games.**
- **United won eight in a row in the 1950s.**
- **United have lost only 11 of 50 league games.**

Blades' top scorers vs Grimsby
Jimmy Dunne 5
Harold Brook, Keith Edwards, Derek Hawksworth,
Colin Morris, Derek Pace, Dennis Thompson 4

Blades hat-tricks vs Grimsby
17 Jan 1948 Dennis Thompson
26 Oct 1982 Keith Edwards (cup)
22 Feb 1997 Jan Aage Fjortoft

Played for both clubs

Charlie Henderson	Grimsby 1892-93	Blades 1896-97
Jack Jones	Grimsby 1893-94	Blades 1894-97
Wilson Greenwood	Blades 1894-95	Grimsby 1898-1900
Hugh Morris	Blades 1893-96	Grimsby 1896-97
William Ross	Blades 1895-97	Grimsby 1904-05
Thomas Jenkinson	Blades 1897-98	Grimsby 1898-1901
Herbert Chapman	Grimsby 1898-99	Blades 1902-03
Bill Forster	Blades 1903-06	Grimsby 1908-09
John Bisby	Blades 1905-06	Grimsby 1906-08
John Pattinson	Blades 1905-07	Grimsby 1907-08
Dicky Leafe	Grimsby 1909-10	Blades 1911-13
William Bell	Blades 1926-27	Grimsby 1930-32
Fred Smith	Blades 1947-52	Grimsby 1952-54
Edward Grant	Blades 1950-51	Grimsby 1952-54
Mick Speight	Blades 1971-80	Grimsby 1982-84
Terry Curran	Blades 1982-83	Grimsby 1987-88
Steve Foley	Grimsby 1984-85	Blades 1985-87
Clive Mendonca	Blades 1986-88/91-92	Grimsby 1991-97
Willie Falconer	Blades 1993-94	Grimsby 2001-02
Kingsley Black	Blades 1994-95	Grimsby 1996-2001
Ian Hamilton	Blades 1997-2000	Grimsby 1999-2000
Des Hamilton	Blades 1998-99	Grimsby 2003-04
Aidan Davison	Grimsby 1997-99/2003-04	Blades 1999-2000
George Santos	Blades 2000-02	Grimsby 2002-03
Mick Boulding	Grimsby 2001-04	Blades 2002-03
Marcel Gas	Blades 2002-03	Grimsby 2003-04
Iffy Onoura	Blades 2002-03	Grimsby 2003-04
Laurens Ten Heuvel	Blades 2002-03	Grimsby 2003-04
Steve Kabba	Grimsby 2002-03	Blades 2002-04
Jack Lester	Grimsby 1994-2000	Blades 2003-04
Alan Fettis	Blades 2003-04	Grimsby 2003-04

v. Halifax Town

				Home				Away		Final Positions	
Season	League	Date	Result	Blades	Halifax	Date	Result	Blades	Halifax	Blades	Halifax
1981-82	Division 4	2 January	Drew	2	2	12 April	Won	5	1	1stP	19th

League Cup

						Date	Result	Blades	Halifax	Division	
1975-76	Round 2					10 September	Won	4	2	Div 1	Div 3

Summary	P	W	D	L	F	A
Blades' home league record:	1	0	1	0	2	2
Blades' away league record:	1	1	0	0	5	1
Blades' cup record:	1	1	0	0	4	2
TOTAL:	3	2	1	0	11	5

Blades' top scorers vs Halifax
Chris Guthrie, Tony Kenworthy 3
Keith Edwards 2

Blades hat-tricks vs Halifax
10 Sep 1975 Chris Guthrie (cup)

Played for both clubs

Percy Oldacre	Blades 1921-23	Halifax 1923-24
Jimmy Shankly	Halifax 1924-25	Blades 1926-28
Harry Green	Blades 1925-26	Halifax 1928-29
Arthur Mercer	Blades 1926-28	Halifax 1933-35
Fred Tunstall	Blades 1920-32	Halifax 1932-36
Reg Baines	Blades 1933-34	Halifax 1939-40
Albert Cox	Blades 1935-52	Halifax 1952-54
Walter Rickett	Blades 1946-48	Halifax 1953-54
George Hutchinson	Blades 1948-53	Halifax 1956-58
Harry Priest	Blades 1956-57	Halifax 1957-59
John Parks	Blades 1963-64	Halifax 1966-68
Willie Carlin	Halifax 1962-65	Blades 1967-69
David Staniforth	Blades 1968-74	Halifax 1982-84
David Ford	Blades 1970-73	Halifax 1973-76
John Connaughton	Halifax 1969-70	Blades 1973-74
Tony Field	Halifax 1963-66	Blades 1973-76
Bobby Campbell	Halifax 1974-75/78-79	Blades 1977-78
Ray McHale	Halifax 1974-77	Blades 1982-85
Russell Black	Blades 1984-86	Halifax 1986-88
Chris Wilder	Blades 1986-92/97-99	Halifax 1999-2001
Peter Duffield	Halifax 1987-88	Blades 1987-92
John Francis	Halifax 1984-85	Blades 1988-90
Richard Lucas	Blades 1990-92	Halifax 1998-2000
Nathan Peel	Blades 1991-92	Halifax 1992-93
Bobby Davison	Halifax 1981-83	Blades 1991-92/93-95
Jonathan Cullen	Blades 1997-99	Halifax 1999-2000
Andy Woodward	Blades 1999-2000	Halifax 2001-02
Grant Smith	Halifax 2001-02	Blades 2001-03
Wayne Allison	Halifax 1986-89	Blades 2002-04

v. Hartlepool United

Season	League	Date	Result	Home Blades	Hartlepool	Date	Result	Away Blades	Hartlepool	Final Positions Blades	Hartlepool
1981-82	Division 4	17 October	Drew	1	1	6 March	Won	3	2	1stP	14th

FA Cup

										Division	
1992-93	Round 4	23 January	Won	1	0					Prem	Div 2

League Cup

1988-89	Round 1	6 September	Won*	2	0	30 August	Drew	2	2	Div 3	Div 4

Summary	P	W	D	L	F	A
Blades' home league record:	1	0	1	0	1	1
Blades' away league record:	1	1	0	0	3	2
Blades' cup record:	3	2	1	0	5	2
TOTAL:	**5**	**3**	**2**	**0**	**9**	**5**

Blades' top scorers vs Hartlepool
Tony Agana, Keith Edwards 2

Played for both clubs

Tucker Mordue	Blades 1926-28	Hartlepool 1928-31
Norman Thompson	Blades 1936-37	Hartlepool 1937-38
Alf Tootill	Blades 1938-39	Hartlepool 1947-48
Harry Hooper	Blades 1930-39	Hartlepool 1947-50
Charles Weatherspoon	Blades 1950-51	Hartlepool 1952-53
John Hope	Blades 1970-74	Hartlepool 1975-76
John McPhail	Blades 1978-83	Hartlepool 1990-95
Paul Williams	Blades 1987-89	Hartlepool 1989-90
Richard Lucas	Blades 1990-92	Hartlepool 1996-98
Carl Muggleton	Hartlepool 1988-89	Blades 1995-96
Don Hutchison	Hartlepool 1989-91	Blades 1995-98
Jonathan Cullen	Hartlepool 1996-98	Blades 1997-99
Michael Brown	Hartlepool 1996-97	Blades 1999-2004
Frank Talia	Hartlepool 1992-93	Blades 2000-01

Frank Talia, the Australian
goalkeeper who made a
handful of appearances for
United and was once on loan
to Hartlepool.

v. Hereford United

Season	League	Date	Result	Home Blades	Hereford	Date	Result	Away Blades	Hereford	Final Positions Blades	Hereford
1976-77	Division 2	28 August	Drew	1	1	23 March	Drew	2	2	11th	22ndR
1981-82	Division 4	29 August	Drew	2	2	17 February	Drew	1	1	1stP	10th

Summary	P	W	D	L	F	A
Blades' home league record:	2	0	2	0	3	3
Blades' away league record:	2	0	2	0	3	3
TOTAL:	**4**	**0**	**4**	**0**	**6**	**6**

FACT FILE

- **Sheffield United have never beaten Hereford.**
- **Hereford have never beaten Sheffield United.**

Blades' top scorers vs Hereford
Keith Edwards 2

Played for both clubs

Ken Mallender	Blades 1961-69	Hereford 1972-74
Alan Birchenall	Blades 1964-68	Hereford 1979-80
Colin Addison	Blades 1967-71	Hereford 1972-74
Gary Jones	Blades 1974-75	Hereford 1980-81
Cliff Powell	Hereford 1987-88	Blades 1987-89
Tony Agana	Blades 1987-92	Hereford 1996-97
Phil Starbuck	Hereford 1989-90	Blades 1994-97

v. Huddersfield Town

Season	League	Date	Result	Blades	Hudd'fd	Date	Result	Blades	Hudd'fd	Blades	Hudd'fd
				Home				**Away**		*Final Positions*	
1920-21	Division 1	29 December	Drew	1	1	29 March	Lost	0	1	20th	17th
1921-22	Division 1	29 August	Drew	1	1	6 September	Drew	1	1	11th	14th
1922-23	Division 1	9 April	Lost	0	2	10 February	Lost	1	2	10th	3rd
1923-24	Division 1	15 March	Lost	0	1	22 March	Lost	0	1	5th	1st
1924-25	Division 1	3 January	Drew	1	1	6 September	Lost	1	2	14th	1st
1925-26	Division 1	5 September	Lost	2	3	16 January	Lost	1	4	5th	1st
1926-27	Division 1	20 November	Drew	3	3	9 April	Won	2	0	8th	2nd
1927-28	Division 1	12 November	Lost	1	7	30 April	Won	1	0	13th	2nd
1928-29	Division 1	6 April	Won	1	0	24 November	Lost	1	6	11th	16th
1929-30	Division 1	17 February	Lost	0	1	21 September	Drew	2	2	20th	10th
1930-31	Division 1	21 March	Lost	0	2	15 November	Drew	1	1	15th	5th
1931-32	Division 1	17 October	Lost	0	2	2 March	Drew	2	2	7th	4th
1932-33	Division 1	17 September	Lost	1	2	1 February	Lost	0	1	10th	6th
1933-34	Division 1	10 February	Lost	1	4	30 September	Lost	1	6	22ndR	2nd
1946-47	Division 1	21 December	Drew	2	2	26 April	Drew	1	1	6th	20th
1947-48	Division 1	17 April	Lost	0	1	29 November	Lost	1	2	12th	19th
1948-49	Division 1	22 January	Drew	0	0	11 September	Drew	0	0	22ndR	20th
1952-53	Division 2	30 August	Lost	0	2	3 January	Drew	1	1	1stP	2ndP
1953-54	Division 1	19 September	Lost	3	6	6 February	Drew	2	2	20th	3rd
1954-55	Division 1	26 March	Drew	2	2	6 November	Won	2	1	13th	12th
1955-56	Division 1	10 March	Won	3	1	29 October	Won	2	1	22ndR	21stR
1956-57	Division 2	16 March	Won	2	0	3 November	Won	4	1	7th	12th

Lee Sandford and Wayne Allison in combat in January 1998.

		Home				Away				Final Positions	
Season	League	Date	Result	Blades	Hudd'fd	Date	Result	Blades	Hudd'fd	Blades	Hudd'fd
1957-58	Division 2	8 March	Won	3	2	26 October	Drew	1	1	6th	9th
1958-59	Division 2	13 September	Drew	0	0	31 January	Won	2	0	3rd	14th
1959-60	Division 2	30 April	Won	2	0	31 October	Won	1	0	4th	6th
1960-61	Division 2	6 September	Won	3	1	14 September	Won	1	0	2ndP	20th
1968-69	Division 2	21 December	Drew	0	0	19 October	Lost	0	1	9th	6th
1969-70	Division 2	23 August	Drew	0	0	26 December	Lost	1	2	6th	1stP
1971-72	Division 1	31 August	Won	3	1	21 March	Drew	0	0	10th	22ndR
1980-81	Division 3	28 February	Drew	2	2	20 September	Lost	0	1	21stR	4th
1982-83	Division 3	7 September	Won	2	0	22 January	Drew	0	0	11th	3rdP
1984-85	Division 2	1 December	Lost	0	2	13 May	Drew	2	2	18th	13th
1985-86	Division 2	14 September	Drew	1	1	11 January	Lost	1	3	7th	16th
1986-87	Division 2	18 October	Drew	0	0	14 March	Drew	1	1	9th	17th
1987-88	Division 2	5 December	Drew	2	2	7 May	Won	2	0	21stR	23rdR
1988-89	Division 3	11 March	Won	5	1	5 November	Lost	2	3	2ndP	14th
1995-96	Division 1	9 December	Lost	0	2	24 September	Won	2	1	9th	8th
1996-97	Division 1	3 December	Won	3	1	31 March	Lost	1	2	5th	20th
1997-98	Division 1	27 January	Drew	1	1	30 August	Drew	0	0	6th	16th
1998-99	Division 1	28 December	Won	2	1	5 September	Lost	0	1	8th	10th
1999-00	Division 1	30 October	Lost	0	1	2 October	Lost	1	4	16th	8th
2000-01	Division 1	17 October	Won	3	0	17 March	Lost	1	2	10th	22ndR

FA Cup										Division	
1912-13	Round 1					15 January	Lost	1	3	Div 1	Div 2
1927-28	Semi-Final	24 March				Old Trafford	Drew*	2	2	Div 1	Div 1
		26 March				Goodison Park (replay)	Drew*	0	0		
		2 April				Maine Road (2nd replay)	Lost	0	1		
1929-30	Round 4					25 January	Lost	1	2	Div 1	Div 1
1945-46	Round 3	7 January	Won	2	0	5 January	Drew	1	1	Div 1	Div 1
1956-57	Round 3	7 January	Drew*	1	1	5 January	Drew	0	0	Div 2	Div 2
		14 January				Maine Road (2nd replay)	Lost	1	2		
1988-89	Round 3					7 January	Won	1	0	Div 3	Div 3

Summary

	P	W	D	L	F	A
Blades' home league record:	42	12	15	15	56	62
Blades' away league record:	42	10	14	18	46	62
Blades' cup record:	11	2	5	4	10	12
TOTAL:	**95**	**24**	**34**	**37**	**112**	**136**

FACT FILE

- From 1929 to 1954, United went 20 games without a league win.
- From 1954 to 1960, United were undefeated in 15 league games.
- United did not win in their first 14 games in the series.
- United's worst home league defeat was the 7-1 to Huddersfield in 1927.

Blades' top scorers vs Huddersfield

Harry Johnson 8
Billy Gillespie 6
Derek Hawksworth 5
Colin Collindridge, Jimmy Dunne 4
Tony Agana, Peter Duffield, Bobby Howitt,
Alf Ringstead, Billy Russell, Fred Tunstall 3

Played for both clubs

Harry Cawthorne	Huddersfield 1921-27	Blades 1926-29
Levi Redfern	Huddersfield 1927-31	Blades 1935-36
Willis Vaughton	Huddersfield 1933-34	Blades 1934-35
George Richardson	Huddersfield 1933-34	Blades 1935-39
Bobby Barclay	Blades 1931-37	Huddersfield 1936-40
Eddie Boot	Blades 1935-37	Huddersfield 1936-52
Albert Nightingale	Blades 1946-48	Huddersfield 1947-52
Graham Bailey	Huddersfield 1946-47	Blades 1947-49
George Hutchinson	Huddersfield 1947-48	Blades 1948-53
Derek Hawksworth	Blades 1950-58	Huddersfield 1958-60
Kevin Lewis	Blades 1957-60	Huddersfield 1963-65
Ron Simpson	Huddersfield 1951-58	Blades 1958-65
Ian Holmes	Blades 1971-73	Huddersfield 1977-80
Keith Edwards	Blades 1975-78/81-86	Huddersfield 1989-91
Paul Garner	Huddersfield 1972-76	Blades 1975-84
Bobby Campbell	Huddersfield 1975-77/78-79	Blades 1977-78
Tommy Smith	Blades 1978-79	Huddersfield 1978-79
Terry Poole	Huddersfield 1968-77	Blades 1979-80
Terry Curran	Blades 1982-83	Huddersfield 1985-86
Mel Eves	Huddersfield 1983-84	Blades 1984-86
Peter Withe	Blades 1985-88	Huddersfield 1988-90
Chris Marsden	Blades 1987-88	Huddersfield 1988-94
Simon Webster	Huddersfield 1984-88	Blades 1987-90
Bobby Davison	Huddersfield 1980-81	Blades 1991-92/93-95
Tom Cowan	Blades 1991-94	Huddersfield 1993-99
Phil Starbuck	Huddersfield 1991-95	Blades 1994-97
Christian Short	Huddersfield 1994-95	Blades 1995-98
Lee Morris	Blades 1997-2000	Huddersfield 2000-01
Rob Kozluk	Blades 1998-2004	Huddersfield 2000-01
Des Hamilton	Blades 1998-99	Huddersfield 1998-99
Martin Smith	Blades 1999-2000	Huddersfield 1999-2003
Darren Bullock	Huddersfield 1993-97	Blades 2000-01
Andrew Morrison	Huddersfield 1996-99	Blades 2000-01
Jon Newby	Blades 2000-01	Huddersfield 2003-04
Peter Ndlovu	Huddersfield 2000-01	Blades 2000-04
Iffy Onoura	Huddersfield 1989-94/2003-04	Blades 2002-03
Steve Yates	Blades 2002-03	Huddersfield 2003-04
Wayne Allison	Huddersfield 1997-2000	Blades 2002-04

v. Hull City

			Home				Away			Final Positions	
Season	League	Date	Result	Blades	Hull	Date	Result	Blades	Hull	Blades	Hull
1934-35	Division 2	8 December	Lost	3	4	20 April	Won	3	0	11th	13th
1935-36	Division 2	21 December	Won	7	0	30 April	Drew	2	2	3rd	22ndR
1949-50	Division 2	29 April	Won	5	0	10 December	Won	4	0	3rd	7th
1950-51	Division 2	25 December	Won	3	1	26 December	Drew	1	1	8th	10th
1951-52	Division 2	25 August	Won	4	1	22 December	Lost	1	2	11th	18th
1952-53	Division 2	29 April	Lost	0	2	27 September	Lost	0	4	1stP	18th
1959-60	Division 2	24 August	Won	6	0	31 August	Won	2	0	4th	21stR
1968-69	Division 2	8 April	Drew	1	1	18 September	Drew	1	1	9th	11th
1969-70	Division 2	4 October	Won	3	0	31 January	Won	3	2	6th	13th
1970-71	Division 2	9 March	Lost	1	2	24 October	Drew	1	1	2ndP	5th
1976-77	Division 2	26 February	Drew	1	1	17 September	Drew	1	1	11th	14th
1977-78	Division 2	23 August	Won	2	0	31 December	Won	3	2	12th	22ndR
1979-80	Division 3	19 January	Drew	1	1	8 September	Lost	1	3	12th	20th
1980-81	Division 3	20 December	Won	3	1	25 April	Drew	1	1	21stR	24thR
1981-82	Division 4	30 January	Drew	0	0	19 September	Lost	1	2	1stP	8th
1983-84	Division 3	17 March	Drew	2	2	8 October	Lost	1	4	3rdP	4th
1985-86	Division 2	2 November	Won	3	1	5 April	Drew	0	0	7th	6th
1986-87	Division 2	26 December	Won	4	2	20 April	Drew	0	0	9th	14th
1987-88	Division 2	3 October	Won	2	1	27 February	Won	2	1	21stR	15th
1989-90	Division 2	23 September	Drew	0	0	3 February	Drew	0	0	2ndP	14th

FA Cup

										Division	
1982-83	Round 1	23 November	Won	2	0	20 November	Drew	1	1	Div 3	Div 4

League Cup

										Division	
1975-76	Round 3					7 October	Lost	0	2	Div 1	Div 2
1982-83	Round 1	31 August	Won	3	1	14 September	Lost	0	1	Div 3	Div 4

Summary	P	W	D	L	F	A
Blades' home league record:	20	11	6	3	51	20
Blades' away league record:	20	6	9	5	28	27
Blades' cup record:	5	2	1	2	6	5
TOTAL:	**45**	**19**	**16**	**10**	**85**	**52**

FACT FILE

- **Hull have not won in their last 12 visits to Bramall Lane.**
- **United are undefeated in their last eight matches.**
- **United have won matches 7-0, 6-0, 5-0, 4-0, 3-0 and 2-0, but never 1-0.**

Brian Marwood.

Blades' top scorers vs Hull

Keith Edwards 10
Harold Brook, Jack Pickering 5
Jimmy Hagan, Fred Smith 4

Blades hat-tricks vs Hull

20 Apr 1935 Mick Killourhy
21 Dec 1935 Jack Pickering
25 Aug 1951 Alf Ringstead
2 Nov 1985 Keith Edwards

Played for both clubs

Jackie Smith	Hull 1905-11	Blades 1910-11
Stan Fazackerley	Hull 1911-13	Blades 1912-21
Joe Kitchen	Blades 1907-21	Hull 1921-23
Dave Mercer	Hull 1913-21	Blades 1920-28
Bobby Hughes	Hull 1919-22	Blades 1922-23
Tucker Mordue	Hull 1923-24	Blades 1926-28
William Bell	Blades 1926-27	Hull 1932-33
Jock Gibson	Hull 1922-29	Blades 1928-33
Jack Pears	Blades 1934-35	Hull 1937-38
Richard Lowe	Blades 1937-38	Hull 1939-40
George Richardson	Blades 1935-39	Hull 1938-48
Jock Smith	Hull 1949-51	Blades 1950-53
Gerry Summers	Blades 1957-64	Hull 1963-66
Alan Warboys	Blades 1972-73	Hull 1977-79
Keith Edwards	Blades 1975-78/81-86	Hull 1978-82/87-90
Terry Curran	Blades 1982-83	Hull 1986-87
John Moore	Hull 1988-89	Blades 1988-89
Billy Whitehurst	Hull 1980-86/88-90	Blades 1989-91
Brian Marwood	Hull 1979-84	Blades 1990-92
Glyn Hodges	Blades 1990-96	Hull 1997-98
Bobby Davison	Blades 1991-92/93-95	Hull 1995-96
Kevin Gage	Blades 1991-96	Hull 1997-99
Gary Ablett	Hull 1986-87	Blades 1995-96
Steve Hawes	Blades 1995-97	Hull 1998-99
Christopher Bettney	Blades 1996-97	Hull 1997-99
Aidan Davison	Hull 1996-97	Blades 1999-2000
Dean Windass	Hull 1991-96	Blades 2002-03
Owen Morrison	Blades 2002-03	Hull 2002-03
Alan Fettis	Hull 1991-96/2002-04	Blades 2003-04

Season	League	Date	Result	Blades	Ipswich	Date	Result	Blades	Ipswich	Blades	Ipswich
		Home						**Away**		*Final Positions*	
1957-58	Division 2	8 April	Drew	1	1	7 April	Lost	0	1	6th	8th
1958-59	Division 2	8 November	Won	2	0	30 April	Lost	0	1	3rd	16th
1959-60	Division 2	7 November	Won	1	0	26 March	Lost	0	2	4th	11th
1960-61	Division 2	7 March	Lost	1	3	15 October	Won	1	0	2ndP	1stP
1961-62	Division 1	14 October	Won	2	1	3 March	Lost	0	4	5th	1st
1962-63	Division 1	25 August	Won	2	1	21 December	Lost	0	1	10th	17th
1963-64	Division 1	9 October	Won	3	1	29 February	Lost	0	1	12th	22ndR
1971-72	Division 1	27 November	Won	7	0	15 April	Drew	0	0	10th	13th
1972-73	Division 1	29 August	Drew	0	0	28 April	Drew	1	1	14th	4th
1973-74	Division 1	12 March	Lost	0	3	27 April	Won	1	0	13th	4th
1974-75	Division 1	31 August	Won	3	1	1 March	Won	1	0	6th	3rd
1975-76	Division 1	20 March	Lost	1	2	29 November	Drew	1	1	22ndR	6th
1986-87	Division 2	4 May	Drew	0	0	6 December	Drew	2	2	9th	5th
1987-88	Division 2	26 March	Won	4	1	24 October	Lost	0	1	21stR	8th
1989-90	Division 2	26 August	Won	2	0	13 January	Drew	1	1	2ndP	9th
1992-93	Premiership	16 January	Won	3	0	26 September	Drew	0	0	14th	16th
1993-94	Premiership	28 August	Drew	1	1	22 February	Lost	2	3	20thR	19th
1995-96	Division 1	30 September	Drew	2	2	16 December	Drew	1	1	9th	7th
1996-97	Division 1	14 September	Lost	1	3	18 March	Lost	1	3	5th	4th
1997-98	Division 1	3 March	Lost	0	1	9 November	Drew	2	2	6th	5th

Action from 2003/04 as Jack Lester of United holds off Matt Elliot of Ipswich.

Season	League	Date	Result	Blades	Ipswich	Date	Result	Blades	Ipswich	Blades	Ipswich
			Home					**Away**		*Final Positions*	
1998-99	Division 1	20 December	Lost	1	2	9 May	Lost	1	4	8th	3rd
1999-00	Division 1	28 August	Drew	2	2	29 January	Drew	1	1	16th	3rdP
2002-03	Division 1	9 November	Drew	0	0	8 February	Lost	2	3	3rd	7th
2003-04	Division 1	30 April	Drew	1	1	22 November	Lost	0	3	8th	5th

Division 1 Play-offs — *Final positions*

Season		Date	Result	Blades	Ipswich	Date	Result	Blades	Ipswich	Blades	Ipswich
1996-97	Semi-Final	10 May	Drew	1	1	14 May	Drew*	2	2	5th	4th

FA Cup — *Division*

Season		Date	Result	Blades	Ipswich	Date	Result	Blades	Ipswich		
1973-74	Round 3					5 January	Lost	2	3	Div 1	Div 1
1997-98	Round 4	3 February	Won	1	0	24 January	Drew	1	1	Div 1	Div 1
2002-03	Round 4	25 January	Won	4	3					Div 1	Div 1

Summary	P	W	D	L	F	A
Blades' home league record:	24	10	8	6	40	26
Blades' away league record:	24	3	9	12	18	36
Blades' cup record:	6	2	3	1	11	10
TOTAL:	**54**	**15**	**20**	**19**	**69**	**72**

FACT FILE

- **United have not won in their last 16 league matches, but have, in this period, beaten Ipswich in the FA Cup twice, and the play-offs once (albeit on away goals).**
- **The Blades scored once in their first eight visits to Portman Road, and have never scored more than two in a game there.**
- **Between 1958 and 1993, United won 10 out of 15 at home.**

Blades' top scorers vs Ipswich

Alan Woodward 7
Brian Deane 5
Billy Russell 4
Derek Pace, Ron Simpson 3

Blades hat-tricks vs Ipswich

27 Nov 1971 Alan Woodward (4)
16 Jan 1993 Brian Deane

Played for both clubs

Mick Hill	Blades 1966-70	Ipswich 1969-73
Les Tibbott	Ipswich 1975-79	Blades 1978-82
David Barnes	Ipswich 1982-84	Blades 1989-94
Brian Gayle	Ipswich 1989-92	Blades 1991-96
Jonathan Hunt	Ipswich 1998-99	Blades 1998-2000
Marcus Bent	Blades 1999-2001	Ipswich 2001-04
Manuel Thetis	Ipswich 1998-2000	Blades 2000-01
Gus Uhlenbeek	Ipswich 1995-98	Blades 2000-02
George Santos	Blades 2000-02	Ipswich 2003-04
Paul Gerrard	Ipswich 2002-03	Blades 2003-04

v. Leeds United

Season	League	Date	Result	Home Blades	Home Leeds	Date	Result	Away Blades	Away Leeds	Final Positions Blades	Final Positions Leeds
1924-25	Division 1	8 November	Drew	1	1	14 March	Drew	1	1	14th	18th
1925-26	Division 1	21 November	Won	2	0	3 April	Lost	0	2	5th	19th
1926-27	Division 1	18 September	Won	1	0	5 February	Drew	1	1	8th	21stR
1928-29	Division 1	1 April	Drew	1	1	2 April	Lost	0	2	11th	13th
1929-30	Division 1	9 November	Won	3	2	15 March	Drew	2	2	20th	5th
1930-31	Division 1	6 April	Drew	1	1	7 April	Lost	0	4	15th	21stR
1932-33	Division 1	22 October	Drew	0	0	4 March	Won	3	1	10th	8th
1933-34	Division 1	9 December	Won	2	1	21 April	Drew	1	1	22ndR	9th
1939-40	Division 1					2 September	Won	1	0		
1946-47	Division 1	4 January	Won	6	2	7 September	Drew	2	2	6th	22ndR
1949-50	Division 2	5 September	Lost	0	1	14 September	Won	1	0	3rd	5th
1950-51	Division 2	23 September	Drew	2	2	3 February	Lost	0	1	8th	5th
1951-52	Division 2	16 February	Won	3	0	6 October	Lost	1	3	11th	6th
1952-53	Division 2	11 October	Won	2	1	28 February	Won	3	0	1stP	10th
1960-61	Division 2	5 November	Won	3	2	25 March	Won	2	1	2ndP	14th
1964-65	Division 1	24 April	Lost	0	3	31 October	Lost	1	4	19th	2nd
1965-66	Division 1	26 February	Drew	1	1	11 September	Drew	2	2	9th	2nd
1966-67	Division 1	27 March	Lost	1	4	28 March	Lost	0	2	10th	4th
1967-68	Division 1	11 November	Won	1	0	6 April	Lost	0	3	21stR	4th
1971-72	Division 1	17 August	Won	3	0	22 January	Lost	0	1	10th	2nd
1972-73	Division 1	15 August	Lost	0	2	11 November	Lost	1	2	14th	3rd
1973-74	Division 1	16 April	Lost	0	2	15 April	Drew	0	0	13th	1st
1974-75	Division 1	1 April	Drew	1	1	21 September	Lost	1	5	6th	9th
1975-76	Division 1	30 August	Lost	0	2	14 April	Won	1	0	22ndR	5th
1984-85	Division 2	23 March	Won	2	1	6 October	Drew	1	1	18th	7th
1985-86	Division 2	22 April	Won	3	2	28 September	Drew	1	1	7th	14th
1986-87	Division 2	7 February	Drew	0	0	30 August	Won	1	0	9th	4th
1987-88	Division 2	31 October	Drew	2	2	19 March	Lost	0	5	21stR	7th
1989-90	Division 2	26 December	Drew	2	2	16 April	Lost	0	4	2ndP	1stP
1990-91	Division 1	23 September	Lost	0	2	8 May	Lost	1	2	13th	4th
1991-92	Division 1	26 April	Lost	2	3	5 October	Lost	3	4	9th	1st
1992-93	Premiership	6 April	Won	2	1	17 October	Lost	1	3	14th	17th
1993-94	Premiership	13 March	Drew	2	2	18 September	Lost	1	2	20thR	5th

FA Cup

Season	Round	Date	Result	Blades	Leeds	Date	Result	Blades	Leeds	Division Blades	Division Leeds
1935-36	Round 5	15 February	Won	3	1					Div 2	Div 1
1967-68	Q'ter Final					30 March	Lost	0	1	Div 1	Div 1
2002-03	Q'ter Final	9 March	Won	1	0					Div 1	Prem

League Cup

Season	Round	Date	Result	Blades	Leeds					Division Blades	Division Leeds
1970-71	Round 2	8 September	Won	1	0					Div 2	Div 1
1978-79	Round 3	10 October	Lost	1	4					Div 2	Div 1
2002-03	Round 3	6 November	Won	2	1					Div 1	Prem

Summary	P	W	D	L	F	A
Blades' home league record:	32	13	11	8	49	44
Blades' away league record:	33	7	9	17	33	62
Blades' cup record:	6	4	0	2	8	7
TOTAL:	**71**	**24**	**20**	**27**	**90**	**113**

FACT FILE

- **The 1936 FA Cup match was watched by Bramall Lane's highest attendance of 68,287.**
- **Between 1987 and 1994, United won once in 13 matches. In 2002-03, however, they knocked Leeds out of both cups.**
- **United were undefeated in their first nine home games.**
- **United won five in a row from 1952 to 1961.**

Blades' top scorers vs Leeds
Harold Brook, Jack Pickering 4
Jimmy Dunne, Jimmy Hagan, George Hutchinson,
Fred Tunstall 3

Robert Page leaping high above Harry Kewell.

Played for both clubs

Norman Wharton	Blades 1928-30	Leeds 1939-40
Alec Stacey	Leeds 1927-34	Blades 1933-37
Charlie Wilkinson	Leeds 1931-34	Blades 1933-38
Albert Nightingale	Blades 1946-48	Leeds 1952-57
Harold Brook	Blades 1946-54	Leeds 1954-58
George Hutchinson	Blades 1948-53	Leeds 1955-56
Ted Burgin	Blades 1949-57	Leeds 1958-61
Len Browning	Leeds 1946-52	Blades 1951-54
Billy Hudson	Leeds 1951-52	Blades 1953-54
Colin Grainger	Blades 1953-57	Leeds 1960-61
Cliff Mason	Blades 1955-62	Leeds 1961-63
Mick Jones	Blades 1962-68	Leeds 1967-74
Tony Currie	Blades 1967-76	Leeds 1976-79
Keith Edwards	Blades 1975-78/81-86	Leeds 1986-88
Gary Hamson	Blades 1976-79	Leeds 1979-86
Imre Varadi	Blades 1978-79	Leeds 1989-93
Alex Sabella	Blades 1978-80	Leeds 1980-81
Tony Agana	Blades 1987-92	Leeds 1991-92
Martin Dickinson	Leeds 1979-86	Blades 1988-89
Brian Deane	Blades 1988-93/97-98	Leeds 1993-97
Vinnie Jones	Leeds 1989-91	Blades 1990-92
John Pemberton	Blades 1990-94	Leeds 1993-96
Paul Beesley	Blades 1990-95	Leeds 1995-97
Mervyn Day	Leeds 1984-93	Blades 1991-92
Chris Kamara	Leeds 1989-92	Blades 1992-94
David White	Leeds 1993-96	Blades 1995-98
Ian Rush	Leeds 1995-97	Blades 1997-98
Bruno Ribeiro	Leeds 1997-99	Blades 1999-2001
Terry Phelan	Leeds 1985-86	Blades 2001-02
Mike Whitlow	Leeds 1988-92	Blades 2003-04
Andy Gray	Leeds 1995-97	Blades 2003-04

Nick Montgomery in action in the FA Cup victory over Leeds in March 2003. Seth Johnson is the Leeds player.

v. Leicester City

Season	League	Date	Result	Home Blades	Home Leicester	Date	Result	Away Blades	Away Leicester	Final Positions Blades	Final Positions Leicester
1908-09	Division 1	27 February	Won	2	1	24 October	Drew	1	1	12th	20thR
1925-26	Division 1	25 December	Lost	2	4	26 December	Drew	2	2	5th	17th
1926-27	Division 1	19 March	Lost	0	3	30 October	Drew	2	2	8th	7th
1927-28	Division 1	5 September	Drew	1	1	29 August	Lost	1	3	13th	3rd
1928-29	Division 1	23 February	Lost	1	4	13 October	Lost	1	3	11th	2nd
1929-30	Division 1	4 January	Won	7	1	7 September	Drew	3	3	20th	8th
1930-31	Division 1	24 September	Lost	0	2	8 September	Drew	2	2	15th	16th
1931-32	Division 1	19 March	Drew	2	2	7 November	Lost	3	4	7th	19th
1932-33	Division 1	31 December	Won	5	2	27 April	Drew	1	1	10th	19th
1933-34	Division 1	4 September	Won	2	1	28 August	Lost	0	4	22ndR	17th
1935-36	Division 2	31 August	Lost	1	2	28 December	Won	3	1	3rd	6th
1936-37	Division 2	1 January	Won	3	1	29 March	Won	2	1	7th	1stP
1949-50	Division 2	18 March	Drew	2	2	29 October	Drew	1	1	3rd	15th
1950-51	Division 2	13 January	Won	2	1	9 September	Drew	2	2	8th	14th
1951-52	Division 2	22 March	Won	5	0	3 November	Drew	5	5	11th	5th
1952-53	Division 2	22 November	Won	7	2	11 April	Drew	0	0	1stP	5th
1954-55	Division 1	25 December	Drew	1	1	27 December	Won	1	0	13th	21stR
1956-57	Division 2	8 September	Drew	1	1	12 January	Lost	0	5	7th	1stP
1961-62	Division 1	24 February	Won	3	1	7 October	Lost	1	4	5th	14th
1962-63	Division 1	26 March	Drew	0	0	27 October	Lost	1	3	10th	4th
1963-64	Division 1	21 March	Lost	0	1	9 November	Won	1	0	12th	11th
1964-65	Division 1	26 March	Lost	0	2	14 November	Won	2	0	19th	18th
1965-66	Division 1	25 September	Drew	2	2	19 March	Lost	0	1	9th	7th

United's Dean Windass and Leicester defender Matty Elliott.

				Home					Away		Final Positions	
Season	League	Date	Result	Blades	Leicester	Date	Result	Blades	Leicester	Blades	Leicester
1966-67	Division 1	26 November	Lost	0	1	22 April	Drew	2	2	10th	8th
1967-68	Division 1	25 November	Drew	0	0	2 March	Lost	1	3	21stR	13th
1969-70	Division 2	6 December	Won	1	0	21 March	Lost	1	2	6th	3rd
1970-71	Division 2	26 December	Won	2	1	10 April	Drew	0	0	2ndP	1stP
1971-72	Division 1	1 January	Drew	1	1	18 September	Won	1	0	10th	12th
1972-73	Division 1	16 December	Won	2	0	24 February	Drew	0	0	14th	16th
1973-74	Division 1	6 October	Drew	1	1	23 February	Drew	1	1	13th	9th
1974-75	Division 1	26 April	Won	4	0	19 October	Lost	0	3	6th	18th
1975-76	Division 1	15 November	Lost	1	2	21 February	Drew	1	1	22ndR	7th
1978-79	Division 2	8 May	Drew	2	2	23 August	Won	1	0	20thR	17th
1987-88	Division 2	17 October	Won	2	1	5 March	Lost	0	1	21stR	13th
1989-90	Division 2	4 November	Drew	1	1	5 May	Won	5	2	2ndP	13th
1995-96	Division 1	21 October	Lost	1	3	30 March	Won	2	0	9th	5thP
2002-03	Division 1	21 April	Won	2	1	7 December	Drew	0	0	3rd	2ndP

FA Cup

Season		Date	Result	Blades	Leicester		Result	Blades	Leicester	Division	
1899-00	Round 1	27 January	Won	1	0					Div 1	Div 2
1929-30	Round 3	11 January	Won	2	1					Div 1	Div 1
1949-50	Round 3	7 January	Won	3	1					Div 2	Div 2
1960-61	Semi-Final	18 March	Elland Road				Drew	0	0	Div 2	Div 1
		23 March	City Ground, Nottingham (replay)				Drew*	0	0		
		27 March	St Andrew's, Birmingham (2nd replay)				Lost*	0	2		
1975-76	Round 3					3 January	Lost	0	3	Div 1	Div 1

League Cup

Season						Date	Result	Blades	Leicester	Division	
1969-70	Round 4					15 October	Lost	0	2	Div 2	Div 2

Summary

	P	W	D	L	F	A
Blades' home league record:	37	15	12	10	69	51
Blades' away league record:	37	9	16	12	50	63
Blades' cup record:	8	3	2	3	6	9
TOTAL:	**82**	**27**	**30**	**25**	**125**	**123**

Blades' top scorers vs Leicester
Jimmy Dunne 11
Alan Woodward 7
Jack Pickering 6
Jimmy Hagan 5
Bobby Barclay, Harold Brook, Harry Johnson,
Gil Reece 4

Blades hat-tricks vs Leicester
7 Sep 1929 Jimmy Dunne
4 Jan 1930 Jimmy Dunne (4)
27 Sep 1930 Jimmy Dunne

FACT FILE

- United's highest scoring draw was 5-5 against Leicester in 1951.
- From 1937 to 1963, United were unbeaten in 10 home games.
- Between 1935 and 1956, United were unbeaten in 14 games.
- United failed to win in their first 10 trips to Filbert Street.

Played for both clubs

Hugh Gallacher	Blades 1892-94	Leicester 1894-96
Harry Hammond	Blades 1892-97	Leicester 1900-01
Fred Milnes	Blades 1902-05	Leicester 1906-07
Jimmy Donnelly	Blades 1902-07	Leicester 1907-10
Albert Trueman	Leicester 1905-08	Blades 1910-13
Johnny Lang	Blades 1902-09	Leicester 1909-10
John Roxburgh	Leicester 1920-23	Blades 1925-27
Pat Carrigan	Leicester 1923-30	Blades 1929-33
Bill Hodgson	Blades 1957-64	Leicester 1963-65
Alan Birchenall	Blades 1964-68	Leicester 1971-77
Willie Carlin	Blades 1967-69	Leicester 1970-72
Geoff Salmons	Blades 1967-74/77-78	Leicester 1977-78
Alan Young	Leicester 1979-82	Blades 1982-83
Brian Deane	Blades 1988-93/97-98	Leicester 2001-04
Colin Hill	Blades 1989-92	Leicester 1991-97
Bobby Davison	Blades 1991-92/93-95	Leicester 1992-93
Franz Carr	Blades 1992-94	Leicester 1994-95
Carl Muggleton	Leicester 1988-93	Blades 1995-96
Stuart Wilson	Leicester 1996-99	Blades 1999-2000
Marcus Bent	Blades 1999-2001	Leicester 2003-04
David Kelly	Leicester 1989-92	Blades 2000-01
Robert Ullathorne	Leicester 1997-99	Blades 2000-03
John Curtis	Blades 2002-03	Leicester 2003-04
Ashley Ward	Leicester 1991-92	Blades 2003-04
Mike Whitlow	Leicester 1991-97	Blades 2003-04
Alan Fettis	Leicester 1999-2000	Blades 2003-04
Dean Sturridge	Leicester 2000-02	Blades 2003-04

Goalmouth action with Curtis and Kenny
keeping Dickov in check.

v. Leyton Orient

Season	League	Date	Result	Home Blades	Leyton O	Date	Result	Away Blades	Leyton O	Final Positions Blades	Leyton O
1956-57	Division 2	27 October	Lost	2	3	9 March	Won	2	1	7th	15th
1957-58	Division 2	14 December	Lost	0	2	26 April	Won	1	0	6th	12th
1958-59	Division 2	7 March	Lost	2	3	18 October	Drew	1	1	3rd	17th
1959-60	Division 2	24 October	Lost	0	2	17 March	Drew	1	1	4th	10th
1960-61	Division 2	14 January	Won	4	1	3 September	Won	4	1	2ndP	19th
1962-63	Division 1	26 April	Won	2	0	8 December	Drew	2	2	10th	22ndR
1970-71	Division 2	17 October	Won	3	1	15 August	Lost	1	3	2ndP	17th
1976-77	Division 2	20 November	Drew	1	1	16 April	Won	2	0	11th	19th
1977-78	Division 2	26 December	Won	2	0	27 March	Lost	1	3	12th	14th
1978-79	Division 2	19 August	Lost	1	2	11 November	Drew	1	1	20thR	11th
1982-83	Division 3	1 January	Won	3	0	14 May	Lost	1	4	11th	20th
1983-84	Division 3	3 March	Won	6	3	18 October	Lost	0	2	3rdP	11th

Summary		P	W	D	L	F	A
Blades' home league record:		12	6	1	5	26	18
Blades' away league record:		12	4	4	4	17	19
TOTAL:		**24**	**10**	**5**	**9**	**43**	**37**

FACT FILE

- United lost their first four home games, but were undefeated in their first six away games.
- United have won six of the last eight at home.
- Only Wimbledon have played United so often in the league without ever meeting them in either cup.

Blades' top scorers vs Orient
Keith Edwards 4
Colin Morris, Derek Pace, Billy Russell 3

Blades hat-tricks vs Orient
3 Mar 1984 Keith Edwards

Played for both clubs

Frank Thacker	Blades 1898-99	Orient 1906-08
Dickie Bourne	Blades 1900-02	Orient 1905-07
Peter Boyle	Blades 1898-1904	Orient 1905-06
Tommy Simons	Orient 1905-07	Blades 1910-12
Alex Forbes	Blades 1946-48	Orient 1956-57
Glenn Cockerill	Blades 1983-86	Orient 1993-96
Chris Wilder	Blades 1986-92/97-99	Orient 1991-92
Richard Cadette	Orient 1984-85	Blades 1987-88
Vaughan Ryan	Blades 1988-89	Orient 1992-95
Andy Sayer	Orient 1989-92	Blades 1990-91
Paul Beesley	Orient 1989-90	Blades 1990-95
Mervyn Day	Orient 1979-83	Blades 1991-92
Mel Rees	Orient 1989-90	Blades 1991-92
Andy Scott	Blades 1992-98	Orient 2003-04

v. Lincoln City

Season	League	Date	Result	Blades	Lincoln	Date	Result	Blades	Lincoln	Blades	Lincoln
			Home				**Away**			*Final Positions*	
1892-93	Division 2	3 September	Won	4	2	1 October	Lost	0	1	2ndP	9th
1952-53	Division 2	20 September	Won	6	1	7 February	Lost	2	3	1stP	15th
1956-57	Division 2	25 December	Won	2	0	26 December	Lost	1	4	7th	18th
1957-58	Division 2	28 December	Won	4	0	31 August	Drew	2	2	6th	20th
1958-59	Division 2	6 December	Won	6	1	25 April	Won	2	1	3rd	19th
1959-60	Division 2	5 March	Won	3	2	17 October	Lost	0	2	4th	13th
1960-61	Division 2	1 October	Won	2	1	22 February	Won	5	0	2ndP	22ndR
1982-83	Division 3	7 May	Lost	0	1	29 September	Lost	0	3	11th	6th
1983-84	Division 3	7 February	Drew	0	0	3 September	Won	2	0	3rdP	14th

FA Cup

Season	Round	Date	Result	Blades	Lincoln	Date	Result	Blades	Lincoln	Division	
1891-92	2nd Qual Rd	24 October	Won	4	1					Non L	Non L
1960-61	Round 4	28 January	Won	3	1					Div 2	Div 2
1963-64	Round 3					4 January	Won	4	0	Div 1	Div 4
1983-84	Round 2	19 December	Won	1	0	10 December	Drew	0	0	Div 3	Div 3

League Cup

Season	Round	Date	Result	Blades	Lincoln	Date	Result	Blades	Lincoln	Division	
2000-01	Round 1	22 August	Won	6	1	5 September	Lost	0	1	Div 1	Div 3

Summary

	P	W	D	L	F	A
Blades' home league record:	9	7	1	1	27	8
Blades' away league record:	9	3	1	5	14	16
Blades' cup record:	7	5	1	1	18	4
TOTAL:	25	15	3	7	59	28

FACT FILE

- **The Blades have won 11 of their 13 home games.**
- **On 3 September 1892, United played their first-ever league match, and beat Lincoln 4-2.**

Steve Cammack made a scattering of appearances for the Blades in the early 1970s. He played for the Imps in the next decade.

Blades' top scorers vs Lincoln
Billy Russell 8
Derek Pace 7
Harry Hammond 4
Marcus Bent, William Hamilton, Alf Ringstead,
Ron Simpson 3

Blades hat-tricks vs Lincoln
3 Sep 1892 Harry Hammond
22 Aug 2000 Marcus Bent (cup)

Played for both clubs

William Egan	Blades 1895-96	Lincoln 1896-97
William Ross	Blades 1895-97	Lincoln 1897-98
Albert Groves	Lincoln 1903-04	Blades 1903-07
Edward Connor	Lincoln 1907-08	Blades 1911-12
George W.R. Richardson	Lincoln 1921-22	Blades 1921-23
Jack Kendall	Lincoln 1922-24/28-30	Blades 1929-34
Wally Webster	Lincoln 1925-26	Blades 1925-30
Chick Reed	Blades 1931-32	Lincoln 1932-35
Ernie Robinson	Blades 1933-34	Lincoln 1935-39
Jock Dodds	Blades 1934-39	Lincoln 1948-50
Tom Johnson	Blades 1929-40	Lincoln 1946-49
Dick Young	Blades 1936-49	Lincoln 1948-54
Harold Brook	Blades 1946-54	Lincoln 1957-58
Fred White	Blades 1947-50	Lincoln 1950-51
Derek Hawksworth	Blades 1950-58	Lincoln 1959-61
Dennis Gratton	Blades 1955-59	Lincoln 1959-61
Jeff Smith	Blades 1956-57	Lincoln 1957-67
Bobby Rooney	Blades 1958-60	Lincoln 1962-64
Steve Cammack	Blades 1971-76	Lincoln 1981-82
Paul Casey	Blades 1979-82	Lincoln 1988-91
Richard Cooper	Blades 1982-85	Lincoln 1985-87
Gary West	Blades 1982-85	Lincoln 1985-87/90-92
Paul Smith	Blades 1982-86	Lincoln 1988-95
Glenn Cockerill	Lincoln 1976-80/81-84	Blades 1983-86
John Burridge	Blades 1984-87	Lincoln 1993-94
Steve Foley	Blades 1985-87	Lincoln 1994-95
Tony Daws	Blades 1986-87	Lincoln 1993-96
Chris Wilder	Blades 1986-92/97-99	Lincoln 1998-99
Andy Leaning	Blades 1987-88	Lincoln 1993-96
Darren Carr	Blades 1987-89	Lincoln 2000-01
Steve Thompson	Lincoln 1980-85/89-90	Blades 1988-89
Alan Roberts	Blades 1988-90	Lincoln 1989-90
Richard Lucas	Blades 1990-92	Lincoln 1994-95
Alan Cork	Lincoln 1977-78	Blades 1991-94
Charlie Hartfield	Blades 1991-97	Lincoln 1998-99
Kingsley Black	Blades 1994-95	Lincoln 2000-03
Mark Foran	Blades 1994-96	Lincoln 1996-97
Tony Battersby	Blades 1995-96	Lincoln 1998-2003
Ian Hamilton	Blades 1997-2000	Lincoln 2001-02
Tyrone Thompson	Blades 2000-01	Lincoln 2002-03
Shane Nicholson	Lincoln 1986-92	Blades 2001-02

v. Liverpool

Season	League	Date	Result	Blades	Liverpool	Date	Result	Blades	Liverpool	Blades	Liverpool
				Home				**Away**		*Final Positions*	
1894-95	Division 1	8 December	Drew	2	2	6 October	Drew	2	2	6th	16thR
1896-97	Division 1	19 October	Drew	1	1	2 January	Drew	0	0	2nd	5th
1897-98	Division 1	29 December	Lost	1	2	5 February	Won	4	0	1st	9th
1898-99	Division 1	2 January	Lost	0	2	29 October	Lost	1	2	16th	2nd
1899-00	Division 1	10 March	Lost	1	2	4 November	Drew	2	2	2nd	10th
1900-01	Division 1	22 April	Lost	0	2	1 December	Won	2	1	14th	1st
1901-02	Division 1	7 December	Won	2	1	5 April	Lost	0	1	10th	11th
1902-03	Division 1	29 November	Won	2	0	28 March	Won	4	2	4th	5th
1903-04	Division 1	14 November	Won	2	1	12 March	Lost	0	3	7th	17thR
1905-06	Division 1	16 December	Lost	1	2	21 April	Lost	1	3	13th	1st
1906-07	Division 1	22 December	Won	1	0	27 April	Drew	2	2	4th	15th
1907-08	Division 1	16 September	Drew	0	0	28 December	Lost	0	3	17th	8th
1908-09	Division 1	14 September	Lost	0	2	19 December	Lost	1	2	12th	16th
1909-10	Division 1	28 December	Won	4	2	25 March	Drew	0	0	6th	2nd
1910-11	Division 1	19 September	Won	2	0	17 December	Lost	0	2	9th	13th
1911-12	Division 1	16 December	Won	3	1	20 April	Lost	0	2	14th	17th
1912-13	Division 1	14 October	Won	4	1	21 December	Drew	2	2	15th	12th
1913-14	Division 1	20 December	Lost	0	1	27 April	Lost	1	2	10th	16th
1914-15	Division 1	21 November	Won	2	1	12 April	Lost	1	2	6th	13th
1919-20	Division 1	3 January	Won	3	2	17 January	Lost	0	2	14th	4th
1920-21	Division 1	16 October	Lost	0	1	9 October	Drew	2	2	20th	4th
1921-22	Division 1	10 September	Lost	0	1	17 September	Drew	1	1	11th	1st
1922-23	Division 1	2 April	Won	4	1	30 March	Lost	1	2	10th	1st
1923-24	Division 1	1 December	Drew	1	1	8 December	Won	3	2	5th	12th
1924-25	Division 1	16 March	Lost	0	1	18 October	Lost	1	4	14th	4th
1925-26	Division 1	19 December	Won	3	1	1 May	Drew	2	2	5th	7th
1926-27	Division 1	7 February	Lost	1	4	11 September	Lost	1	5	8th	9th
1927-28	Division 1	27 August	Drew	1	1	31 December	Lost	1	2	13th	16th
1928-29	Division 1	10 September	Lost	1	3	5 September	Won	2	1	11th	5th
1929-30	Division 1	25 December	Won	4	0	26 December	Lost	0	2	20th	12th
1930-31	Division 1	4 April	Won	4	1	29 November	Lost	1	6	15th	9th
1931-32	Division 1	31 October	Won	3	0	12 March	Lost	1	2	7th	10th
1932-33	Division 1	29 August	Won	6	2	7 September	Drew	2	2	10th	14th
1933-34	Division 1	6 January	Drew	2	2	2 September	Lost	2	3	22ndR	18th
1939-40	Division 1	26 August	Won	2	1						
1946-47	Division 1	31 August	Lost	0	1	28 December	Won	2	1	6th	1st
1947-48	Division 1	8 September	Won	3	1	26 March	Lost	0	4	12th	11th
1948-49	Division 1	30 August	Lost	1	2	25 August	Drew	3	3	22ndR	12th
1953-54	Division 1	13 March	Won	3	1	24 October	Lost	0	3	20th	22ndR
1956-57	Division 2	13 April	Won	3	0	1 December	Lost	1	5	7th	3rd
1957-58	Division 2	30 November	Drew	1	1	12 April	Lost	0	1	6th	4th
1958-59	Division 2	15 September	Won	2	0	10 September	Lost	1	2	3rd	4th
1959-60	Division 2	5 September	Won	2	1	16 January	Lost	0	3	4th	3rd
1960-61	Division 2	1 April	Drew	1	1	26 November	Lost	2	4	2ndP	3rd

| | | Home | | | | | Away | | | Final Positions | |
Season	League	Date	Result	Blades	Liverpool	Date	Result	Blades	Liverpool	Blades	Liverpool
1962-63	Division 1	11 May	Drew	0	0	1 September	Lost	0	2	10th	8th
1963-64	Division 1	21 September	Won	3	0	1 February	Lost	1	6	12th	1st
1964-65	Division 1	13 March	Won	3	0	7 October	Lost	1	3	19th	7th
1965-66	Division 1	1 September	Drew	0	0	25 August	Won	1	0	9th	1st
1966-67	Division 1	28 April	Lost	0	1	3 December	Lost	0	1	10th	5th
1967-68	Division 1	15 April	Drew	1	1	12 April	Won	2	1	21stR	3rd
1971-72	Division 1	30 October	Drew	1	1	19 February	Lost	0	2	10th	3rd
1972-73	Division 1	26 December	Lost	0	3	23 September	Lost	0	5	14th	1st
1973-74	Division 1	8 April	Won	1	0	27 October	Lost	0	1	13th	2nd
1974-75	Division 1	28 September	Won	1	0	15 March	Drew	0	0	6th	2nd
1975-76	Division 1	17 January	Drew	0	0	6 September	Lost	0	1	22ndR	1st
1990-91	Division 1	25 August	Lost	1	3	15 December	Lost	0	2	13th	2nd
1991-92	Division 1	28 March	Won	2	0	1 January	Lost	1	2	9th	6th
1992-93	Premiership	12 September	Won	1	0	19 August	Lost	1	2	14th	6th
1993-94	Premiership	26 December	Drew	0	0	2 April	Won	2	1	20thR	8th

FA Cup

									Division	
1898-99	Semi-Final	18 March	City Ground, Nottingham		Drew	2	2		Div 1	Div 1
		23 March	Burnden Park, Bolton (replay)		Drew*	4	4			
		30 March	Baseball Ground, Derby (2nd replay)		Won	1	0			
1914-15	Round 2	30 January	Won	1	0				Div 1	Div 1
1922-23	Round 3					24 February	Won	2	1	Div 1	Div 1
1937-38	Round 4	22 January	Drew	1	1	26 January	Lost	0	1	Div 2	Div 1

League Cup

1968-69	Round 2					4 September	Lost	0	4	Div 2	Div 1
1978-79	Round 2	28 August	Won	1	0					Div 2	Div 1
1992-93	Round 3	28 October	Drew	0	0	11 November	Lost	0	3	Prem	Prem
2002-03	Semi-Final	8 January	Won	2	1	21 January	Lost*	0	2	Div 1	Prem

Michael Tonge brings the ball away from Jamie Carragher in the League Cup semi-final.

Summary	P	W	D	L	F	A
Blades' home league record:	59	28	14	17	93	62
Blades' away league record:	58	9	12	37	61	126
Blades' cup record:	13	5	4	4	14	19
TOTAL:	**130**	**42**	**30**	**58**	**168**	**207**

FACT FILE

- Between 1953 and 1965, the Blades lost all nine matches at Anfield, but were unbeaten at home throughout this period.
- United failed to win in their first six home games.
- United have twice gone over 10 games at Anfield without a win, but then, historically, very few sides have done well at Anfield.
- United have lost only one of their 10 games at home since 1972.
- United's first ever League Cup semi-final came against Liverpool in 2003, when Liverpool came out on top in a very close, and sometimes controversial, tie.
- The second replay in the 1899 cup tie was originally played on 27 March at Fallowfield in Manchester, but was abandoned at half-time due to crowd trouble with Liverpool leading 1-0.

Blades' top scorers vs Liverpool
Jimmy Dunne 10
Joe Kitchen, Fred Tunstall 8
Billy Gillespie, Harry Johnson 7
Brian Deane, Jimmy Hagan, Jack Pickering 5

Blades hat-tricks vs Liverpool
4 Apr 1931 Jimmy Dunne (4)

Played for both clubs

Jack Drummond	Blades 1892-94	Liverpool 1894-95
Rabbi Howell	Blades 1892-98	Liverpool 1897-1901
Frank Becton	Liverpool 1894-98	Blades 1898-99
Jimmy Harrop	Liverpool 1907-12	Blades 1920-22
Bert Pearson	Blades 1912-14	Liverpool 1919-21
Harold Barton	Liverpool 1929-34	Blades 1934-39
Archie McPherson	Liverpool 1929-35	Blades 1934-36
Kevin Lewis	Blades 1957-60	Liverpool 1960-63
Willie Carlin	Liverpool 1959-60	Blades 1967-69
Phil Thompson	Liverpool 1971-83	Blades 1984-86
Gary Ablett	Liverpool 1986-92	Blades 1995-96
Don Hutchison	Liverpool 1991-94	Blades 1995-98
Nigel Spackman	Liverpool 1986-89	Blades 1996-97
Ian Rush	Liverpool 1980-87/88-96	Blades 1997-98
Dean Saunders	Liverpool 1991-93	Blades 1997-99
John Newby	Liverpool 1999-2000	Blades 2000-01

v. Loughborough Town

FA Cup		Date	Result	Away Blades	Loughb'gh	Division Blades	Loughb'gh
1890-91 4th Qual Rd		6 December	Won	6	1	Non L	Non L

Summary	P	W	D	L	F	A
Blades' cup record:	1	1	0	0	6	1
TOTAL:	**1**	**1**	**0**	**0**	**6**	**1**

FACT FILE

- **United's last six-goal haul in the FA Cup came in this match in 1890.**

Blades' top scorers vs Loughborough
W. Robertson, Arthur Watson 2

Played for both clubs

Billy Mellor	Blades 1892-93	Loughborough 1895-96

v. Luton Town

			Home					Away		Final Positions	
Season	League	Date	Result	Blades	Luton	Date	Result	Blades	Luton	Blades	Luton
1937-38	Division 2	11 September	Won	2	0	2 February	Won	3	2	3rd	12th
1938-39	Division 2	28 January	Drew	2	2	24 September	Lost	0	2	2ndP	7th
1949-50	Division 2	27 August	Drew	2	2	24 December	Won	3	1	3rd	17th
1950-51	Division 2	20 January	Won	2	1	16 September	Drew	0	0	8th	19th
1951-52	Division 2	20 August	Won	3	0	29 August	Lost	1	2	11th	8th
1952-53	Division 2	7 March	Drew	1	1	18 October	Lost	1	4	1stP	3rd
1955-56	Division 1	26 December	Lost	0	4	27 December	Lost	1	2	22ndR	10th
1960-61	Division 2	11 February	Won	2	1	24 September	Won	4	1	2ndP	13th
1970-71	Division 2	6 February	Won	2	1	5 December	Lost	1	2	2ndP	6th
1974-75	Division 1	1 February	Drew	1	1	9 November	Won	1	0	6th	20thR
1976-77	Division 2	22 January	Lost	0	3	21 August	Lost	0	2	11th	6th
1977-78	Division 2	25 March	Won	4	1	27 December	Lost	0	4	12th	13th
1978-79	Division 2	30 September	Drew	1	1	10 February	Drew	1	1	20thR	18th
1990-91	Division 1	30 March	Won	2	1	26 December	Won	1	0	13th	18th
1991-92	Division 1	30 November	Drew	1	1	22 February	Lost	1	2	9th	20thR
1994-95	Division 1	22 October	Lost	1	3	3 December	Won	6	3	8th	16th
1995-96	Division 1	23 March	Won	1	0	31 January	Lost	0	1	9th	24thR

FA Cup

										Division	
1990-91	Round 3	5 January	Lost	1	3					Div 1	Div 1
1991-92	Round 3	4 January	Won	4	0					Div 1	Div 1

League Cup

1969-70	Round 3	23 September	Won	3	0					Div 2	Div 3
1974-75	Round 3	8 October	Won	2	0					Div 1	Div 1
1985-86	Round 2	24 September	Lost	1	2	7 October	Lost	1	3	Div 2	Div 1

Summary	P	W	D	L	F	A
Blades' home league record:	17	8	6	3	27	23
Blades' away league record:	17	6	2	9	24	29
Blades' cup record:	6	3	0	3	12	8
TOTAL:	40	17	8	15	63	60

FACT FILE

- United were undefeated in their first six home games.
- Other than this, there are no real sequences to speak of in a very even series.

Blades' top scorers vs Luton

Alan Woodward 6

Harold Brook, Ian Bryson, Glyn Hodges 3

Played for both clubs

Bernie Harris	Blades 1924-27	Luton 1928-29
Jock Gibson	Blades 1928-33	Luton 1933-34
Harry Gooney	Blades 1930-35	Luton 1935-36
Willie Boyd	Blades 1933-35	Luton 1935-36
Alan Birchenall	Blades 1964-68	Luton 1978-80
Peter Anderson	Luton 1970-76	Blades 1978-79
Bruce Rioch	Luton 1964-69	Blades 1978-79
Imre Varadi	Blades 1978-79	Luton 1991-92
Ian Benjamin	Blades 1978-80	Luton 1992-94
Viv Busby	Luton 1969-73	Blades 1979-80
Barry Butlin	Luton 1972-75	Blades 1979-81
Don Givens	Luton 1970-72	Blades 1980-81
John Ryan	Luton 1969-76	Blades 1980-82
Bob Hatton	Luton 1978-80	Blades 1980-83
Mervyn Day	Luton 1991-92	Blades 1991-92
Chris Kamara	Luton 1991-93	Blades 1992-94
Kingsley Black	Luton 1987-92	Blades 1994-95
Steve Kabba	Luton 2001-02	Blades 2002-03

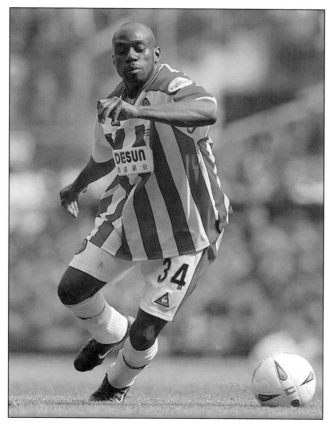

Steve Kabba, Hatter then Blade.

v. Macclesfield Town

						Away		Division	

League Cup

	Date	Result	Blades	Macclesfield	Blades	Macclesfield
2003-04 Round 1	12 August	Won	**2**	**1**	Div 1	Div 3

Summary	P	W	D	L	F	A
Blades' cup record:	1	1	0	0	2	1
TOTAL:	**1**	**1**	**0**	**0**	**2**	**1**

Blades' top scorers vs Macclesfield

Jack Lester 2

Played for both clubs

Tony Philliskirk	Blades 1983-88	Macclesfield 1997-98
Nathan Peel	Blades 1991-92	Macclesfield 1997-98
Christopher Bettney	Blades 1996-97	Macclesfield 2002-01

v. Maidstone United

FA Cup	Date	Result	Blades Maidstone					Division Blades Maidstone
1987-88 Round 3	9 January	Won	**1** **0**					Div 2 Non L

Summary	P	W	D	L	F	A
Blades' cup record:	1	1	0	0	1	0
TOTAL:	**1**	**1**	**0**	**0**	**1**	**0**

FACT FILE

● Mark Dempsey scored the only goal of the game.

Played for both clubs

Nicky Johns   Blades 1978-79   Maidstone 1989-91

Goalkeeper Nicky Johns made just one loan appearance at Sheffield United and turned out for Maidstone 10 years later.

v. Manchester City

Season	League	Date	Result	Home Blades	Man C	Date	Result	Away Blades	Man C	Final Positions Blades	Man C
1892-93	Division 2	25 March	Won	2	1	4 March	Won	3	2	2ndP	5th
1899-00	Division 1	7 October	Won	3	0	25 December	Won	2	1	2nd	7th
1900-01	Division 1	26 December	Drew	1	1	22 December	Lost	1	2	14th	11th
1901-02	Division 1	23 November	Won	5	0	22 March	Lost	0	4	10th	18thR
1903-04	Division 1	28 December	Won	5	3	3 October	Won	1	0	7th	2nd
1904-05	Division 1	21 January	Lost	0	3	24 September	Drew	1	1	6th	3rd
1905-06	Division 1	4 November	Lost	1	3	10 March	Won	2	1	13th	5th
1906-07	Division 1	23 March	Lost	1	4	17 November	Won	2	0	4th	17th
1907-08	Division 1	28 March	Lost	1	2	11 March	Won	2	0	17th	3rd
1908-09	Division 1	12 December	Won	4	0	17 April	Won	3	1	12th	19thR
1910-11	Division 1	11 February	Drew	2	2	8 October	Won	4	0	9th	17th
1911-12	Division 1	26 February	Won	6	2	30 September	Drew	0	0	14th	15th
1912-13	Division 1	5 October	Drew	1	1	8 February	Lost	0	3	15th	6th
1913-14	Division 1	13 September	Lost	1	3	3 January	Lost	1	2	10th	13th
1914-15	Division 1	29 March	Drew	0	0	7 November	Drew	0	0	6th	5th
1919-20	Division 1	6 September	Won	3	1	30 August	Drew	3	3	14th	7th
1920-21	Division 1	16 April	Drew	1	1	9 April	Lost	1	2	20th	2nd
1921-22	Division 1	1 April	Won	1	0	8 April	Drew	2	2	11th	10th
1922-23	Division 1	26 August	Won	2	0	2 September	Drew	3	3	10th	8th
1923-24	Division 1	1 September	Won	3	0	25 August	Lost	1	2	5th	11th
1924-25	Division 1	27 September	Lost	0	5	23 February	Lost	1	2	14th	10th
1925-26	Division 1	26 October	Won	8	3	4 November	Won	4	2	5th	21stR
1928-29	Division 1	1 December	Lost	1	3	13 April	Lost	1	3	11th	8th
1929-30	Division 1	23 November	Lost	1	2	29 March	Lost	1	2	20th	3rd
1930-31	Division 1	28 January	Drew	2	2	20 September	Won	4	0	15th	8th
1931-32	Division 1	15 February	Won	2	1	3 October	Drew	1	1	7th	14th
1932-33	Division 1	5 November	Lost	2	5	22 March	Lost	0	1	10th	16th
1933-34	Division 1	28 October	Drew	1	1	10 March	Lost	1	4	22ndR	5th
1938-39	Division 2	25 February	Won	1	0	22 October	Lost	2	3	2ndP	5th
1947-48	Division 1	1 May	Won	2	1	13 December	Lost	3	4	12th	10th
1948-49	Division 1	9 October	Lost	0	2	5 March	Lost	0	1	22ndR	7th
1950-51	Division 2	28 April	Drew	0	0	9 December	Lost	3	5	8th	2ndP
1953-54	Division 1	25 December	Drew	2	2	26 December	Lost	1	2	20th	17th
1954-55	Division 1	30 August	Lost	0	2	25 August	Lost	2	5	13th	7th
1955-56	Division 1	8 October	Drew	1	1	11 April	Lost	1	3	22ndR	4th
1961-62	Division 1	11 November	Won	3	1	31 March	Drew	1	1	5th	12th
1962-63	Division 1	3 April	Won	3	1	24 April	Won	3	1	10th	21stR
1966-67	Division 1	1 April	Won	1	0	6 May	Drew	1	1	10th	15th
1967-68	Division 1	20 January	Lost	0	3	16 September	Lost	2	5	21stR	1st
1971-72	Division 1	12 February	Drew	3	3	23 October	Lost	1	2	10th	4th
1972-73	Division 1	9 December	Drew	1	1	14 April	Lost	1	3	14th	11th
1973-74	Division 1	20 October	Lost	1	2	16 March	Won	1	0	13th	14th
1974-75	Division 1	11 January	Drew	1	1	7 December	Lost	2	3	6th	8th
1975-76	Division 1	1 November	Drew	2	2	6 March	Lost	0	4	22ndR	8th

Season	League	Date	Result	Home Blades	Man C	Date	Result	Away Blades	Man C	Final Positions Blades	Man C
1984-85	Division 2	17 November	Drew	0	0	20 April	Lost	0	2	18th	3rdP
1987-88	Division 2	8 March	Lost	1	2	10 October	Won	3	2	21stR	9th
1990-91	Division 1	8 September	Drew	1	1	19 January	Lost	0	2	13th	5th
1991-92	Division 1	8 February	Won	4	2	26 October	Lost	2	3	9th	5th
1992-93	Premiership	9 April	Drew	1	1	26 December	Lost	0	2	14th	9th
1993-94	Premiership	25 September	Lost	0	1	19 March	Drew	0	0	20thR	16th
1996-97	Division 1	28 September	Won	2	0	29 January	Drew	0	0	5th	14th
1997-98	Division 1	15 November	Drew	1	1	21 March	Drew	0	0	6th	22ndR
1999-00	Division 1	22 January	Won	1	0	21 August	Lost	0	6	16th	2ndP
2001-02	Division 1	1 January	Lost	1	3	16 October	Drew	0	0	13th	1stP

FA Cup

Season	Round	Date	Result	Home Blades	Man C	Date	Result	Away Blades	Man C	Division Blades	Man C
1905-06	Round 1	13 January	Won	4	1					Div 1	Div 1
1913-14	Q'ter-Final	12 March	Drew	0	0	7 March	Drew	0	0	Div 1	Div 1
		16 March		Villa Park (2nd replay)			Won	1	0		
1938-39	Round 4	21 January	Won	2	0					Div 2	Div 2

League Cup

Season	Round	Date	Result	Home Blades	Man C	Date	Result	Away Blades	Man C	Division Blades	Man C
1988-89	Round 3					2 November	Lost	2	4	Div 3	Div 2

Summary	P	W	D	L	F	A
Blades' home league record:	54	20	18	16	93	82
Blades' away league record:	54	13	13	28	74	104
Blades' cup record:	6	3	2	1	9	5
TOTAL:	114	36	33	45	176	191

FACT FILE

- Between 1933 and 1956, United lost nine games in a row at Maine Road.
- United did not score in their last six visits to Maine Road, and will no doubt be relieved that they will not have to go back there.
- In the first decade of the 20th century, there was a strange sequence of seven successive away wins.
- City have scored only one goal in five FA Cup matches.

Blades' top scorers vs Manchester City
Billy Gillespie, Joe Kitchen 9
Arthur Brown 8
Jimmy Dunne, Harry Johnson 7
Fred Tunstall 6
Walter Bennett, Alf Common, Brian Deane,
Billy Dearden, Mick Jones, Derek Pace,
Jack Pickering 4

Blades hat-tricks vs Manchester City
13 Jan 1906 Arthur Brown (cup)
26 Feb 1912 Billy Gillespie
26 Oct 1925 Harry Johnson (4)
10 Sep 1930 Jimmy Dunne
3 Apr 1963 Derek Pace

Played for both clubs

Hugh Morris	Man City 1892-94/95-96	Blades 1893-96
Jimmy Yates	Man City 1892-94	Blades 1893-97
Joe Davies	Man City 1892-94/95-96/1900-01	Blades 1894-96
William Egan	Man City 1893-94	Blades 1895-96
Robert Hill	Blades 1892-96	Man City 1895-97
George Utley	Blades 1913-22	Man City 1922-23
James McCourt	Blades 1920-24	Man City 1924-25
Jack Harrison	Man City 1929-30	Blades 1930-31
Roy Warhurst	Blades 1946-50	Man City 1957-59
Fred Smith	Blades 1947-52	Man City 1952-53
Imre Varadi	Blades 1978-79	Man City 1986-89
John Ryan	Blades 1980-82	Man City 1981-82
John Burridge	Blades 1984-87	Man City 1994-95
Ken McNaught	Man City 1984-85	Blades 1985-86
Peter Beagrie	Blades 1986-88	Man City 1993-97
Simon Tracey	Blades 1988-2002	Man City 1994-95
Carl Bradshaw	Man City 1988-89	Blades 1989-94
Jamie Hoyland	Man City 1983-85	Blades 1990-95
Paul Beesley	Blades 1990-95	Man City 1996-98
Brian Gayle	Man City 1988-90	Blades 1991-96
Adrian Heath	Man City 1989-92	Blades 1995-96
David White	Man City 1986-94	Blades 1995-98
Michel Vonk	Man City 1991-95	Blades 1995-98
Gareth Taylor	Blades 1995-99	Man City 1998-2000
Paul Simpson	Man City 1982-89	Blades 1996-97
Earl Barrett	Man City 1985-87	Blades 1997-98
Michael Brown	Man City 1995-99	Blades 1999-2004
Andrew Morrison	Man City 1998-2001	Blades 2000-01
Keith Curle	Man City 1991-96	Blades 2000-02
Terry Phelan	Man City 1992-96	Blades 2001-02
Richard Edghill	Man City 1993-2002	Blades 2002-03
Ashley Ward	Man City 1898-90	Blades 2003-04

v. Manchester United

Season	League	Date	Result	Home Blades	Man U	Date	Result	Away Blades	Man U	Final Positions Blades	Man U
1893-94	Division 1	25 November	Won	3	1	10 March	Won	2	0	10th	16thR
1906-07	Division 1	15 September	Lost	0	2	19 January	Lost	0	2	4th	8th
1907-08	Division 1	18 January	Won	2	0	21 September	Lost	1	2	17th	1st
1908-09	Division 1	13 February	Drew	0	0	10 October	Lost	1	2	12th	13th
1909-10	Division 1	23 October	Lost	0	1	5 March	Lost	0	1	6th	5th
1910-11	Division 1	10 December	Won	2	0	15 April	Drew	1	1	9th	1st
1911-12	Division 1	13 April	Won	6	1	9 December	Lost	0	1	14th	13th
1912-13	Division 1	12 April	Won	2	1	7 December	Lost	0	4	15th	4th
1913-14	Division 1	22 November	Won	2	0	22 April	Lost	1	2	10th	14th
1914-15	Division 1	17 April	Won	3	1	12 December	Won	2	1	6th	18th
1919-20	Division 1	25 October	Drew	2	2	1 November	Lost	0	3	14th	12th
1920-21	Division 1	13 November	Drew	0	0	6 November	Lost	1	2	20th	13th
1921-22	Division 1	2 January	Won	3	0	17 April	Lost	2	3	11th	22ndR
1925-26	Division 1	24 April	Won	2	0	12 December	Won	2	1	5th	9th
1926-27	Division 1	30 August	Drew	2	2	1 January	Lost	0	5	8th	15th
1927-28	Division 1	10 December	Won	2	1	21 April	Won	3	2	13th	18th
1928-29	Division 1	26 December	Won	6	1	25 December	Drew	1	1	11th	12th
1929-30	Division 1	7 October	Won	3	1	3 May	Won	5	1	20th	17th
1930-31	Division 1	22 November	Won	3	1	28 March	Won	2	1	15th	22ndR
1934-35	Division 2	1 September	Won	3	2	5 January	Drew	3	3	11th	5th
1935-36	Division 2	22 February	Drew	1	1	19 October	Lost	1	3	3rd	1stP
1937-38	Division 2	17 February	Lost	1	2	2 October	Won	1	0	3rd	2ndP
1946-47	Division 1	12 October	Drew	2	2	26 May	Lost	2	6	6th	2nd
1947-48	Division 1	31 January	Won	2	1	13 September	Won	1	0	12th	2nd
1948-49	Division 1	18 September	Drew	2	2	4 May	Lost	2	3	22ndR	2nd
1953-54	Division 1	24 April	Lost	1	3	5 December	Drew	2	2	20th	4th
1954-55	Division 1	13 November	Won	3	0	2 April	Lost	0	5	13th	5th
1955-56	Division 1	10 September	Won	1	0	14 January	Lost	1	3	22ndR	1st
1961-62	Division 1	24 April	Lost	2	3	23 April	Won	1	0	5th	15th
1962-63	Division 1	1 December	Drew	1	1	20 April	Drew	1	1	10th	19th
1963-64	Division 1	30 November	Lost	1	2	13 April	Lost	1	2	12th	2nd
1964-65	Division 1	26 December	Lost	0	1	28 December	Drew	1	1	19th	1st
1965-66	Division 1	16 April	Won	3	1	20 November	Lost	1	3	9th	4th
1966-67	Division 1	26 December	Won	2	1	27 December	Lost	0	2	10th	1st
1967-68	Division 1	14 October	Lost	0	3	20 April	Lost	0	1	21stR	2nd
1971-72	Division 1	4 April	Drew	1	1	2 October	Lost	0	2	10th	8th
1972-73	Division 1	30 September	Won	1	0	23 April	Won	2	1	14th	18th
1973-74	Division 1	2 March	Lost	0	1	26 December	Won	2	1	13th	21stR
1975-76	Division 1	13 December	Lost	1	4	23 August	Lost	1	5	22ndR	3rd
1990-91	Division 1	26 February	Won	2	1	17 November	Lost	0	2	13th	6th
1991-92	Division 1	14 March	Lost	1	2	2 November	Lost	0	2	9th	2nd
1992-93	Premiership	15 August	Won	2	1	6 February	Lost	1	2	14th	1st
1993-94	Premiership	7 December	Lost	0	3	18 August	Lost	0	3	20thR	1st

FA Cup		Date	Result	Home Blades	Man U					Division Blades	Man U
1989-90	Q'ter-Final	11 March	Lost	0	1					Div 2	Div 1
1992-93	Round 5	14 February	Won	2	1					Prem	Prem
1993-94	Round 3	9 January	Lost	0	1					Prem	Prem
1994-95	Round 3	9 January	Lost	0	2					Div 1	Prem

Summary	P	W	D	L	F	A
Blades' home league record:	43	22	9	12	76	53
Blades' away league record:	43	11	6	26	48	88
Blades' cup record:	4	1	0	3	2	5
TOTAL:	**90**	**34**	**15**	**41**	**126**	**146**

FACT FILE

- In August 1992, Brian Deane scored the first-ever Premier League goal when he scored against eventual champions Manchester United after five minutes.
- From 1909 to 1936, the Blades were unbeaten in an impressive 16 home games.
- The men from Yorkshire have lost their last seven matches at Old Trafford, including cup semi-finals to Newcastle and Arsenal.

Blades' top scorers vs Manchester United
Fred Tunstall 8
Harry Johnson 7
Jimmy Dunne 6
Willie Boyd, Brian Deane, George Jones,
Jack Pickering, Jimmy Simmons, Alan Woodward 4

Blades hat-tricks vs Manchester United
13 Apr 1912 Dicky Leafe
26 Dec 1928 Harry Johnson
22 Nov 1930 Jimmy Dunne

Played for both clubs

John Peden	Man United 1893-94	Blades 1894-95
Wilson Greenwood	Blades 1894-95	Man United 1900-01
John Cunningham	Blades 1897-98	Man United 1898-99
Ralph Gaudie	Blades 1897-98	Man United 1903-04
Edward Connor	Man United 1909-11	Blades 1911-12
Thomas Boyle	Blades 1921-29	Man United 1928-30
Wallie Boyd	Blades 1933-35	Man United 1934-35
Roy John	Blades 1934-36	Man United 1936-37
Dick Gardner	Man United 1935-37	Blades 1937-38
John Connaughton	Man United 1971-72	Blades 1973-74
Don Givens	Man United 1969-70	Blades 1980-81
Stewart Houston	Man United 1973-80	Blades 1980-83
Mark Dempsey	Man United 1985-86	Blades 1986-88
Paul Parker	Man United 1991-96	Blades 1996-97
Paul McGrath	Man United 1982-89	Blades 1997-98
Andy Goram	Blades 1998-99	Man United 2000-01
Steve Bruce	Man United 1987-96	Blades 1998-99
John Curtis	Man United 1997-2000	Blades 2002-03

v. Mansfield Town

Season	League	Date	Result	Blades	Mansfield	Date	Result	Blades	Mansfield	Final Positions Blades	Mansfield
			Home					**Away**		*Final Positions*	
1977-78	Division 2	4 March	Won	2	0	8 October	Drew	1	1	12th	21stR
1979-80	Division 3	9 February	Won	1	0	22 September	Won	4	3	12th	23rdR
1981-82	Division 4	20 October	Won	4	1	8 March	Drew	1	1	1stP	20th
1988-89	Division 3	25 April	Lost	1	2	4 April	Won	1	0	2ndP	15th

FA Cup

Season	Round	Date	Result	Blades	Mansfield	Date	Result	Blades	Mansfield	Division Blades	Mansfield
1950-51	Round 4	27 January	Drew	0	0	31 January	Lost*	1	2	Div 2	Div 3N
1968-69	Round 3					4 January	Lost	1	2	Div 2	Div 3
1988-89	Round 1	22 November	Won	2	1	19 November	Drew	1	1	Div 3	Div 3

Summary

Summary	P	W	D	L	F	A
Blades' home league record:	4	3	0	1	8	3
Blades' away league record:	4	2	2	0	7	5
Blades' cup record:	5	1	2	2	5	6
TOTAL:	**13**	**6**	**4**	**3**	**20**	**14**

FACT FILE

● **United went nine games without defeat from 1977 to 1989.**

Blades' top scorers vs Mansfield
Keith Edwards 3
Tony Kenworthy 2

Played for both clubs

Walter Hoyland	Blades 1921-27	Mansfield 1932-33
Harry Johnson	Blades 1919-31	Mansfield 1931-36
Chick Reed	Blades 1931-32	Mansfield 1937-38
Lloyd Barke	Blades 1934-37	Mansfield 1937-47
Alf Ringstead	Blades 1950-59	Mansfield 1959-60
Billy Hudson	Blades 1953-54	Mansfield 1954-55
Glyn Jones	Blades 1955-58	Mansfield 1959-61
Sam Kemp	Blades 1956-58	Mansfield 1958-59
Graeme Crawford	Blades 1969-71	Mansfield 1971-72
Ian MacKenzie	Blades 1969-75	Mansfield 1975-78
Paul Garner	Blades 1975-84	Mansfield 1984-89
Tony Kenworthy	Blades 1975-86	Mansfield 1985-90
Dennis Longhorn	Mansfield 1971-74	Blades 1976-78
Imre Varadi	Blades 1978-79	Mansfield 1995-96
John Matthews	Blades 1978-82	Mansfield 1982-84
Steve Charles	Blades 1979-85	Mansfield 1987-93
Mel Eves	Blades 1984-86	Mansfield 1987-88
David Frain	Blades 1985-88	Mansfield 1994-95

Mark Todd	Blades 1987-91	Mansfield 1995-96
John Moore	Mansfield 1986-87	Blades 1988-89
Phil Kite	Blades 1990-92	Mansfield 1991-92
Nathan Peel	Blades 1991-92	Mansfield 1995-96
John Reed	Blades 1991-96	Mansfield 1993-94
Paul Holland	Mansfield 1990-95	Blades 1995-96
Carl Muggleton	Blades 1995-96	Mansfield 1999-2000
Ben Doane	Blades 1999-2003	Mansfield 2002-03
David Kelly	Blades 2000-01	Mansfield 2001-02
Keith Curle	Blades 2000-02	Mansfield 2002-03
Mick Boulding	Mansfield 1999-2001	Blades 2002-03
Iffy Onoura	Mansfield 1994-96	Blades 2002-03

Imre Varadi.

v. Matlock Town

FA Cup	Date	Result	Home					Division	
			Blades	Matlock				Blades	Matlock
1890-91 3rd Qual Rd	15 November	Won	**3**	**0**				Non L	Non L

Summary	P	W	D	L	F	A
Blades' cup record:	1	1	0	0	3	0
TOTAL:	**1**	**1**	**0**	**0**	**3**	**0**

Blades' top scorers vs Matlock

Bernard Shaw 2

v. Middlesbrough

				Home				Away		Final Positions	
Season	League	Date	Result	Blades	M'boro	Date	Result	Blades	M'boro	Blades	M'boro
1902-03	Division 1	7 March	Lost	1	3	8 November	Won	2	0	4th	13th
1903-04	Division 1	28 March	Won	3	0	7 November	Lost	1	4	7th	10th
1904-05	Division 1	25 February	Lost	0	1	29 October	Won	1	0	6th	15th
1905-06	Division 1	18 November	Won	1	0	24 March	Won	1	0	13th	18th
1906-07	Division 1	24 November	Drew	1	1	30 March	Won	1	0	4th	11th
1907-08	Division 1	25 December	Drew	0	0	1 February	Lost	0	2	17th	6th
1908-09	Division 1	10 April	Won	2	0	5 December	Won	2	1	12th	9th
1909-10	Division 1	1 January	Won	2	0	1 September	Won	2	0	6th	17th
1910-11	Division 1	27 March	Won	2	1	19 November	Lost	1	3	9th	16th
1911-12	Division 1	18 November	Drew	1	1	23 March	Drew	1	1	14th	7th
1912-13	Division 1	31 March	Won	1	0	23 November	Lost	1	4	15th	16th
1913-14	Division 1	25 December	Won	3	1	10 April	Won	3	2	10th	3rd
1914-15	Division 1	31 October	Lost	0	1	17 March	Drew	2	2	6th	12th
1919-20	Division 1	20 September	Won	5	1	13 September	Lost	0	1	14th	13th
1920-21	Division 1	15 January	Drew	1	1	22 January	Drew	2	2	20th	8th
1921-22	Division 1	31 December	Won	6	1	14 January	Drew	1	1	11th	8th
1922-23	Division 1	11 November	Won	4	1	4 November	Lost	2	3	10th	18th
1923-24	Division 1	29 December	Lost	0	1	5 January	Won	1	0	5th	22ndR
1927-28	Division 1	17 March	Won	4	1	5 November	Lost	0	3	13th	22ndR
1929-30	Division 1	9 September	Lost	1	3	4 September	Lost	1	3	20th	16th
1930-31	Division 1	20 December	Won	4	2	25 April	Lost	1	4	15th	7th
1931-32	Division 1	16 April	Won	2	1	5 December	Lost	3	4	7th	18th
1932-33	Division 1	27 March	Won	2	0	27 December	Drew	2	2	10th	17th
1933-34	Division 1	31 March	Won	3	1	18 November	Lost	3	10	22ndR	16th
1946-47	Division 1	28 September	Won	2	1	1 February	Won	4	2	6th	11th
1947-48	Division 1	25 August	Drew	1	1	3 September	Lost	0	3	12th	16th
1948-49	Division 1	4 December	Won	1	0	30 April	Lost	1	3	22ndR	19th
1953-54	Division 1	27 February	Drew	2	2	10 October	Lost	0	2	20th	21stR
1956-57	Division 2	8 December	Won	2	1	20 April	Lost	1	3	7th	6th
1957-58	Division 2	19 April	Won	3	2	7 December	Won	2	1	6th	7th
1958-59	Division 2	25 August	Lost	0	1	3 September	Drew	0	0	3rd	13th
1959-60	Division 2	19 April	Drew	0	0	18 April	Won	2	1	4th	5th
1960-61	Division 2	29 April	Won	4	1	29 October	Lost	1	3	2ndP	5th
1968-69	Division 2	12 October	Lost	1	3	28 January	Lost	1	3	9th	4th
1969-70	Division 2	9 August	Won	3	0	17 March	Lost	0	1	6th	4th
1970-71	Division 2	19 September	Drew	1	1	24 April	Drew	1	1	2ndP	7th
1974-75	Division 1	14 September	Won	1	0	26 December	Lost	0	1	6th	7th
1975-76	Division 1	26 December	Drew	1	1	17 April	Lost	0	3	22ndR	13th
1984-85	Division 2	13 October	Lost	0	3	16 March	Lost	0	1	18th	19th
1985-86	Division 2	21 September	Lost	0	1	18 March	Won	2	1	7th	21stR
1987-88	Division 2	7 November	Lost	0	2	2 April	Lost	0	6	21stR	3rdP
1989-90	Division 2	20 January	Won	1	0	2 September	Drew	3	3	2ndP	21st
1992-93	Premiership	9 February	Won	2	0	5 September	Lost	0	2	14th	21stR
1994-95	Division 1	26 December	Drew	1	1	17 April	Drew	1	1	8th	1stP

		Home					Away		Final Positions	
Season	League	Date	Result		Date	Result				
			Blades	M'boro			Blades	M'boro	Blades	M'boro
1997-98	Division 1	7 April	Won	1	0	5 October	Won	2	1	6th	2ndP

FA Cup

Division

Season	League	Date	Result		Date	Result				
1922-23	Round 2	8 February	Won	3	0	3 February	Drew	1	1	Div 1	Div 1

Summary

	P	W	D	L	F	A
Blades' home league record:	45	25	10	10	76	43
Blades' away league record:	45	13	9	23	55	94
Blades' cup record:	2	1	1	0	4	1
TOTAL:	92	39	20	33	135	138

FACT FILE

- In November 1933 at Ayresome Park, the Blades conceded 10 in a league match for the first and only time.
- From 1930 to 1958, United were unbeaten in 10 home games.

Blades' top scorers vs Middlesbrough
Joe Kitchen 11
Jimmy Dunne 9
Billy Gillespie, Harry Johnson 8
Stan Fazackerley, Derek Pace 5
Walter Hardinge, Jack Pickering, Fred Tunstall 4

Blades hat-tricks vs Middlesbrough
20 Sep 1919 Joe Kitchen
31 Dec 1921 Harry Johnson
20 Dec 1930 Jimmy Dunne
5 Dec 1931 Jimmy Dunne

Played for both clubs

Martin Moran	Blades 1899-1900	Middlesbrough 1900-02
Billy Brawn	Blades 1899-1902	Middlesbrough 1905-08
Alf Common	Blades 1901-04	Middlesbrough 1904-10
Fred Priest	Blades 1896-1906	Middlesbrough 1906-07
Albert Groves	Blades 1903-07	Middlesbrough 1907-10
Arthur Brown	Blades 1902-08	Middlesbrough 1912-13
Arthur Stevenson	Middlesbrough 1923-24	Blades 1924-28
Ronnie Waldock	Blades 1954-57	Middlesbrough 1959-62
William Hamilton	Blades 1956-61	Middlesbrough 1960-62
Terry Garbett	Middlesbrough 1965-66	Blades 1973-76
Joe Bolton	Middlesbrough 1981-83	Blades 1983-86
Dean Glover	Blades 1986-87	Middlesbrough 1987-89
Peter Beagrie	Middlesbrough 1984-86	Blades 1986-88
Alan Roberts	Middlesbrough 1982-86	Blades 1988-90
Brian Deane	Blades 1988-93/97-98	Middlesbrough 1998-2002
John Gannon	Blades 1988-96	Middlesbrough 1993-94
Phil Kite	Middlesbrough 1985-86	Blades 1990-92
Brian Marwood	Blades 1990-92	Middlesbrough 1991-92
Chris Kamara	Middlesbrough 1992-93	Blades 1992-94
Willie Falconer	Middlesbrough 1991-93	Blades 1993-94
Jan Aage Fjortoft	Middlesbrough 1994-97	Blades 1996-98
Andy Campbell	Middlesbrough 1995-2002	Blades 1998-99
Dean Windass	Middlesbrough 2000-03	Blades 2002-03
Alan Wright	Middlesbrough 2003-04	Blades 2003-04

v. Millwall

			Home					Away		Final Positions	
Season	League	Date	Result	Blades	Millwall	Date	Result	Blades	Millwall	Blades	Millwall
1938-39	Division 2	15 October	Won	2	1	18 February	Lost	0	4	2ndP	13th
1968-69	Division 2	24 August	Won	1	0	14 March	Lost	0	1	9th	10th
1969-70	Division 2	31 March	Won	3	1	25 October	Lost	0	1	6th	10th
1970-71	Division 2	13 April	Won	2	0	14 September	Won	2	1	2ndP	8th
1976-77	Division 2	3 May	Drew	1	1	27 November	Won	1	0	11th	10th
1977-78	Division 2	18 March	Won	5	2	22 October	Drew	1	1	12th	16th
1978-79	Division 2	24 February	Lost	0	2	14 October	Drew	1	1	20thR	21stR
1979-80	Division 3	27 October	Lost	0	1	8 March	Drew	1	1	12th	14th
1980-81	Division 3	28 March	Lost	2	3	25 October	Won	4	1	21stR	16th
1982-83	Division 3	30 October	Drew	1	1	12 March	Won	2	1	11th	17th
1983-84	Division 3	4 February	Won	2	0	1 October	Won	2	1	3rdP	9th
1985-86	Division 2	5 October	Lost	1	3	8 March	Lost	0	3	7th	9th
1986-87	Division 2	2 September	Won	2	1	14 February	Lost	0	1	9th	16th
1987-88	Division 2	19 September	Lost	1	2	28 December	Lost	1	3	21stR	1stP
1994-95	Division 1	14 January	Drew	1	1	29 October	Lost	1	2	8th	12th
1995-96	Division 1	13 February	Won	2	0	16 March	Lost	0	1	9th	22ndR
2001-02	Division 1	19 March	Won	3	2	22 September	Lost	0	2	13th	4th
2002-03	Division 1	27 August	Won	3	1	1 February	Lost	0	1	3rd	9th
2003-04	Division 1	2 March	Won	2	1	18 October	Lost	0	2	8th	10th

FA Cup

										Division	
1894-95	Round 1	2 February	Won	3	1					Div 1	Non L
1913-14	Round 3					21 February	Won	4	0	Div 1	Non L

League Cup

										Division	
1967-68	Round 2					13 September	Lost	2	3	Div 1	Div 2

Action from the game against Millwall in March 2004, when both sides were vying for a play-off place.

Robbie Kozluk in action against Millwall in 2003/04.

Summary	P	W	D	L	F	A
Blades' home league record:	19	11	3	5	34	23
Blades' away league record:	19	5	3	11	16	28
Blades' cup record:	3	2	0	1	9	4
TOTAL:	**41**	**18**	**6**	**17**	**59**	**55**

FACT FILE

- Between 1970 and 1983, United were unbeaten in eight visits to Millwall, but have lost all eight since.
- United were unbeaten in their first seven at home.
- The sides have never produced a goalless draw.

Blades' top scorers vs Millwall
Peter Ndlovu, Alan Woodward 3

Played for both clubs

Jock Smith	Blades 1950-53	Millwall 1952-56
Colin Rawson	Blades 1953-56	Millwall 1955-59
Chris Guthrie	Blades 1975-77	Millwall 1979-80
Nicky Johns	Millwall 1976-78	Blades 1978-79
Peter Anderson	Blades 1978-79	Millwall 1980-83
Tony Towner	Millwall 1978-80	Blades 1982-83
Richard Cadette	Blades 1987-88	Millwall 1994-97
Alan McLeary	Millwall 1982-93/96-99	Blades 1992-93
David Tuttle	Blades 1993-96	Millwall 1999-2003
Kingsley Black	Blades 1994-95	Millwall 1995-96
Carl Veart	Blades 1994-96	Millwall 1997-98
Scott Fitzgerald	Blades 1995-96	Millwall 1996-2001
Mark Beard	Millwall 1993-95	Blades 1995-98
Aidan Davison	Millwall 1991-93	Blades 1999-2000
Paul Shaw	Millwall 1997-2000	Blades 2003-04

v. New Brighton

	Home						Division
FA Cup	*Date*	*Result*	Blades N Brighton				Blades N Brighton
1948-49　Round 3	8 January	Won	**5**　**2**				Div 1 Div 3N

Summary	*P*	*W*	*D*	*L*	*F*	*A*
Blades' cup record:	1	1	0	0	5	2
TOTAL:	**1**	**1**	**0**	**0**	**5**	**2**

Blades' top scorers vs New Brighton
George Jones 3

Blades hat-tricks vs New Brighton
8 Jan 1949 George Jones (cup)

Played for both clubs
Jimmy Dunne	New Brighton 1925-26	Blades 1926-34
Willis Vaughton	Blades 1934-35	New Brighton 1936-39
Harry Hitchen	New Brighton 1946-48	Blades 1948-53

v. Newcastle United

		Home				Away				Final Positions	
Season	League	Date	Result	Blades	Newcastle	Date	Result	Blades	Newcastle	Blades	Newcastle
1898-99	Division 1	26 September	Drew	2	2	15 October	Won	2	1	16th	13th
1899-00	Division 1	26 March	Won	3	1	21 October	Drew	0	0	2nd	5th
1900-01	Division 1	8 December	Won	2	0	13 April	Lost	0	3	14th	6th
1901-02	Division 1	12 April	Won	1	0	14 December	Drew	1	1	10th	3rd
1902-03	Division 1	15 November	Won	2	1	14 March	Drew	0	0	4th	14th
1903-04	Division 1	25 December	Drew	2	2	24 October	Won	1	0	7th	4th
1904-05	Division 1	11 February	Lost	1	3	15 October	Drew	1	1	6th	1st
1905-06	Division 1	2 December	Won	2	0	4 April	Lost	1	2	13th	4th
1906-07	Division 1	8 December	Drew	0	0	13 April	Drew	0	0	4th	1st
1907-08	Division 1	1 January	Drew	1	1	26 December	Won	3	2	17th	4th
1908-09	Division 1	14 November	Drew	1	1	20 March	Lost	0	4	12th	1st
1909-10	Division 1	18 December	Won	4	0	30 April	Drew	0	0	6th	4th
1910-11	Division 1	3 April	Drew	0	0	5 November	Drew	1	1	9th	8th
1911-12	Division 1	1 January	Won	2	1	26 December	Drew	2	2	14th	3rd
1912-13	Division 1	30 December	Drew	1	1	25 December	Won	2	1	15th	14th
1913-14	Division 1	18 April	Won	2	0	13 December	Lost	1	2	10th	11th
1914-15	Division 1	27 February	Won	1	0	24 October	Lost	3	4	6th	15th
1919-20	Division 1	6 December	Won	2	1	13 December	Lost	1	2	14th	8th
1920-21	Division 1	2 October	Lost	0	3	25 September	Lost	0	3	20th	5th
1921-22	Division 1	24 September	Drew	1	1	1 October	Lost	1	2	11th	7th
1922-23	Division 1	16 September	Won	2	0	9 September	Lost	0	3	10th	4th
1923-24	Division 1	15 September	Won	2	1	8 September	Drew	2	2	5th	9th
1924-25	Division 1	13 April	Lost	1	2	1 January	Drew	0	0	14th	6th
1925-26	Division 1	10 April	Won	4	3	9 December	Lost	1	3	5th	10th
1926-27	Division 1	12 February	Won	2	1	25 September	Lost	0	2	8th	1st
1927-28	Division 1	23 April	Drew	1	1	22 October	Lost	0	1	13th	9th
1928-29	Division 1	1 September	Won	3	1	5 January	Lost	2	4	11th	10th
1929-30	Division 1	5 October	Won	1	0	8 February	Won	5	3	20th	19th
1930-31	Division 1	25 October	Won	3	1	28 February	Lost	0	1	15th	17th
1931-32	Division 1	30 April	Lost	0	3	19 December	Lost	3	5	7th	11th
1932-33	Division 1	8 October	Won	3	1	18 February	Lost	0	2	10th	5th
1933-34	Division 1	17 March	Won	4	0	4 November	Lost	1	3	22ndR	21stR
1934-35	Division 2	10 November	Won	5	1	23 March	Lost	1	4	11th	6th
1935-36	Division 2	23 November	Won	5	1	28 March	Lost	0	3	3rd	8th
1936-37	Division 2	5 September	Won	2	1	2 January	Lost	0	4	7th	4th
1937-38	Division 2	15 January	Won	4	0	4 September	Lost	0	6	3rd	19th
1938-39	Division 2	3 September	Drew	0	0	31 December	Drew	0	0	2ndP	9th
1948-49	Division 1	7 May	Drew	0	0	11 December	Lost	2	3	22ndR	4th
1953-54	Division 1	31 October	Won	3	1	20 March	Lost	1	4	20th	15th
1954-55	Division 1	1 January	Won	6	2	28 August	Won	2	1	13th	8th
1955-56	Division 1	17 December	Won	2	1	20 August	Lost	2	4	22ndR	11th
1965-66	Division 1	27 November	Won	3	2	23 April	Won	2	0	9th	15th
1966-67	Division 1	23 August	Lost	0	1	31 August	Lost	0	1	10th	20th
1967-68	Division 1	23 September	Won	2	1	3 February	Lost	0	1	21stR	10th

		Home					**Away**			*Final Positions*	
Season	*League*	*Date*	*Result*	Blades	Newcastle	*Date*	*Result*	Blades	Newcastle	Blades	Newcastle
1971-72	Division 1	1 April	Won	1	0	27 December	Won	2	1	10th	11th
1972-73	Division 1	19 August	Lost	1	2	30 December	Lost	1	4	14th	9th
1973-74	Division 1	8 September	Drew	1	1	29 December	Lost	0	1	13th	15th
1974-75	Division 1	27 August	Won	2	1	21 August	Drew	2	2	6th	15th
1975-76	Division 1	19 April	Won	1	0	27 December	Drew	1	1	22ndR	15th
1978-79	Division 2	26 December	Won	1	0	14 April	Won	3	1	20thR	8th
1989-90	Division 2	24 February	Drew	1	1	25 November	Lost	0	2	2ndP	3rd
1993-94	Premiership	30 April	Won	2	0	24 November	Lost	0	4	20thR	3rd

FA Cup

										Division	
1893-94	Round 1					27 January	Lost	0	2	Div 1	Div 2
1901-02	Q'ter Final	27 February	Won	2	1	22 February	Drew	1	1	Div 1	Div 1
1913-14	Round 1					10 January	Won	5	0	Div 1	Div 1
1946-47	Q'ter Final	1 March	Lost	0	2					Div 1	Div 2
1960-61	Q'ter Final					4 March	Won	3	1	Div 2	Div 1
1976-77	Round 3	8 January	Drew	0	0	24 January	Lost	1	3	Div 2	Div 1
1997-98	Semi-Final	5 April		Old Trafford			Lost	0	1	Div 1	Prem
1999-00	Round 4					8 January	Lost	1	4	Div 1	Prem

League Cup

1961-62	Round 2	2 October	Drew	2	2	11 October	Won	2	0	Div 1	Div 2
1969-70	Round 2	2 September	Won	2	0					Div 2	Div 1
1988-89	Round 2	27 September	Won	3	0	12 October	Lost	0	2	Div 3	Div 1

Summary	*P*	*W*	*D*	*L*	*F*	*A*
Blades' home league record:	52	33	13	6	98	48
Blades' away league record:	52	9	13	30	53	107
Blades' cup record:	15	6	3	6	22	19
TOTAL:	**119**	**48**	**29**	**42**	**173**	**174**

FACT FILE

- **Twelve consecutive matches from 1932 to 1938 ended in home wins.**
- **United were unbeaten in 12 home games in the league from 1932 to 1965.**
- **From 1926 to 1949, United won one and lost 14 of 16 visits to Tyneside.**
- **Newcastle won just four times in the teams' first 30 league matches.**

Blades' top scorers vs Newcastle

Harry Johnson 9
Fred Tunstall 8
Jimmy Dunne 7
Bob Evans, Billy Gillespie 6
Jock Dodds, Joe Kitchen, Fred Priest 5
Walter Bennett, Jack Pickering 4

Blades hat-tricks vs Newcastle

1 Sep 1928 Harry Johnson
23 Nov 1935 Jock Dodds
4 Mar 1961 Billy Russell (cup)

Played for both clubs

Bob Benson	Newcastle 1902-03	Blades 1905-14
James Raine	Blades 1904-05	Newcastle 1905-06
Wally Hardinge	Newcastle 1905-06	Blades 1907-13
Jack Peart	Blades 1907-10	Newcastle 1911-13
Jack Alderson	Newcastle 1912-13	Blades 1925-29
Tom Phillipson	Newcastle 1919-21	Blades 1927-30
Tucker Mordue	Newcastle 1925-26	Blades 1926-28
Bert Chandler	Newcastle 1925-27	Blades 1926-29
Jack Dryden	Newcastle 1932-34	Blades 1935-36
Arthur Bottom	Blades 1948-54	Newcastle 1957-59
Jim Iley	Blades 1954-58	Newcastle 1962-69
Keith Kettleborough	Blades 1960-66	Newcastle 1965-67
Bill Punton	Newcastle 1953-58	Blades 1966-68
John Tudor	Blades 1968-71	Newcastle 1970-77
David Ford	Newcastle 1969-71	Blades 1970-73
Trevor Hockey	Newcastle 1963-66	Blades 1970-73
John Hope	Newcastle 1968-69	Blades 1970-74
Chris Guthrie	Newcastle 1971-72	Blades 1975-77
Imre Varadi	Blades 1978-79	Newcastle 1981-83
Viv Busby	Newcastle 1971-72	Blades 1979-80
Gary Brazil	Blades 1980-85	Newcastle 1988-90
John Burridge	Blades 1984-87	Newcastle 1989-91
Peter Withe	Newcastle 1978-80	Blades 1985-88
Billy Whitehurst	Newcastle 1985-87	Blades 1989-91
Glyn Hodges	Newcastle 1987-88	Blades 1990-96
Franz Carr	Newcastle 1991-93	Blades 1992-94
Andy Walker	Newcastle 1991-92	Blades 1995-98
Wayne Quinn	Blades 1997-2001/02-03	Newcastle 2000-01
Ian Rush	Newcastle 1997-98	Blades 1997-98
Des Hamilton	Newcastle 1997-98	Blades 1998-99
David Kelly	Newcastle 1991-93	Blades 2000-01
Gary Kelly	Newcastle 1986-90	Blades 2002-03

v. Newport County

Season	League	Date	Result	Home Blades	Newport	Date	Result	Away Blades	Newport	Final Positions Blades	Newport
1980-81	Division 3	14 October	Won	2	0	3 January	Lost	0	4	21stR	12th
1982-83	Division 3	1 March	Won	2	0	2 November	Lost	1	3	11th	4th
1983-84	Division 3	12 May	Won	2	0	17 December	Won	2	0	3rdP	13th

FA Cup										Division	
1951-52	Round 3	12 January	Won	2	0					Div 2 Div 3S	
1952-53	Round 3					10 January	Won	4	1	Div 2 Div 3S	

Summary	P	W	D	L	F	A
Blades' home league record:	3	3	0	0	6	0
Blades' away league record:	3	1	0	2	3	7
Blades' cup record:	2	2	0	0	6	1
TOTAL:	8	6	0	2	15	8

FACT FILE

- United have won every one of their home games 2-0 (and, just for good measure, repeated the scoreline in Wales in 1983).

Blades' top scorers vs Newport
Keith Edwards 4
Arthur Bottom, Bob Hatton 2

Played for both clubs

George Hall	Blades 1932-35	Newport 1936-37	
Roy John	Blades 1934-36	Newport 1936-37	
Gil Reece	Newport 1963-65	Blades 1965-73	
John McGeady	Blades 1975-77	Newport 1978-79	
Wally Downes	Newport 1987-88	Blades 1987-88	
Darren Carr	Newport 1987-88	Blades 1987-89	
Paul Williams	Newport 1987-88	Blades 1987-89	
John Moore	Newport 1985-86	Blades 1988-89	

v. Northampton Town

Season	League	Date	Result	Home Blades	North'ton	Date	Result	Away Blades	North'ton	Final Positions Blades	North'ton
1965-66	Division 1	1 January	Drew	2	2	9 October	Won	1	0	9th	21stR
1981-82	Division 4	16 March	Won	7	3	3 November	Won	2	1	1stP	22nd
1988-89	Division 3	20 September	Won	4	0	15 April	Won	2	1	2ndP	20th

FA Cup

Season	Round	Date	Result			Date	Result			Division	
1901-02	Round 1					25 January	Won	2	0	Div 1	Non L

League Cup

Season	Round	Date	Result	Home Blades	North'ton	Date	Result	Away Blades	North'ton	Division	
1990-91	Round 2	10 October	Won	2	1	25 September	Won	1	0	Div 1	Div 4

Summary	P	W	D	L	F	A
Blades' home league record:	3	2	1	0	13	5
Blades' away league record:	3	3	0	0	5	2
Blades' cup record:	3	3	0	0	5	1
TOTAL:	**9**	**8**	**1**	**0**	**23**	**8**

FACT FILE

- No side has faced the Blades more often without winning at least once.
- United have won their last seven.

Blades' top scorers vs Northampton
Brian Deane 4
Keith Edwards 3

Blades hat-tricks vs Northampton
16 Mar 1982 Keith Edwards

Played for both clubs

Thomas Boyle	Blades 1921-29	Northampton 1930-35
Albert Partridge	Blades 1923-29	Northampton 1933-34
Jesse Bennett	Blades 1929-30	Northampton 1933-36
Bernard Radford	Blades 1929-31	Northampton 1931-32
George Henson	Northampton 1932-35	Blades 1938-40
Jack Cross	Northampton 1953-54	Blades 1953-56
Ian Benjamin	Blades 1978-80	Northampton 1984-88
Bob Hatton	Northampton 1968-69	Blades 1980-83
Chris Wilder	Blades 1986-92/97-99	Northampton 1998-99
Colin Hill	Blades 1989-92	Northampton 1997-99
Rob Scott	Blades 1994-96	Northampton 1995-96
Doug Hodgson	Blades 1994-97	Northampton 1998-99
Tony Battersby	Blades 1995-96	Northampton 1999-2000
Martin Smith	Blades 1999-2000	Northampton 2003-04
Robert Ullathorne	Blades 2000-03	Northampton 2003-04

v. Northwich Victoria

				Home					Away		Final Positions	
Season	League	Date	Result	Blades	Northwich	Date	Result	Blades	Northwich		Blades	Northwich
1892-93	Division 2	23 January	Drew	1	1	18 February	Won	3	1		2ndP	7th

Summary	P	W	D	L	F	A
Blades' home league record:	1	0	1	0	1	1
Blades' away league record:	1	1	0	0	3	1
TOTAL:	**2**	**1**	**1**	**0**	**4**	**2**

Season	League	Date	Result	Home Blades	Norwich	Date	Result	Away Blades	Norwich	Final Positions Blades	Norwich
1934-35	Division 2	16 March	Drew	1	1	3 November	Lost	1	3	11th	14th
1935-36	Division 2	1 February	Won	3	2	28 September	Won	1	0	3rd	11th
1936-37	Division 2	26 December	Won	2	0	29 August	Drew	1	1	7th	17th
1937-38	Division 2	4 December	Won	4	1	16 April	Drew	2	2	3rd	14th
1938-39	Division 2	17 September	Won	4	0	2 February	Won	2	1	2ndP	21stR
1960-61	Division 2	17 December	Drew	1	1	20 August	Drew	1	1	2ndP	4th
1968-69	Division 2	29 March	Won	1	0	7 September	Lost	0	2	9th	13th
1969-70	Division 2	6 September	Won	1	0	20 December	Drew	1	1	6th	11th
1970-71	Division 2	3 April	Drew	0	0	29 August	Lost	0	1	2ndP	10th
1972-73	Division 1	27 January	Won	2	0	9 September	Drew	1	1	14th	20th
1973-74	Division 1	22 September	Won	1	0	9 February	Lost	1	2	13th	22ndR
1975-76	Division 1	27 September	Lost	0	1	3 April	Won	3	1	22ndR	10th
1985-86	Division 2	22 March	Lost	2	5	7 September	Lost	0	4	7th	1stP
1990-91	Division 1	11 May	Won	2	1	3 November	Lost	0	3	13th	15th
1991-92	Division 1	18 January	Won	1	0	17 August	Drew	2	2	9th	18th
1992-93	Premiership	10 March	Lost	0	1	6 November	Lost	1	2	14th	3rd
1993-94	Premiership	21 November	Lost	1	2	23 April	Won	1	0	20thR	12th
1995-96	Division 1	9 September	Won	2	1	28 February	Drew	0	0	9th	16th
1996-97	Division 1	9 February	Lost	2	3	30 October	Drew	1	1	5th	13th
1997-98	Division 1	11 April	Drew	2	2	6 December	Lost	1	2	6th	15th
1998-99	Division 1	19 September	Won	2	1	27 February	Drew	1	1	8th	9th
1999-00	Division 1	19 October	Drew	0	0	29 April	Lost	1	2	16th	12th
2000-01	Division 1	10 April	Drew	1	1	21 October	Lost	2	4	10th	15th
2001-02	Division 1	29 September	Won	2	1	3 February	Lost	1	2	13th	6th
2002-03	Division 1	22 February	Lost	0	1	7 September	Won	3	2	3rd	8th
2003-04	Division 1	23 August	Won	1	0	31 January	Lost	0	1	8th	1stP

FA Cup

Season	Round	Date	Result	Blades	Norwich	Date	Result	Blades	Norwich	Division	
1958-59	Q'ter Final	28 February	Drew	1	1	4 March	Lost	2	3	Div 2	Div 3
1961-62	Round 5	17 February	Won	3	1					Div 1	Div 2
1988-89	Round 5					18 February	Lost	2	3	Div 3	Div 1
1996-97	Round 3					4 January	Lost	0	1	Div 1	Div 1

League Cup

Season	Round	Date	Result	Blades	Norwich	Date	Result	Blades	Norwich	Division	
1974-75	Round 4	12 November	Drew	2	2	27 November	Lost*	1	2	Div 1	Div 2

Summary

	P	W	D	L	F	A
Blades' home league record:	26	14	6	6	38	25
Blades' away league record:	26	5	9	12	28	42
Blades' cup record:	7	1	2	4	11	13
TOTAL:	**59**	**20**	**17**	**22**	**77**	**80**

FACT FILE

- United were unbeaten in their first 13 home games in the series.
- United were unbeaten in 10 games from 1935 to 1959.
- United have lost on all four cup visits to Carrow Road.
- From 1996 to 2002, United failed to win in eight away games.

Blades' top scorers vs Norwich
Jock Dodds 12
Tony Agana, Michael Brown, Brian Deane,
Billy Dearden, John Tudor 3

Played for both clubs

Jack Peart	Blades 1907-10	Norwich 1922-23
Tommy Simons	Blades 1910-12	Norwich 1920-21
Albert Sturgess	Blades 1908-23	Norwich 1923-25
Norman Wharton	Blades 1928-30	Norwich 1931-35
Paddy Sloan	Blades 1947-48	Norwich 1951-52
Ken Mallender	Blades 1961-69	Norwich 1968-71
Bill Punton	Norwich 1959-67	Blades 1966-68
Trevor Hockey	Blades 1970-73	Norwich 1972-73
Jim Bone	Norwich 1971-73	Blades 1972-74
Viv Busby	Norwich 1976-78	Blades 1979-80
Martin Peters	Norwich 1974-80	Blades 1980-81
John Ryan	Norwich 1976-80	Blades 1980-82
Roger Hansbury	Norwich 1974-81	Blades 1987-88
Graham Benstead	Norwich 1984-88	Blades 1987-89
Simon Tracey	Blades 1988-2002	Norwich 1994-95
Carl Bradshaw	Blades 1989-94	Norwich 1994-98
Steve Bruce	Norwich 1984-88	Blades 1998-99
Des Hamilton	Blades 1998-99	Norwich 1999-2000
Alex Notman	Blades 1999-2000	Norwich 2000-04
Robert Ullathorne	Norwich 1990-96	Blades 2000-03
Paul Peschisolido	Norwich 2000-01	Blades 2000-04
Ashley Ward	Norwich 1994-96	Blades 2003-04

v. Nottingham Forest

Season	League	Date	Result	Home Blades	Home Forest	Date	Result	Away Blades	Away Forest	Final Positions Blades	Final Positions Forest
1893-94	Division 1	1 January	Lost	0	2	18 November	Drew	1	1	10th	7th
1894-95	Division 1	29 September	Won	3	2	17 November	Lost	0	3	6th	7th
1895-96	Division 1	23 November	Won	2	1	14 December	Lost	1	3	12th	13th
1896-97	Division 1	20 February	Lost	0	3	26 September	Drew	2	2	2th	11th
1897-98	Division 1	4 December	Drew	1	1	18 September	Drew	1	1	1st	8th
1898-99	Division 1	5 November	Drew	2	2	4 March	Lost	1	2	16th	11th
1899-00	Division 1	25 November	Won	3	0	31 March	Lost	0	4	2nd	8th
1900-01	Division 1	5 January	Lost	0	1	8 September	Lost	0	2	14th	4th
1901-02	Division 1	4 January	Drew	2	2	7 September	Lost	1	2	10th	5th
1902-03	Division 1	13 October	Won	2	0	27 December	Drew	2	2	4th	10th
1903-04	Division 1	2 April	Won	2	0	5 December	Drew	1	1	7th	9th
1904-05	Division 1	3 December	Won	4	0	1 April	Won	2	1	6th	16th
1905-06	Division 1	3 March	Lost	1	4	28 October	Lost	1	4	13th	19thR
1907-08	Division 1	14 September	Drew	2	2	20 April	Drew	1	1	17th	9th
1908-09	Division 1	5 September	Lost	1	2	2 January	Won	2	0	12th	14th
1909-10	Division 1	12 February	Lost	1	4	2 October	Won	3	2	6th	14th
1910-11	Division 1	1 October	Lost	0	1	4 February	Won	2	1	9th	20thR
1922-23	Division 1	30 September	Drew	0	0	23 September	Lost	0	1	10th	20th
1923-24	Division 1	24 November	Drew	0	0	17 November	Won	2	1	5th	20th
1924-25	Division 1	11 October	Lost	1	2	14 February	Won	3	2	14th	22ndR
1934-35	Division 2	27 April	Won	2	1	15 December	Lost	1	2	11th	9th
1935-36	Division 2	5 October	Won	1	0	8 February	Won	1	0	3rd	19th
1936-37	Division 2	14 November	Won	4	1	20 March	Drew	1	1	7th	18th
1937-38	Division 2	28 August	Won	2	1	1 January	Lost	1	2	3rd	20th
1938-39	Division 2	24 December	Lost	0	1	27 August	Won	2	0	2ndP	20th
1951-52	Division 2	10 November	Lost	1	4	29 March	Won	2	0	11th	4th
1952-53	Division 2	22 September	Won	2	0	6 April	Drew	1	1	1stP	7th
1956-57	Division 2	27 April	Lost	0	4	22 April	Lost	1	2	7th	2ndP
1961-62	Division 1	22 December	Won	2	0	26 August	Lost	0	2	5th	19th
1962-63	Division 1	15 December	Won	3	1	18 August	Lost	1	2	10th	9th
1963-64	Division 1	28 December	Lost	1	2	26 December	Drew	3	3	12th	13th
1964-65	Division 1	20 April	Lost	0	2	19 April	Drew	0	0	19th	5th
1965-66	Division 1	11 December	Drew	1	1	8 January	Lost	0	1	9th	18th
1966-67	Division 1	27 August	Lost	1	2	31 December	Lost	1	3	10th	2nd
1967-68	Division 1	19 August	Lost	1	3	16 December	Lost	0	1	21stR	11th
1971-72	Division 1	18 December	Won	2	1	4 September	Won	3	2	10th	21stR
1976-77	Division 2	19 March	Won	2	0	9 October	Lost	1	6	11th	3rdP
1990-91	Division 1	22 December	Won	3	2	1 April	Lost	0	2	13th	8th
1991-92	Division 1	19 October	Won	4	2	1 February	Won	5	2	9th	8th
1992-93	Premiership	24 October	Drew	0	0	1 May	Won	2	0	14th	22ndR
1997-98	Division 1	13 September	Won	1	0	1 April	Lost	0	3	6th	1stP
1999-00	Division 1	16 October	Won	2	1	22 April	Drew	0	0	16th	14th
2000-01	Division 1	10 March	Lost	1	3	29 November	Lost	0	2	10th	11th
2001-02	Division 1	19 January	Drew	0	0	11 August	Drew	1	1	13th	16th

| | | | Home | | | | Away | | | Final Positions | |
Season	League	Date	Result	Blades	Forest	Date	Result	Blades	Forest	Blades	Forest
2002-03	Division 1	15 April	Won	1	0	2 November	Lost	0	3	3rd	6th
2003-04	Division 1	3 April	Lost	1	2	13 September	Lost	1	3	8th	14th

Division 1 Play-offs

										Final positions	
2002-03	Semi-Final	15 May	Won*	4	3	10 May	Drew	1	1	3rd	6th

FA Cup

Season	League	Date	Result	Blades	Forest	Date	Result	Blades	Forest	Division	
1898-99	Q'ter Final					25 February	Won	1	0	Div 1	Div 1
1904-05	Round 1					4 February	Lost	0	2	Div 1	Div 1
1909-10	Round 1					15 January	Lost	2	3	Div 1	Div 1
1922-23	Round 1	18 January	Drew*	0	0	13 January	Drew	0	0	Div 1	Div 1
		22 January	Meadow Lane, Nottingham (2nd replay) Drew*					1	1		
		25 January	Hillsborough (3rd replay)				Won	1	0		
1927-28	Q'ter Final	3 March	Won	3	0					Div 1	Div 2
1936-37	Round 3					16 January	Won	4	2	Div 2	Div 2
1954-55	Round 3	8 January	Lost	1	3					Div 1	Div 2
1959-60	Round 4	30 January	Won	3	0					Div 2	Div 1
2001-02	Round 3	5 January	Won	1	0					Div 1	Div 1
2003-04	Round 4					25 January	Won	3	0	Div 1	Div 1

Summary

	P	W	D	L	F	A
Blades' home league record:	46	20	9	17	65	63
Blades' away league record:	46	12	12	22	54	80
Blades' cup record:	15	8	4	3	25	15
TOTAL:	**107**	**40**	**25**	**42**	**144**	**158**

Action from 2002/03 as Steve Kabba tussles with former England defender Des Walker.

FACT FILE

- United failed to win in their first 11 away league games.
- From 1906 to 1924, United failed to win in nine home games.
- Between 1970 and 1999, United won six and drew one of their seven home games.
- United's victory in May 1993 confirmed Forest's relegation in Brian Clough's last season as manager there.

Blades' top scorers vs Forest
Jock Dodds 9
Arthur Brown, Derek Pace 7
Harry Johnson, Alf Ringstead 6
Mick Jones 5
Jack Almond, Ian Bryson 4

Blades hat-tricks vs Forest
30 Jan 1960 Derek Pace (cup)

Played for both clubs

Harry Rothery	Blades 1905-06	Forest 1906-07
Jackie Smith	Blades 1910-11	Forest 1910-11
Harry Green	Blades 1925-26	Forest 1927-28
Sid Gibson	Forest 1921-29	Blades 1928-32
Colin Collindridge	Blades 1946-50	Forest 1950-54
Colin Rawson	Forest 1946-47	Blades 1953-56
Jim Iley	Blades 1954-58	Forest 1959-63
Colin Addison	Forest 1960-67	Blades 1967-71
John Barnwell	Forest 1963-70	Blades 1970-71
Trevor Hockey	Forest 1961-64	Blades 1970-73
Barry Butlin	Forest 1974-77	Blades 1979-81
Paul Richardson	Forest 1967-77	Blades 1981-83
Terry Curran	Forest 1975-77	Blades 1982-83
Steve Wigley	Forest 1982-86	Blades 1985-87
Peter Withe	Forest 1976-79	Blades 1985-88
Hans Segers	Forest 1984-88	Blades 1987-88
Glyn Hodges	Blades 1990-96	Forest 1998-99
Franz Carr	Forest 1985-91	Blades 1992-94
Kingsley Black	Forest 1991-96	Blades 1994-95
Phil Starbuck	Forest 1986-91	Blades 1994-97
Gareth Taylor	Blades 1995-99	Forest 2003-04
Carl Tiler	Forest 1991-95	Blades 1996-98
Dean Saunders	Forest 1996-98	Blades 1997-99
Alan Fettis	Forest 1996-97	Blades 2003-04
Andy Gray	Forest 1998-2002	Blades 2003-04
Jack Lester	Forest 1999-2003	Blades 2003-04
Paul Gerrard	Forest 2003-04	Blades 2003-04

v. Notts County

		Home						Away			Final Positions	
Season	League	Date	Result	Blades	Notts C	Date	Result	Blades	Notts C	Blades	Notts C
1897-98	Division 1	19 February	Lost	0	1	1 January	Won	3	1	1st	13th
1898-99	Division 1	7 January	Drew	2	2	10 September	Drew	2	2	16th	5th
1899-00	Division 1	3 February	Drew	1	1	30 September	Won	2	1	2nd	15th
1900-01	Division 1	9 March	Won	4	2	3 November	Won	4	2	14th	3rd
1901-02	Division 1	9 November	Won	3	0	8 March	Lost	0	4	10th	13th
1902-03	Division 1	10 April	Won	3	0	25 October	Drew	1	1	4th	15th
1903-04	Division 1	10 October	Won	3	1	4 April	Lost	1	2	7th	13th
1904-05	Division 1	1 October	Won	2	1	28 January	Won	5	1	6th	18th
1905-06	Division 1	1 January	Won	1	0	26 December	Won	3	2	13th	16th
1906-07	Division 1	26 December	Won	2	1	1 April	Lost	0	4	4th	18th
1907-08	Division 1	23 November	Lost	0	1	21 March	Won	3	0	17th	18th
1908-09	Division 1	13 March	Won	3	2	7 November	Lost	1	3	12th	15th
1909-10	Division 1	18 October	Drew	2	2	11 December	Won	2	1	6th	9th
1910-11	Division 1	8 April	Lost	0	2	3 December	Won	3	0	9th	11th
1911-12	Division 1	30 March	Lost	1	3	25 November	Lost	0	2	14th	16th
1912-13	Division 1	30 November	Won	2	0	5 April	Won	1	0	15th	19thR
1914-15	Division 1	28 December	Won	1	0	2 April	Lost	1	3	6th	16th
1919-20	Division 1	1 September	Won	3	0	2 October	Drew	2	2	14th	21stR
1923-24	Division 1	7 April	Won	3	1	5 April	Won	2	0	5th	10th
1924-25	Division 1	18 April	Won	2	0	13 December	Lost	0	2	14th	9th
1925-26	Division 1	13 March	Won	3	0	31 October	Lost	0	2	5th	22ndR
1934-35	Division 2	13 October	Won	3	0	23 February	Won	1	0	11th	22ndR
1950-51	Division 2	7 October	Lost	1	2	24 February	Lost	0	3	8th	17th
1951-52	Division 2	26 December	Won	1	0	25 December	Lost	1	3	11th	15th
1952-53	Division 2	4 April	Won	2	1	15 November	Won	3	0	1stP	19th
1956-57	Division 2	13 October	Won	5	1	23 February	Drew	2	2	7th	20th
1957-58	Division 2	24 August	Won	1	0	21 December	Lost	0	1	6th	21stR
1976-77	Division 2	6 November	Won	1	0	28 March	Lost	1	2	11th	8th
1977-78	Division 2	4 October	Won	4	1	25 April	Won	2	1	12th	15th
1978-79	Division 2	10 April	Won	5	1	13 March	Lost	1	4	20thR	6th
1984-85	Division 2	15 September	Won	3	0	12 January	Drew	0	0	18th	20thR
1988-89	Division 3	27 March	Drew	1	1	26 December	Won	4	1	2ndP	9th
1991-92	Division 1	17 September	Lost	1	3	20 April	Won	3	1	9th	21stR
1994-95	Division 1	27 August	Lost	1	3	11 March	Lost	1	2	8th	24thR

FA Cup

										Division	
1890-91	Round 1	17 January	Lost	1	9					Non L Div 1	
1927-28	Round 3					14 January	Won	3	2	Div 1 Div 2	
1930-31	Round 4	24 January	Won	4	1					Div 1 Div 3S	
1998-99	Round 3	2 January	Drew	1	1	23 January	Won*	4	3	Div 1 Div 2	

Summary	P	W	D	L	F	A
Blades' home league record:	34	23	4	7	70	33
Blades' away league record:	34	15	5	14	55	55
Blades' cup record:	5	3	1	1	13	16
TOTAL:	**73**	**41**	**10**	**22**	**138**	**104**

FACT FILE

- **United have had winning runs at home of eight matches (twice) and seven matches.**
- **Neither side has won more than two in a row in Nottingham.**
- **Having been knocked out of their first FA Cup 13-0 by Bolton, United were knocked out of their second 9-1 by Notts County. Just seven years later, however, they were champions.**

Blades' top scorers vs Notts County
Joe Kitchen 7
Arthur Brown, Bert Lipsham 6
Keith Edwards, Harry Johnson 5
Walter Bennett, Jimmy Donnelly 4

Blades hat-tricks vs Notts County
24 Jan 1931 Jimmy Dunne (cup)

Played for both clubs

William Ross	Blades 1895-97	Notts Co 1900-04
Thomas Clinch	Blades 1899-1900	Notts Co 1904-05
Herbert Chapman	Blades 1902-03	Notts Co 1903-04
Mark Mellors	Notts Co 1902-04	Blades 1907-08
Jack Peart	Blades 1907-10	Notts Co 1912-20
Chick Reed	Blades 1931-32	Notts Co 1938-39
Derek Pace	Blades 1957-65	Notts Co 1964-66
Dennis Shiels	Blades 1958-64	Notts Co 1965-66
Alan Birchenall	Blades 1964-68	Notts Co 1975-76/77-78
Willie Carlin	Blades 1967-69	Notts Co 1971-74
Barry Butlin	Notts Co 1968-70	Blades 1979-81
Jeff King	Notts Co 1975-76	Blades 1981-83
Alan Young	Blades 1982-83	Notts Co 1984-86
Tony Daws	Notts Co 1984-86	Blades 1986-87
Martin Kuhl	Blades 1986-88	Notts Co 1994-95
Chris Wilder	Blades 1986-92/97-99	Notts Co 1995-97
Chris Marsden	Blades 1987-88	Notts Co 1994-96
Tony Agana	Blades 1987-92	Notts Co 1991-97
Paul Rogers	Blades 1991-96	Notts Co 1995-97
Tony Battersby	Blades 1995-96	Notts Co 1995-97
Brett Angell	Blades 1995-96	Notts Co 1999-2000
Christian Short	Notts Co 1990-96	Blades 1995-98
Shaun Derry	Notts Co 1995-98	Blades 1997-2000
Ian Hamilton	Blades 1997-2000	Notts Co 2000-02
Paul Devlin	Notts Co 1991-96/98-99	Blades 1997-2002
Andy Goram	Blades 1998-99	Notts Co 1998-99
Aidan Davison	Notts Co 1988-89	Blades 1999-2000
Shaun Murphy	Notts Co 1992-97	Blades 1999-2003
Marcel Cas	Notts Co 2001-03	Blades 2002-03
Andy Parkinson	Notts Co 2003-04	Blades 2003-04

v. Oldham Athletic

Season	League	Date	Result	Home Blades	Home Oldham	Date	Result	Away Blades	Away Oldham	Final Positions Blades	Final Positions Oldham
1910-11	Division 1	26 December	Lost	1	2	17 April	Lost	0	3	9th	7th
1911-12	Division 1	30 December	Won	4	0	2 September	Won	3	2	14th	18th
1912-13	Division 1	7 September	Drew	1	1	28 December	Lost	0	2	15th	9th
1913-14	Division 1	21 March	Won	2	1	15 November	Won	2	1	10th	4th
1914-15	Division 1	5 December	Won	3	0	10 April	Lost	0	3	6th	2nd
1919-20	Division 1	8 November	Won	1	0	15 November	Lost	0	4	14th	17th
1920-21	Division 1	1 January	Won	3	0	18 December	Drew	0	0	20th	19th
1921-22	Division 1	25 February	Won	1	0	18 February	Won	2	0	11th	19th
1922-23	Division 1	18 November	Drew	2	2	25 November	Won	2	0	10th	22ndR
1934-35	Division 2	2 February	Won	2	1	22 September	Lost	2	3	11th	21stR
1976-77	Division 2	5 April	Won	2	1	27 December	Won	2	1	11th	13th
1977-78	Division 2	12 November	Won	1	0	17 December	Lost	0	3	12th	8th
1978-79	Division 2	21 October	Won	4	2	3 March	Drew	1	1	20thR	14th
1984-85	Division 2	12 February	Won	2	0	8 September	Drew	2	2	18th	14th
1985-86	Division 2	12 April	Won	2	0	9 November	Won	5	1	7th	8th
1986-87	Division 2	18 April	Won	2	0	1 January	Lost	1	3	9th	3rd
1987-88	Division 2	2 January	Lost	0	5	12 September	Lost	2	3	21stR	10th
1989-90	Division 2	26 September	Won	2	1	28 March	Won	2	0	2ndP	8th
1991-92	Division 1	4 April	Won	2	0	7 September	Lost	1	2	9th	17th
1992-93	Premiership	22 February	Won	2	0	13 April	Drew	1	1	14th	19th
1993-94	Premiership	1 January	Won	2	1	3 May	Drew	1	1	20thR	21stR
1994-95	Division 1	1 October	Won	2	0	25 February	Drew	3	3	8th	14th
1995-96	Division 1	3 February	Won	2	1	26 August	Lost	1	2	9th	18th
1996-97	Division 1	28 December	Drew	2	2	7 September	Won	2	0	5th	23rdR

FA Cup

Season	Round	Date	Result	Home Blades	Home Oldham	Date	Result	Away Blades	Away Oldham	Division Blades	Division Oldham
1914-15	Q'ter Final	13 March	Won	3	0	6 March	Drew	0	0	Div 1	Div 1

Summary	P	W	D	L	F	A
Blades' home league record:	24	19	3	2	47	20
Blades' away league record:	24	8	6	10	35	41
Blades' cup record:	2	1	1	0	3	0
TOTAL:	**50**	**28**	**10**	**12**	**85**	**61**

FACT FILE

- United have won 20 and lost one of their last 24 home matches – a superb record. However, the one defeat (in 1988) was a heavy one.
- Neither side has won more than two in a row in Oldham.

Blades' top scorers vs Oldham

Joe Kitchen 10

Brian Deane, Keith Edwards, Colin Morris 4

Blades hat-tricks vs Oldham

2 Sep 1911 Joe Kitchen

Played for both clubs

Walter Davies	Oldham 1912-13	Blades 1913-15
Ollie Tummon	Oldham 1912-15	Blades 1919-20
Harold Gough	Blades 1913-24	Oldham 1926-27
Seth King	Blades 1922-29	Oldham 1929-32
Jack Pears	Oldham 1930-34	Blades 1934-35
Eddie Shimwell	Blades 1946-47	Oldham 1957-58
Roy Warhurst	Blades 1946-50	Oldham 1960-61
Eric Over	Blades 1954-55	Oldham 1957-58
Barry Hartle	Blades 1960-66	Oldham 1970-71
Billy Dearden	Oldham 1964-67	Blades 1970-76
David Irving	Blades 1975-76	Oldham 1976-78
Simon Stainrod	Blades 1975-79	Oldham 1978-81
Alan Young	Oldham 1974-79	Blades 1982-83
Tony Philliskirk	Blades 1983-88	Oldham 1988-89
Simon Webster	Blades 1987-90	Oldham 1994-95
John Gannon	Blades 1988-96	Oldham 1995-97
Adrian Littlejohn	Blades 1991-95/2001-02	Oldham 1997-99
Mark Foran	Blades 1994-96	Oldham 1996-97
Doug Hodgson	Blades 1994-97	Oldham 1996-99
Phil Starbuck	Blades 1994-97	Oldham 1997-98
Michel Vonk	Oldham 1995-96	Blades 1995-98
Nick Henry	Oldham 1987-97	Blades 1996-99
Earl Barrett	Oldham 1987-92	Blades 1997-98
Andy Goram	Oldham 1981-88/2001-02	Blades 1998-99
Gary Kelly	Oldham 1996-2003	Blades 2002-03
Paul Gerrard	Oldham 1992-96	Blades 2003-04
Andy Gray	Oldham 1998-99	Blades 2003-04
Chris Armstrong	Oldham 2001-03	Blades 2003-04

v. Oxford United

Season	League	Home Date	Result	Blades	Oxford	Away Date	Result	Blades	Oxford	Final Positions Blades	Oxford
1968-69	Division 2	14 September	Lost	1	2	19 April	Lost	0	1	9th	20th
1969-70	Division 2	15 April	Won	5	1	17 September	Drew	0	0	6th	15th
1970-71	Division 2	28 November	Won	3	0	30 January	Won	2	1	2ndP	14th
1979-80	Division 3	29 September	Won	3	1	16 February	Drew	1	1	12th	17th
1980-81	Division 3	23 August	Won	1	0	31 January	Lost	0	2	21stR	14th
1982-83	Division 3	19 March	Won	3	2	6 November	Drew	0	0	11th	5th
1983-84	Division 3	6 March	Lost	1	2	5 November	Drew	2	2	3rdP	1stP
1984-85	Division 2	9 March	Drew	1	1	20 October	Lost	1	5	18th	1stP
1989-90	Division 2	14 April	Won	2	1	1 January	Lost	0	3	2ndP	17th
1996-97	Division 1	15 March	Won	3	1	14 December	Lost	1	4	5th	17th
1997-98	Division 1	7 February	Won	1	0	20 September	Won	4	2	6th	12th
1998-99	Division 1	26 March	Lost	1	2	24 October	Won	2	0	8th	23rdR

League Cup

										Division	
1986-87	Round 3					29 October	Lost	1	3	Div 2	Div 1

Summary

	P	W	D	L	F	A
Blades' home league record:	12	8	1	3	25	13
Blades' away league record:	12	3	4	5	13	21
Blades' cup record:	1	0	0	1	1	3
TOTAL:	**25**	**11**	**5**	**9**	**39**	**37**

FACT FILE

- **The Blades won eight of their 10 home games from 1970 to 1998.**
- **United failed to win in eight away games from 1980 to 1996.**

Blades' top scorers vs Oxford
Alan Woodward 4

Played for both clubs

Geoffrey Denial	Blades 1952-55	Oxford 1962-63
Imre Varadi	Blades 1978-79	Oxford 1992-93
Billy Whitehurst	Oxford 1986-88	Blades 1989-91
Andy Scott	Blades 1992-98	Oxford 2000-04
Paul Simpson	Oxford 1988-92	Blades 1996-97
Bobby Ford	Oxford 1993-98/2002-03	Blades 1997-2002
Dean Saunders	Oxford 1986-89	Blades 1997-99
Dean Windass	Oxford 1998-99	Blades 2002-03
Paul Gerrard	Oxford 1998-99	Blades 2003-04

v. Peterborough United

				Home			Away		Final Positions	
Season	League	Date	Result	Blades Pet'borough	Date	Result	Blades Pet'borough		Blades	Pet'borough
1981-82	Division 4	8 May	Won	4 0	21 April	Won	4 0		1stP	5th

FA Cup

									Division	
1961-62	Round 4				27 January	Won	3 1		Div 1	Div 3

League Cup

1984-85	Round 1	28 August	Won	1 0	5 September	Drew*	2 2		Div 2	Div 4

Summary	P	W	D	L	F	A
Blades' home league record:	1	1	0	0	4	0
Blades' away league record:	1	1	0	0	4	0
Blades' cup record:	3	2	1	0	6	3
TOTAL:	5	4	1	0	14	3

FACT FILE

- **United won the first four matches in the series.**

Blades' top scorers vs Peterborough
Keith Edwards 5
Colin Morris 3
Billy Russell 2

Played for both clubs

Jim Walker	Blades 1949-54	Peterborough 1960-65	
Jim Iley	Blades 1954-58	Peterborough 1968-73	
John Turley	Blades 1957-58	Peterborough 1961-64	
Harry Orr	Blades 1958-64	Peterborough 1964-65	
Dennis Shiels	Blades 1958-64	Peterborough 1964-65	
David Bradford	Blades 1974-77	Peterborough 1976-77	
Ian Benjamin	Blades 1978-80	Peterborough 1982-84	
Barry Butlin	Peterborough 1977-79	Blades 1979-81	
Keith Waugh	Peterborough 1976-81	Blades 1981-85	
Tony Philliskirk	Blades 1983-88	Peterborough 1992-94	
Martin Pike	Peterborough 1983-86	Blades 1986-90	
Tom Cowan	Blades 1991-94	Peterborough 2001-02	
David Tuttle	Peterborough 1992-93	Blades 1993-96	
Mark Blount	Blades 1994-96	Peterborough 1995-96	
Mark Foran	Blades 1994-96	Peterborough 1995-98	
Jonathan Cullen	Blades 1997-99	Peterborough 1999-2002	
Curtis Woodhouse	Blades 1997-2001	Peterborough 2003-04	
Paul Shaw	Peterborough 1995-96	Blades 2003-04	

v. Plymouth Argyle

Season	League	Date	Result	Blades	Plymouth	Date	Result	Blades	Plymouth	Blades	Plymouth
				Home			**Away**			*Final Positions*	
1934-35	Division 2	27 October	Lost	1	2	9 March	Lost	0	2	11th	8th
1935-36	Division 2	7 December	Drew	0	0	11 March	Drew	1	1	3rd	7th
1936-37	Division 2	27 March	Won	2	0	21 November	Lost	0	2	7th	5th
1937-38	Division 2	12 March	Drew	0	0	30 October	Lost	0	2	3rd	13th
1938-39	Division 2	1 October	Lost	0	1	4 February	Won	1	0	2ndP	15th
1949-50	Division 2	8 October	Drew	1	1	25 February	Won	1	0	3rd	21stR
1952-53	Division 2	17 January	Won	5	0	6 September	Lost	2	5	1stP	4th
1959-60	Division 2	2 January	Won	4	0	29 August	Drew	1	1	4th	19th
1960-61	Division 2	23 August	Won	3	0	31 August	Lost	0	2	2ndP	11th
1976-77	Division 2	7 May	Won	1	0	11 December	Drew	0	0	11th	21stR
1979-80	Division 3	1 December	Won	3	2	19 April	Lost	1	4	12th	15th
1980-81	Division 3	4 October	Drew	0	0	14 April	Lost	0	1	21stR	7th
1982-83	Division 3	18 September	Won	3	1	16 April	Lost	1	3	11th	8th
1983-84	Division 3	28 February	Won	2	0	29 October	Won	1	0	3rdP	19th
1986-87	Division 2	21 February	Won	2	1	14 October	Lost	0	1	9th	7th
1987-88	Division 2	19 April	Won	1	0	31 August	Lost	0	1	21stR	16th
1989-90	Division 2	10 February	Won	1	0	16 September	Drew	0	0	2ndP	16th

League Cup *Division*

						Date	Result	Blades	Plymouth		
1964-65	Round 2					23 September	Lost	1	2	Div 1	Div 2

Summary

	P	W	D	L	F	A
Blades' home league record:	17	11	4	2	29	8
Blades' away league record:	17	3	4	10	9	25
Blades' cup record:	1	0	0	1	1	2
TOTAL:	**35**	**14**	**8**	**13**	**39**	**35**

FACT FILE

- The Blades have won 10 of their last 11 games at home, keeping eight clean sheets in the process.
- In total, they are unbeaten in 12 at home since their last defeat in 1938.
- In contrast, United have won just one of the last 12 away from home.
- The last four meetings have produced only three goals.

Blades' top scorers vs Plymouth
Arthur Bottom, Len Browning, Colin Morris, Derek Pace 3

Blades hat-tricks vs Plymouth
17 Jan 1953 Arthur Bottom

Played for both clubs

Len Birks	Blades 1924-31	Plymouth 1930-33
Bernard Oxley	Blades 1928-34	Plymouth 1935-36
Harry Gooney	Blades 1930-35	Plymouth 1935-36
Arthur Eggleston	Plymouth 1935-37	Blades 1937-39
Alf Tootill	Plymouth 1936-38	Blades 1938-39
Jack Chisholm	Blades 1948-50	Plymouth 1949-54
Ronnie Waldock	Blades 1954-57	Plymouth 1959-60
Keith Edwards	Blades 1975-78/81-86	Plymouth 1990-91
John Matthews	Blades 1978-82	Plymouth 1985-89
Neil Ramsbottom	Plymouth 1976-77	Blades 1979-80
Mike Trusson	Plymouth 1976-80	Blades 1980-84
Julian Broddle	Blades 1981-82	Plymouth 1989-90
Phil Kite	Blades 1990-92	Plymouth 1992-93
Adrian Littlejohn	Blades 1991-95/2001-02	Plymouth 1995-98
Doug Hodgson	Blades 1994-97	Plymouth 1995-96
Graham Anthony	Blades 1994-97	Plymouth 1997-98
Phil Starbuck	Blades 1994-97	Plymouth 1997-98
David Lee	Plymouth 1991-92	Blades 1997-98
Nicky Marker	Plymouth 1987-93/98-99	Blades 1997-99
Andrew Morrison	Plymouth 1987-93	Blades 2000-01
Jean-Philippe Javary	Plymouth 2000-01	Blades 2001-03
Grant Smith	Blades 2001-03	Plymouth 2002-03

Grant Smith, who went on loan to Argyle.

v. Portsmouth

Season	League	Date	Result	Blades	Portsm'th	Date	Result	Blades	Portsm'th	Blades	Portsm'th
			Home				**Away**			*Final Positions*	
1927-28	Division 1	2 January	Won	3	1	9 April	Lost	1	4	13th	20th
1928-29	Division 1	15 December	Won	3	0	29 April	Won	3	2	11th	20th
1929-30	Division 1	5 April	Lost	2	3	30 November	Lost	1	3	20th	13th
1930-31	Division 1	27 September	Won	3	1	31 January	Won	3	2	15th	4th
1931-32	Division 1	29 August	Lost	1	2	2 January	Lost	1	2	7th	8th
1932-33	Division 1	3 September	Lost	2	3	7 January	Lost	0	1	10th	9th
1933-34	Division 1	23 September	Lost	0	1	3 February	Drew	1	1	22ndR	10th
1946-47	Division 1	10 May	Won	3	1	12 April	Drew	0	0	6th	12th
1947-48	Division 1	1 January	Lost	1	2	17 September	Lost	0	6	12th	8th
1948-49	Division 1	19 February	Won	3	1	25 September	Lost	0	3	22ndR	1st
1953-54	Division 1	19 December	Won	3	1	22 August	Won	4	3	20th	14th
1954-55	Division 1	2 May	Won	5	2	9 October	Lost	2	6	13th	3rd
1955-56	Division 1	5 November	Lost	1	3	17 March	Drew	1	1	22ndR	12th
1959-60	Division 2	16 April	Drew	0	0	12 December	Won	2	0	4th	20th
1960-61	Division 2	20 September	Won	3	1	3 April	Won	2	1	2ndP	21stR
1968-69	Division 2	11 January	Won	2	0	2 November	Lost	1	2	9th	15th
1969-70	Division 2	7 October	Won	5	0	16 August	Won	5	1	6th	17th
1970-71	Division 2	9 January	Won	2	0	30 September	Won	5	1	2ndP	16th
1980-81	Division 3	6 December	Won	1	0	10 January	Lost	0	1	21stR	6th
1982-83	Division 3	15 January	Won	2	1	28 August	Lost	1	4	11th	1stP
1984-85	Division 2	29 December	Won	4	1	2 October	Lost	1	2	18th	4th
1985-86	Division 2	26 April	Drew	0	0	23 November	Won	3	0	7th	4th
1986-87	Division 2	13 December	Won	1	0	9 May	Won	2	1	9th	2ndP
1989-90	Division 2	31 October	Won	2	1	7 April	Lost	2	3	2ndP	12th
1994-95	Division 1	31 December	Won	3	1	8 April	Lost	0	1	8th	18th
1995-96	Division 1	4 November	Won	4	1	8 April	Won	2	1	9th	21st
1996-97	Division 1	7 December	Won	1	0	1 March	Drew	1	1	5th	7th
1997-98	Division 1	23 August	Won	2	1	31 January	Drew	1	1	6th	20th
1998-99	Division 1	3 October	Won	2	1	9 March	Lost	0	1	8th	19th
1999-00	Division 1	4 December	Won	1	0	7 August	Lost	0	2	16th	18th
2000-01	Division 1	12 August	Won	2	0	23 December	Drew	0	0	10th	20th
2001-02	Division 1	9 February	Won	4	3	20 October	Lost	0	1	13th	17th
2002-03	Division 1	13 August	Drew	1	1	13 January	Won	2	1	3rd	1stP

FA Cup

										Division	
1959-60	Round 3	9 January	Won	3	0					Div 2	Div 2
1970-71	Round 3					2 January	Lost	0	2	Div 2	Div 2
1987-88	Round 4					1 February	Lost	1	2	Div 2	Div 1

League Cup

										Division	
1961-62	Round 3	13 November	Won	1	0					Div 1	Div 3

Summary	P	W	D	L	F	A
Blades' home	33	24	3	6	72	33
Blades' away league record:	33	11	6	16	47	59
Blades' cup record:	4	2	0	2	5	4
TOTAL:	70	37	9	24	124	96

FACT FILE

- Portsmouth clearly hate travelling to Bramall Lane. The Blades have drawn three and won 19 at the ground since Pompey's last win in 1955.
- All four cup matches have resulted in victory for the home side.
- In 1969 and 1970, United scored five against Portsmouth in three consecutive games.
- Portsmouth won five games in a row from 1931 to 1933.

Blades' top scorers vs Portsmouth
Alan Woodward 7
Jimmy Dunne 6
Derek Hawksworth, Harry Johnson, Jack Pickering 5
Derek Pace, Gil Reece 4

Blades hat-tricks vs Portsmouth
7 Oct 1969 Gil Reece
30 Sep 1970 Alan Woodward

Played for both clubs

Bob Widdowson	Blades 1961-68	Portsmouth 1969-70
David Munks	Blades 1961-68	Portsmouth 1969-74
Jeff King	Portsmouth 1975-76	Blades 1981-83
Trevor Ross	Portsmouth 1982-83	Blades 1982-84
Steve Wigley	Blades 1985-87	Portsmouth 1988-92
Martin Kuhl	Blades 1986-88	Portsmouth 1988-93
Paul Wood	Portsmouth 1983-87/93-96	Blades 1989-92
Chris Kamara	Portsmouth 1975-77/81-82	Blades 1992-94
Lee Sandford	Portsmouth 1985-90	Blades 1996-2002
Carl Tiler	Blades 1996-98	Portsmouth 2000-03
Shaun Derry	Blades 1997-2000	Portsmouth 1999-2002
David Lee	Portsmouth 1994-95	Blades 1997-98
Paul Hall	Portsmouth 1993-98	Blades 1999-2000
Michael Brown	Portsmouth 1999-2000	Blades 1999-2004
Steve Lovell	Portsmouth 1999-2002	Blades 2001-02
John Curtis	Blades 2002-03	Portsmouth 2003-04
Carl Robinson	Portsmouth 2002-04	Blades 2003-04

v. Port Vale

Season	League	Date	Result	Blades	Port Vale	Date	Result	Blades	Port Vale	Blades	Port Vale
			Home				**Away**			*Final Positions*	
1892-93	Division 2	17 December	Won	4	0	10 December	Won	10	0	2ndP	11th
1934-35	Division 2	29 December	Won	3	0	25 August	Lost	0	2	11th	18th
1935-36	Division 2	26 October	Won	4	0	11 April	Drew	1	1	3rd	21stR
1956-57	Division 2	25 August	Won	4	2	25 March	Won	6	0	7th	22ndR
1981-82	Division 4	27 February	Won	2	1	10 October	Won	2	0	1stP	7th
1983-84	Division 3	24 April	Won	3	1	27 December	Lost	0	2	3rdP	23rdR
1988-89	Division 3	28 February	Drew	0	0	24 October	Drew	3	3	2ndP	3rdP
1989-90	Division 2	21 April	Won	2	1	16 December	Drew	1	1	2ndP	11th
1994-95	Division 1	4 March	Drew	1	1	24 September	Won	2	0	8th	17th
1995-96	Division 1	4 May	Drew	1	1	11 November	Won	3	2	9th	12th
1996-97	Division 1	4 March	Won	3	0	16 November	Drew	0	0	5th	8th
1997-98	Division 1	28 March	Won	2	1	22 November	Drew	0	0	6th	19th
1998-99	Division 1	20 March	Won	3	0	31 October	Won	3	2	8th	21st
1999-00	Division 1	23 November	Lost	1	3	11 March	Won	3	2	16th	23rdR

FA Cup

Season	League	Date	Result	Blades	Port Vale	Date	Result	Blades	Port Vale	Division	
1897-98	Round 1	29 January	Drew	1	1	2 February	Lost*	1	2	Div 1	Non L
1962-63	Round 4					13 March	Won	2	1	Div 1	Div 3

Summary

	P	W	D	L	F	A
Blades' home league record:	14	10	3	1	33	11
Blades' away league record:	14	7	5	2	34	15
Blades' cup record:	3	1	1	1	4	4
TOTAL:	**31**	**18**	**9**	**4**	**71**	**30**

Blades' top scorers vs Port Vale
Harry Hammond 5
Nathan Blake, Derek Hawksworth 3

Blades hat-tricks vs Port Vale
10 Dec 1892 Harry Hammond (4)
25 Mar 1957 Derek Hawksworth

Michael Twiss had an extended loan at Bramall Lane in 1998-99 and later joined Port Vale.

FACT FILE

- In 1892, Hammond (4), Watson (2), Davies (2), Drummond and Wallace scored as United beat Burslem Port Vale, as they were known at the time, 10-0. United had been three up after only five minutes. Little could the 1,500 or so spectators have imagined that well over 100 years later they would remain the only people to have seen an away team score 10 in any English league match. Worryingly for Vale, they had to face United at Bramall Lane just seven days later, and may have been somewhat relieved with a 4-0 defeat.
- In 1898, United's championship year, they were knocked out of the FA Cup at the first hurdle. In the replay, Vale took the lead but United were utterly dominant for the remainder of the game. United's 'keeper, the eccentric but brilliant William 'Fatty' Foulke, got bored and ventured upfield to see more action. Port Vale broke away and scored the winning goal.
- After 13 attempts over more than a century, Port Vale won at Bramall Lane for the first time in 1999.
- This defeat ended United's 15-match unbeaten run against Port Vale.

Played for both clubs

Jack Peart	Blades 1907-10	Port Vale 1921-22	
Bert Pearson	Blades 1912-14	Port Vale 1921-22	
Harry Wainwright	Port Vale 1919-20	Blades 1924-26	
Percy Oldacre	Blades 1921-23	Port Vale 1926-27	
Len Birks	Port Vale 1920-25	Blades 1924-31	
Percy Thorpe	Blades 1930-33	Port Vale 1934-35	
Colin Grainger	Blades 1953-57	Port Vale 1961-64	
Jack Wilkinson	Blades 1955-57	Port Vale 1957-60	
Steve Cammack	Blades 1971-76	Port Vale 1985-86	
John Connaughton	Blades 1973-74	Port Vale 1974-80	
Gary Hamson	Blades 1976-79	Port Vale 1986-88	
Gary Brazil	Blades 1980-85	Port Vale 1984-85	
Gary West	Blades 1982-85	Port Vale 1988-90	
Paul Smith	Blades 1982-86	Port Vale 1986-88	
Dean Glover	Blades 1986-87	Port Vale 1988-98	
Paul Beesley	Blades 1990-95	Port Vale 1997-99	
Adrian Littlejohn	Blades 1991-95/2001-02	Port Vale 2002-04	
Brett Angell	Blades 1995-96	Port Vale 2002-03	
Gareth Taylor	Blades 1995-99	Port Vale 1999-2000	
Michael Twiss	Blades 1998-99	Port Vale 2000-01	
Marcus Bent	Port Vale 1998-2000	Blades 1999-2001	

v. Preston North End

Season	League	Date	Result	Home Blades	Home Preston NE	Date	Result	Away Blades	Away Preston NE	Final Positions Blades	Final Positions Preston NE
1893-94	Division 1	20 November	Drew	1	1	7 April	Lost	0	3	10th	14th
1894-95	Division 1	13 October	Lost	0	1	8 September	Lost	1	2	6th	4th
1895-96	Division 1	30 September	Won	2	1	30 November	Lost	3	4	12th	9th
1896-97	Division 1	13 March	Lost	0	2	24 October	Lost	0	1	2nd	4th
1897-98	Division 1	23 October	Won	2	1	4 September	Won	3	1	1st	12th
1898-99	Division 1	22 October	Drew	1	1	18 February	Lost	0	1	16th	15th
1899-00	Division 1	24 March	Won	1	0	18 November	Won	1	0	2nd	16th
1900-01	Division 1	10 November	Won	2	1	16 March	Lost	1	3	14th	17thR
1904-05	Division 1	22 October	Won	1	0	21 April	Lost	0	4	6th	8th
1905-06	Division 1	31 March	Drew	0	0	25 November	Drew	1	1	13th	2nd
1906-07	Division 1	2 February	Won	3	1	1 December	Lost	1	2	4th	14th
1907-08	Division 1	7 December	Won	2	0	4 April	Drew	0	0	17th	12th
1908-09	Division 1	28 November	Won	2	1	3 April	Drew	1	1	12th	10th
1909-10	Division 1	4 December	Won	5	1	16 April	Drew	1	1	6th	12th
1910-11	Division 1	26 November	Won	5	0	1 April	Drew	1	1	9th	14th
1911-12	Division 1	28 December	Won	4	2	5 April	Lost	0	3	14th	19thR
1913-14	Division 1	6 December	Won	2	0	11 April	Won	4	2	10th	19thR
1919-20	Division 1	1 January	Won	2	1	2 April	Lost	0	2	14th	19th
1920-21	Division 1	5 February	Won	1	0	7 February	Lost	0	2	20th	16th
1921-22	Division 1	19 November	Won	3	0	26 November	Lost	0	3	11th	16th
1922-23	Division 1	16 December	Drew	2	2	23 December	Won	3	2	10th	16th
1923-24	Division 1	13 October	Won	4	0	6 October	Drew	1	1	5th	18th
1924-25	Division 1	25 October	Won	3	0	28 February	Won	1	0	14th	21stR

Mark Rankine in action against the Deepdale club.

Season	League	Home Date	Result	Blades	Preston NE	Away Date	Result	Blades	Preston NE	Blades	Preston NE
										Final Positions	
1939-40	Division 1					30 August	Drew	0	0		
1946-47	Division 1	24 May	Lost	2	3	4 September	Won	2	1	6th	7th
1947-48	Division 1	20 September	Won	3	1	7 April	Drew	3	3	12th	7th
1948-49	Division 1	6 November	Won	3	2	2 April	Lost	1	4	22ndR	21stR
1949-50	Division 2	27 December	Won	1	0	26 December	Lost	1	4	3rd	6th
1950-51	Division 2	17 March	Lost	2	3	28 October	Drew	1	1	8th	1stP
1953-54	Division 1	10 April	Drew	1	1	21 November	Lost	1	2	20th	11th
1954-55	Division 1	25 September	Lost	0	5	12 February	Won	2	1	13th	14th
1955-56	Division 1	4 February	Won	3	1	24 September	Won	2	0	22ndR	19th
1968-69	Division 2	23 November	Won	4	0	17 March	Drew	2	2	9th	14th
1969-70	Division 2	17 January	Won	2	0	27 September	Lost	1	2	6th	22ndR
1978-79	Division 2	18 November	Lost	0	1	26 August	Drew	2	2	20thR	7th
1982-83	Division 3	4 September	Won	2	1	12 April	Lost	0	1	11th	16th
1983-84	Division 3	10 September	Drew	1	1	31 January	Drew	2	2	3rdP	16th
1988-89	Division 3	8 April	Won	3	1	31 December	Lost	0	2	2ndP	6th
2000-01	Division 1	30 December	Won	3	2	19 August	Lost	0	3	10th	4th
2001-02	Division 1	1 December	Drew	2	2	23 October	Lost	0	3	13th	8th
2002-03	Division 1	21 December	Won	1	0	19 April	Lost	0	2	3rd	12th
2003-04	Division 1	29 November	Won	2	0	9 May	Drew	3	3	8th	15th

FA Cup

Season	Round	Home Date	Result	Blades	Preston NE	Away Date	Result	Blades	Preston NE	Division Blades	Division Preston NE
1898-99	Round 2	16 February	Won	2	1	11 February	Drew	2	2	Div 1	Div 1
1935-36	Round 4	30 January	Won	2	0	25 January	Drew	0	0	Div 2	Div 1
2001-02	Round 4					26 January	Lost	1	2	Div 1	Div 1

League Cup

Season	Round	Home Date	Result	Blades	Preston NE	Away Date	Result	Blades	Preston NE	Division Blades	Division Preston NE
1999-00	Round 2	14 September	Won	2	0	21 September	Lost	0	3	Div 1	Div 2

Summary	P	W	D	L	F	A
Blades' home league record:	41	28	7	6	83	40
Blades' away league record:	42	8	13	21	46	78
Blades' cup record:	7	3	2	2	9	8
TOTAL:	**90**	**39**	**22**	**29**	**138**	**126**

FACT FILE

- **United were unbeaten in 21 home games, including 10 straight wins, between 1897 and 1936.**
- **United's last win at Deepdale was in 1955.**
- **Bizarrely, United played Preston away in April seven seasons in succession, between 1908 and 1920.**
- **Preston have not done the double over Sheffield United since 1897.**
- **United are unbeaten in their last eight homes games against Preston.**

Blades' top scorers vs Preston

Jimmy Hagan, Joe Kitchen 6
Harry Johnson 5
Colin Collindridge, Bob Evans, Billy Gillespie,
Bert Menlove, Fred Priest 4

Played for both clubs

Billy Hendry	Preston 1889-91	Blades 1892-95
Sammy Dobson	Preston 1890-91	Blades 1892-93
Jack Drummond	Preston 1890-91	Blades 1892-94
Hugh Gallacher	Preston 1890-93	Blades 1892-94
Frank Becton	Preston 1891-95/1900-01	Blades 1898-99
John Cunningham	Preston 1893-97	Blades 1897-98
Rabbi Howell	Blades 1892-98	Preston 1901-04
Peter McIntyre	Preston 1898-1901	Blades 1901-02
Dickie Bourne	Blades 1900-02	Preston 1902-05
Joe Walton	Preston 1901-03	Blades 1909-11
Alf Common	Blades 1901-04	Preston 1912-14
Jack English	Preston 1910-12	Blades 1913-15
Norman Wharton	Preston 1925-27	Blades 1928-30
Jack Kendall	Preston 1927-28	Blades 1929-34
Jack Pears	Preston 1933-35	Blades 1934-35
Andy McLaren	Preston 1946-49	Blades 1948-51
Gary Brazil	Blades 1980-85	Preston 1984-89
Bob Atkins	Blades 1982-85	Preston 1984-90
Tony Philliskirk	Blades 1983-88	Preston 1988-89
Paul Williams	Preston 1986-87	Blades 1987-89
Ian Bryson	Blades 1988-93	Preston 1993-97
Richard Lucas	Blades 1990-92	Preston 1992-94
Nathan Peel	Preston 1990-91	Blades 1991-92
Kevin Gage	Blades 1991-96	Preston 1995-97
Alan Kelly	Preston 1985-92	Blades 1992-99
Brett Angell	Blades 1995-96	Preston 1999-2000
Mark Patterson	Preston 1988-90	Blades 1995-98
Mark Rankine	Preston 1996-2003	Blades 2002-04
Andy Gray	Preston 1998-99	Blades 2003-04

v. Queen's Park Rangers

Season	League	Date	Result	Home Blades	Home QPR	Date	Result	Away Blades	Away QPR	Final Positions Blades	Final Positions QPR
1949-50	Division 2	1 October	Drew	1	1	18 February	Won	3	1	3rd	20th
1950-51	Division 2	31 March	Won	2	0	11 November	Lost	1	2	8th	16th
1951-52	Division 2	3 May	Lost	1	2	14 April	Lost	2	4	11th	22ndR
1969-70	Division 2	24 February	Won	2	0	8 November	Lost	1	2	6th	9th
1970-71	Division 2	14 November	Drew	1	1	13 March	Drew	2	2	2ndP	11th
1973-74	Division 1	20 April	Drew	1	1	8 December	Drew	0	0	13th	8th
1974-75	Division 1	17 August	Drew	1	1	14 December	Lost	0	1	6th	11th
1975-76	Division 1	28 February	Drew	0	0	25 October	Lost	0	1	22ndR	2nd
1990-91	Division 1	1 January	Won	1	0	13 April	Won	2	1	13th	12th
1991-92	Division 1	29 February	Drew	0	0	7 December	Lost	0	1	9th	11th
1992-93	Premiership	30 January	Lost	1	2	22 August	Lost	2	3	14th	5th
1993-94	Premiership	16 March	Drew	1	1	1 September	Lost	1	2	20thR	9th
1996-97	Division 1	26 October	Drew	1	1	30 November	Lost	0	1	5th	9th
1997-98	Division 1	18 October	Drew	2	2	25 February	Drew	2	2	6th	21st
1998-99	Division 1	17 April	Won	2	0	21 November	Won	2	1	8th	20th
1999-00	Division 1	5 March	Drew	1	1	30 November	Lost	1	3	16th	10th
2000-01	Division 1	30 September	Drew	1	1	3 March	Won	3	1	10th	23rdR

FA Cup

										Division	
1922-23	Q'ter Final					10 March	Won	1	0	Div 1	Div 3S

League Cup

2003-04	Round 2	23 September	Lost	0	2					Div 1	Div 2

Summary	P	W	D	L	F	A
Blades' home league record:	17	4	11	2	19	14
Blades' away league record:	17	4	3	10	22	38
Blades' cup record:	2	1	0	1	1	2
TOTAL:	**36**	**9**	**14**	**13**	**42**	**44**

FACT FILE

- Eleven of the 17 league meetings in Sheffield have ended in draws. There were five draws in succession (at both venues) from 1970 to 1974.
- United won one of 13 matches at Loftus Road from 1950 to 1996.
- United have lost one of the last 14 in the league at home.

Blades' top scorers vs QPR
Brian Deane 4
Harold Brook, Marcelo 3

Played for both clubs

Fred Hawley	Blades 1912-15	QPR 1926-28
Bob Bolam	Blades 1919-22	QPR 1924-25
Bernie Harris	Blades 1924-27	QPR 1929-32
Tony Currie	Blades 1967-76	QPR 1979-83
Simon Stainrod	Blades 1975-79	QPR 1980-85
Nicky Johns	Blades 1978-79	QPR 1987-89
Derek Richardson	QPR 1976-79	Blades 1979-81
Don Givens	QPR 1972-78	Blades 1980-81
John Burridge	QPR 1980-82	Blades 1984-87
Vinnie Jones	Blades 1990-92	QPR 1997-99
Brett Angell	Blades 1995-96	QPR 2002-03
Gareth Taylor	Blades 1995-99	QPR 1999-2000
Paul Parker	QPR 1987-91	Blades 1996-97
Nigel Spackman	QPR 1988-90	Blades 1996-97
Paul Peschisolido	QPR 2000-01	Blades 2000-04
Paul Furlong	QPR 2000-01/02-04	Blades 2001-02
Steve Yates	QPR 1993-99	Blades 2002-03
Richard Edghill	Blades 2002-03	QPR 2003-04

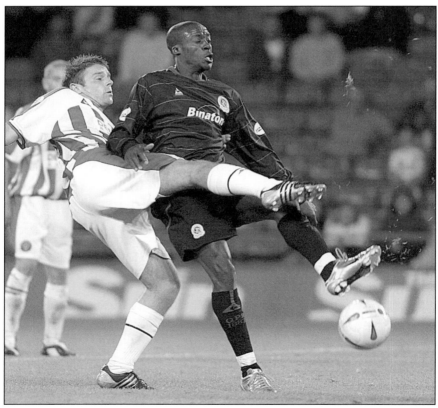

Colin Cryan of United tries to get the ball from Paul Furlong in the League Cup tie in September 2004.

Season	League	Home Date	Result	Blades	Reading	Away Date	Result	Blades	Reading	Final Positions Blades	Reading
1979-80	Division 3	13 October	Won	2	0	23 February	Lost	1	2	12th	7th
1980-81	Division 3	7 February	Won	2	0	13 September	Lost	0	1	21stR	10th
1982-83	Division 3	19 October	Drew	1	1	23 February	Lost	0	2	11th	21stR
1986-87	Division 2	11 October	Drew	3	3	21 March	Lost	0	2	9th	13th
1987-88	Division 2	21 November	Won	4	1	30 April	Lost	1	2	21stR	22ndR
1988-89	Division 3	18 March	Won	1	0	27 August	Won	3	1	2ndP	18th
1994-95	Division 1	25 March	Drew	1	1	17 September	Lost	0	1	8th	2nd
1995-96	Division 1	25 November	Drew	0	0	27 April	Won	3	0	9th	19th
1996-97	Division 1	29 March	Won	2	0	17 August	Lost	0	1	5th	18th
1997-98	Division 1	14 March	Won	4	0	4 November	Won	1	0	6th	24thR
2002-03	Division 1	18 February	Lost	1	3	14 December	Won	2	0	3rd	4th
2003-04	Division 1	24 October	Lost	1	2	28 February	Lost	1	2	8th	9th

FA Cup

										Division	
1997-98	Round 5	13 February	Won	1	0					Div 1	Div 1

Summary	P	W	D	L	F	A
Blades' home league record:	12	6	4	2	22	11
Blades' away league record:	12	4	0	8	12	14
Blades' cup record:	1	1	0	0	1	0
TOTAL:	25	11	4	10	35	25

FACT FILE

- Reading's first win at Bramall Lane came in 2003.
- United lost their first five matches at Reading's former home, Elm Park.

Jack Lester takes a tumble as Reading defender James Harper challenges.

Blades' top scorers vs Reading
Andy Walker 3
Brian Deane, Paul Stancliffe, Peter Withe 2

Played for both clubs
Percy Thorpe	Reading 1928-30	Blades 1930-33
Bert Oswald	Reading 1928-30	Blades 1930-34
Jim Holmes	Blades 1931-36	Reading 1937-40
Jack Cross	Blades 1953-56	Reading 1955-56
John Docherty	Blades 1960-66	Reading 1967-70
Tony Wagstaff	Blades 1960-69	Reading 1969-74
Barry Wagstaff	Blades 1964-69	Reading 1969-75
Barry Butlin	Reading 1976-77	Blades 1979-81
Francis Joseph	Reading 1987-88	Blades 1988-89
Billy Whitehurst	Reading 1987-89	Blades 1989-91
Lee Sandford	Blades 1996-2002	Reading 1997-98
David Lee	Reading 1991-92	Blades 1997-98
Keith Curle	Reading 1987-89	Blades 2000-02
Carl Asaba	Reading 1997-99	Blades 2000-03

Tony Wagstaff who, like his elder brother Barry, started out with the Blades and moved to Reading in 1969.

v. Rochdale

Season	League	Date	Result	Home Blades	Rochdale	Date	Result	Away Blades	Rochdale	Final Positions Blades	Rochdale
1981-82	Division 4	4 May	Won	3	1	16 January	Won	1	0	1stP	21st

Summary	P	W	D	L	F	A
Blades' home league record:	1	1	0	0	3	1
Blades' away league record:	1	1	0	0	1	0
TOTAL:	2	2	0	0	4	1

Blades' top scorers vs Rochdale
Keith Edwards 3

Played for both clubs

Jack Peart	Blades 1907-10	Rochdale 1922-24
Bert Pearson	Blades 1912-14	Rochdale 1923-26
Bobby Hughes	Blades 1922-23	Rochdale 1924-28
Wally Webster	Blades 1925-30	Rochdale 1933-34
Levi Redfern	Rochdale 1934-35	Blades 1935-36
Harry Mills	Blades 1946-47	Rochdale 1950-51
Andy McLaren	Blades 1948-51	Rochdale 1955-57
Ralph Morement	Blades 1949-50	Rochdale 1955-56
George Underwood	Blades 1949-51	Rochdale 1954-55
Ted Burgin	Blades 1949-57	Rochdale 1960-66
Roy Ridge	Blades 1953-61	Rochdale 1964-66
Brian Richardson	Blades 1955-65	Rochdale 1966-67
John Turley	Blades 1957-58	Rochdale 1964-65
Billy Russell	Blades 1957-63	Rochdale 1966-68
Graeme Crawford	Blades 1969-71	Rochdale 1980-83
Steve Conroy	Blades 1977-83	Rochdale 1983-85
Tony Moore	Blades 1979-82	Rochdale 1984-85
Alan Young	Blades 1982-83	Rochdale 1986-87
Tony Towner	Blades 1982-83	Rochdale 1985-86
Ray McHale	Blades 1982-85	Rochdale 1986-87
Paddy McGaaney	Blades 1984-86	Rochdale 1986-87
David Frain	Blades 1985-88	Rochdale 1988-89
Paul Wood	Blades 1987-88	Rochdale 1988-89
Paul Williams	Blades 1987-89	Rochdale 1993-96
John Moore	Rochdale 1987-88	Blades 1988-89
Ian Bryson	Blades 1988-93	Rochdale 1997-99
John Pemberton	Rochdale 1984-85	Blades 1990-94
Christopher Bettney	Blades 1996-97	Rochdale 1999-2000
Paul Simpson	Blades 1996-97	Rochdale 2001-03

v. Rotherham Town

	Home					Away			Division	
FA Cup	*Date*	*Result*	Blades	Roth'am T	*Date*	*Result*	Blades	Roth'am T	Blades	Roth'am T
1889-90 4th Qual Rd	21 December	Won	2	1	7 December	Drew	2	2	Non L	Non L

Summary	P	W	D	L	F	A
Blades' cup record:	2	1	1	0	4	3
TOTAL:	2	1	1	0	4	3

FACT FILE

- **This team merged with Rotherham County in 1925 to form Rotherham United.**

Blades' top scorers vs Rotherham Town
Dugald Galbraith 2

Played for both clubs

William Croxon	Blades 1892-94	Rotherham T 1894-95
Will Lilley	Blades 1892-94	Rotherham T 1894-95
Arthur Wharton	Rotherham T 1893-94/95-96	Blades 1894-95
Harry Thickett	Rotherham T 1893-94	Blades 1893-1904

v. Rotherham United

Season	League	Date	Result	Blades	Roth'am U	Date	Result	Blades	Roth'am U	Blades	Roth'am U
				Home				**Away**		*Final Positions*	
1951-52	Division 2	13 October	Won	1	0	1 March	Lost	1	3	11th	9th
1952-53	Division 2	1 January	Lost	1	4	13 December	Won	2	0	1stP	12th
1956-57	Division 2	15 December	Lost	2	7	18 August	Won	4	0	7th	17th
1957-58	Division 2	19 October	Won	2	0	1 March	Won	6	1	6th	18th
1958-59	Division 2	27 September	Won	2	0	15 April	Drew	2	2	3rd	20th
1959-60	Division 2	3 October	Lost	2	3	2 March	Drew	0	0	4th	8th
1960-61	Division 2	19 November	Won	3	1	8 April	Won	2	1	2ndP	15th
1979-80	Division 3	15 March	Won	1	0	6 October	Won	2	1	12th	13th
1980-81	Division 3	27 September	Lost	1	2	21 February	Lost	1	2	21stR	1stP
1983-84	Division 3	26 December	Won	3	0	21 April	Won	1	0	3rdP	18th
2001-02	Division 1	22 December	Drew	2	2	23 August	Drew	1	1	13th	21st
2002-03	Division 1	14 September	Won	1	0	28 February	Won	2	1	3rd	15th
2003-04	Division 1	16 September	Won	5	0	16 March	Drew	1	1	8th	17th

League Cup

Season	Round	Date	Result	Blades	Roth'am U	Date	Result	Blades	Roth'am U	Division	
1985-86	Round 1	3 September	Won	5	1	20 August	Won	3	1	Div 2	Div 3
1989-90	Round 1	22 August	Drew	1	1	29 August	Lost	0	1	Div 2	Div 3

Summary

	P	W	D	L	F	A
Blades' home league record:	13	8	1	4	26	19
Blades' away league record:	13	7	4	2	25	13
Blades' cup record:	4	2	1	1	9	4
TOTAL:	**30**	**17**	**6**	**7**	**60**	**36**

FACT FILE

- United have not lost in their last eight league meetings.
- United have scored in 25 of the 26 league matches between the teams.

Billy Hodgson, who ran out for both
Blades and local rivals Rotherham
during his career.

Blades' top scorers vs Rotherham
Derek Pace, Alf Ringstead 6
Joe Bolton, Peter Ndlovu, Billy Russell 3

Played for both clubs

Joe Kitchen	Blades 1907-21	Rotherham 1920-21
Bernie Harris	Rotherham 1922-23	Blades 1924-27
Charles Sutcliffe	Rotherham 1920-25	Blades 1924-27
Harry Pantling	Blades 1914-26	Rotherham 1926-27
George Davis	Blades 1928-30	Rotherham 1931-34
Walter Spicer	Blades 1930-31	Rotherham 1931-34
Jack Pears	Rotherham 1928-29	Blades 1934-35
Harry Mills	Blades 1946-47	Rotherham 1947-48
Walter Rickett	Blades 1946-48	Rotherham 1952-53
Joe Cockroft	Rotherham 1930-32	Blades 1948-49
Peter Wragg	Rotherham 1948-53	Blades 1952-56
Colin Rawson	Rotherham 1949-53	Blades 1953-56
Glyn Jones	Blades 1955-58	Rotherham 1957-59
Bill Hodgson	Blades 1957-64	Rotherham 1967-68
Keith Kettleborough	Rotherham 1955-61	Blades 1960-66
Barry Wagstaff	Blades 1964-69	Rotherham 1974-77
Pat Buckley	Blades 1967-71	Rotherham 1972-73
John Flynn	Blades 1969-78	Rotherham 1978-80
Tom McAlister	Blades 1971-76	Rotherham 1975-79
Steve Conroy	Blades 1977-83	Rotherham 1982-83
Imre Varadi	Blades 1978-79	Rotherham 1992-95
Mike Trusson	Blades 1980-84	Rotherham 1983-87
Tony Towner	Rotherham 1980-83	Blades 1982-83
Kevin Arnott	Rotherham 1982-83	Blades 1982-87
Tony Philliskirk	Blades 1983-88	Rotherham 1986-87
Paul Stancliffe	Rotherham 1975-83/90-91	Blades 1983-91
Clive Mendonca	Blades 1986-88/91-92	Rotherham 1987-91
Andy Barnsley	Rotherham 1985-86/88-91	Blades 1986-89
Chris Wilder	Blades 1986-92/97-99	Rotherham 1992-96
Darren Carr	Blades 1987-89	Rotherham 2000-01
Mark Todd	Blades 1987-91	Rotherham 1991-95
Peter Duffield	Blades 1987-92	Rotherham 1990-91
Phil Kite	Blades 1990-92	Rotherham 1992-93
Nathan Peel	Blades 1991-92	Rotherham 1994-95
Bobby Davison	Blades 1991-92/93-95	Rotherham 1994-96
Brian Gayle	Blades 1991-96	Rotherham 1996-97
Scott Marshall	Rotherham 1993-94	Blades 1994-95
Billy Mercer	Rotherham 1989-95	Blades 1994-96
Mark Foran	Rotherham 1994-95	Blades 1994-96
Rob Scott	Blades 1994-96	Rotherham 1998-2004
Carl Muggleton	Blades 1995-96	Rotherham 1995-96
Curtis Woodhouse	Blades 1997-2001	Rotherham 2002-03
Carl Robinson	Rotherham 2003-04	Blades 2003-04

v. Rushden & Diamonds

FA Cup		Date	Result	Home Blades	R & D	Date	Result	Away Blades	R & D	Division Blades	R & D
1999-00	Round 3	12 December	Drew	1	1	21 December	Drew*	1	1	Div 1	Non L
							(won 6-5 pens)				

Summary	P	W	D	L	F	A	
Blades' cup record:	2	0	2	0	2	2	
TOTAL:	2	0	2	0	2	2 (+one penalty shoot-out victory)	

FACT FILE

● **Non-league Diamonds made United fight all the way to a fourth-round tie against Newcastle.**

Played for both clubs

Darren Carr	Blades 1987-89	Rushden 2001-02
Tony Battersby	Blades 1995-96	Rushden 2002-03
Brett Angell	Blades 1995-96	Rushden 2001-02
Paul Hall	Blades 1999-2000	Rushden 2001-04

Action as the Blades take on Rushden. Marcus Bent surges through the defence.

v. Scarborough

							Away		Division	
FA Cup				*Date*		*Result*	Blades	Scarb'gh	Blades	Scarb'gh
1889-90 1st Qual Rd				5 October		Won	**6**	**1**	Non L	Non L

Summary	*P*	*W*	*D*	*L*	*F*	*A*
Blades' cup record:	1	1	0	0	6	1
TOTAL:	1	1	0	0	6	1

FACT FILE

● **This was United's first-ever FA Cup match.**

Blades' top scorers vs Scarborough
Donald Fraser, Dugald Galbraith 2

Played for both clubs

Steve Charles	Blades 1979-85	Scarborough 1992-96
Colin Morris	Blades 1981-88	Scarborough 1988-90
Ray McHale	Blades 1982-85	Scarborough 1987-88
John Burridge	Blades 1984-87	Scarborough 1993-94
Tony Daws	Blades 1986-87	Scarborough 1996-97
Mark Todd	Blades 1987-91	Scarborough 1995-96
Chris Downes	Scarborough 1987-88	Blades 1988-89
John Moore	Blades 1988-89	Scarborough 1991-92
Richard Lucas	Blades 1990-92	Scarborough 1995-97
Jamie Hoyland	Blades 1990-95	Scarborough 1998-99
Glyn Hodges	Blades 1990-96	Scarborough 1998-99
John Reed	Scarborough 1990-92	Blades 1991-96
Rob Scott	Scarborough 1994-95	Blades 1994-96
Graham Anthony	Blades 1994-97	Scarborough 1995-96
Christian Short	Scarborough 1988-90	Blades 1995-98
Tommy Mooney	Scarborough 1990-93	Blades 2002-03

Jamie Hoyland.

v. Scunthorpe United

Season	League	Date	Result	Blades	Scunth'pe	Date	Result	Blades	Scunth'pe	Blades	Scunth'pe
			Home				**Away**			*Final Positions*	
1958-59	Division 2	11 October	Won	4	1	28 March	Won	3	1	3rd	18th
1959-60	Division 2	13 February	Won	2	1	26 September	Drew	1	1	4th	15th
1960-61	Division 2	8 October	Won	2	0	25 February	Drew	1	1	2ndP	9th
1981-82	Division 4	26 September	Won	1	0	20 February	Lost	1	2	1stP	23rd
1983-84	Division 3	1 November	Won	5	3	27 March	Drew	1	1	3rdP	21stR

Summary	P	W	D	L	F	A
Blades' home league record:	5	5	0	0	14	5
Blades' away league record:	5	1	3	1	7	6
TOTAL:	10	6	3	1	21	11

FACT FILE

- **United have a 100% record at home against Scunthorpe United.**

Blades' top scorers vs Scunthorpe
Derek Pace 5
Alf Ringstead 3
Keith Edwards, Tony Kenworthy, Tony Philliskirk, Ron Simpson 2

Blades hat-tricks vs Scunthorpe
11 Oct 1958 Alf Ringstead

Played for both clubs

George Underwood	Blades 1949-51	Scunthorpe 1953-54
George Luke	Blades 1953-55	Scunthorpe 1956-57
Ronnie Waldock	Blades 1954-57	Scunthorpe 1956-60
Cliff Mason	Blades 1955-62	Scunthorpe 1963-64
Andy Wilson	Blades 1959-61	Scunthorpe 1961-65
Micky Ash	Blades 1963-64	Scunthorpe 1965-67
Bill Punton	Blades 1966-68	Scunthorpe 1967-69
Graeme Crawford	Blades 1969-71	Scunthorpe 1977-80
Steve Cammack	Blades 1971-76	Scunthorpe 1979-87
Andy Keeley	Blades 1977-81	Scunthorpe 1981-83
Imre Varadi	Blades 1978-79	Scunthorpe 1995-96
Steve Charles	Blades 1979-85	Scunthorpe 1992-93
Julian Broddle	Blades 1981-82	Scunthorpe 1983-88
Brian Smith	Blades 1984-89	Scunthorpe 1986-87
Tony Daws	Blades 1986-87	Scunthorpe 1987-93
Peter Beagrie	Blades 1986-88	Scunthorpe 2001-04
John Francis	Blades 1988-90	Scunthorpe 1996-97
Carl Bradshaw	Blades 1989-94	Scunthorpe 2001-02
Ian Hamilton	Scunthorpe 1988-92	Blades 1997-2000
Andy Woodward	Blades 1999-2000	Scunthorpe 2000-01

v. Sheffield FC

FA Cup	Date	Result	Home Blades	Sheff FC					Division Blades	Sheff FC
1889-90 3rd Qual Rd	11 November	Won	3	0					Non L	Non L

Summary	P	W	D	L	F	A
Blades' cup record:	1	1	0	0	3	0
TOTAL:	**1**	**1**	**0**	**0**	**3**	**0**

FACT FILE

- **Sheffield FC are the oldest football club in the world, and are still in existence. Sadly, they have not got past the qualifying rounds of the FA Cup since 1887. They were established on 24 October 1857.**

v. Sheffield Heeley

FA Cup					Date		Result	Away Blades	Sheff H	Division Blades	Sheff H
1889-90 2nd Qual Rd					26 October		Won	1	0	Non L	Non L

Summary	P	W	D	L	F	A
Blades' cup record:	1	1	0	0	1	0
TOTAL:	**1**	**1**	**0**	**0**	**1**	**0**

v. Sheffield Wednesday

Season	League	Date	Result	Blades	Sheff W	Date	Result	Blades	Sheff W	Blades	Sheff W
			Home				**Away**			*Final Positions*	
1893-94	Division 1	16 October	Drew	1	1	13 November	Won	2	1	10th	12th
1894-95	Division 1	12 January	Won	1	0	27 October	Won	3	2	6th	8th
1895-96	Division 1	26 December	Drew	1	1	7 September	Lost	0	1	12th	7th
1896-97	Division 1	26 December	Won	2	0	2 March	Drew	1	1	2nd	6th
1897-98	Division 1	27 December	Drew	1	1	16 October	Won	1	0	1st	5th
1898-99	Division 1	26 December	Won	2	1	3 October	Drew	1	1	16th	18thR
1900-01	Division 1	15 December	Won	1	0	29 April	Lost	0	1	14th	8th
1901-02	Division 1	1 March	Won	3	0	2 November	Lost	0	1	10th	9th
1902-03	Division 1	1 September	Lost	2	3	11 October	Won	1	0	4th	1st
1903-04	Division 1	12 December	Drew	1	1	9 April	Lost	0	3	7th	1st
1904-05	Division 1	8 April	Won	4	2	10 December	Won	3	1	6th	9th
1905-06	Division 1	21 October	Lost	0	2	18 April	Lost	0	1	13th	3rd
1906-07	Division 1	4 April	Won	2	1	3 November	Drew	2	2	4th	13th
1907-08	Division 1	9 November	Lost	1	3	7 March	Lost	0	2	17th	5th
1908-09	Division 1	26 December	Won	2	1	25 December	Lost	0	1	12th	5th
1909-10	Division 1	6 November	Drew	3	3	19 March	Won	3	1	6th	11th
1910-11	Division 1	25 February	Lost	0	1	22 October	Lost	0	2	9th	6th
1911-12	Division 1	4 November	Drew	1	1	9 March	Drew	1	1	14th	5th
1912-13	Division 1	1 March	Lost	0	2	26 October	Lost	0	1	15th	3rd
1913-14	Division 1	25 October	Lost	0	1	28 February	Lost	1	2	10th	18th
1914-15	Division 1	5 September	Lost	0	1	2 January	Drew	1	1	6th	7th
1919-20	Division 1	4 October	Won	3	0	27 September	Lost	1	2	14th	22ndR
1926-27	Division 1	15 January	Won	2	0	28 August	Won	3	2	8th	16th
1927-28	Division 1	24 September	Drew	1	1	4 February	Drew	3	3	13th	14th
1928-29	Division 1	2 February	Drew	1	1	22 September	Lost	2	5	11th	1st
1929-30	Division 1	28 September	Drew	2	2	1 February	Drew	1	1	20th	1st
1930-31	Division 1	6 September	Drew	1	1	3 January	Won	3	1	15th	3rd
1931-32	Division 1	2 April	Drew	1	1	21 November	Lost	1	2	7th	3rd
1932-33	Division 1	4 February	Lost	2	3	24 September	Drew	3	3	10th	3rd
1933-34	Division 1	3 March	Won	5	1	21 October	Won	1	0	22ndR	11th
1937-38	Division 2	26 February	Won	2	1	16 October	Won	1	0	3rd	17th
1938-39	Division 2	29 October	Drew	0	0	4 March	Lost	0	1	2ndP	3rd
1949-50	Division 2	21 January	Won	2	0	17 September	Lost	1	2	3rd	2ndP
1951-52	Division 2	8 September	Won	7	3	5 January	Won	3	1	11th	1stP
1953-54	Division 1	12 September	Won	2	0	23 January	Lost	2	3	20th	19th
1954-55	Division 1	18 September	Won	1	0	5 February	Won	2	1	13th	22ndR
1958-59	Division 2	21 February	Won	1	0	4 October	Lost	0	2	3rd	1stP
1961-62	Division 1	16 September	Won	1	0	3 February	Won	2	1	5th	6th
1962-63	Division 1	6 October	Drew	2	2	15 May	Lost	1	3	10th	6th
1963-64	Division 1	14 September	Drew	1	1	18 January	Lost	0	3	12th	6th
1964-65	Division 1	2 January	Lost	2	3	5 September	Won	2	0	19th	8th
1965-66	Division 1	18 September	Won	1	0	12 March	Drew	2	2	9th	17th
1966-67	Division 1	4 February	Won	1	0	24 September	Drew	2	2	10th	11th
1967-68	Division 1	1 September	Lost	0	1	6 January	Drew	1	1	21stR	19th

Season	League	Date	Result	Blades	Sheff W	Date	Result	Blades	Sheff W	Blades	Sheff W
			Home					**Away**		*Final Positions*	
1970-71	Division 2	3 October	Won	3	2	12 April	Drew	0	0	2ndP	15th
1979-80	Division 3	5 April	Drew	1	1	26 December	Lost	0	4	12th	3rdP
1991-92	Division 1	17 November	Won	2	0	11 March	Won	3	1	9th	3rd
1992-93	Premiership	8 November	Drew	1	1	21 April	Drew	1	1	14th	7th
1993-94	Premiership	23 October	Drew	1	1	22 January	Lost	1	3	20thR	7th
2000-01	Division 1	16 December	Drew	1	1	1 April	Won	2	1	10th	17th
2001-02	Division 1	29 January	Drew	0	0	7 October	Drew	0	0	13th	20th
2002-03	Division 1	17 January	Won	3	1	1 September	Lost	0	2	3rd	22ndR

FA Cup

Season	Round	Date	Result	Blades	Sheff W	Date	Result	Blades	Sheff W	Division Blades	Sheff W
1899-00	Round 2	17 February	Drew	1	1	19 February	Won	2	0	Div 1	Div 2
1924-25	Round 2	31 January	Won	3	2					Div 1	Div 2
1927-28	Round 5	22 February	Won	4	1	18 February	Drew	1	1	Div 1	Div 1
1953-54	Round 3	13 January	Lost	1	3	9 January	Drew	1	1	Div 1	Div 1
1959-60	Q'ter Final	12 March	Lost	0	2					Div 2	Div 1
1992-93	Semi-Final	3 April	Wembley				Lost*	1	2	Prem	Prem

League Cup

Season	Round	Date	Result	Blades	Sheff W	Date	Result	Blades	Sheff W	Division Blades	Sheff W
1980-81	Round 1	12 August	Drew	1	1	9 August	Lost	0	2	Div 3	Div 2
2000-01	Round 3					1 November	Lost*	1	2	Div 1	Div 1

Summary	P	W	D	L	F	A
Blades' home league record:	52	23	19	10	81	54
Blades' away league record:	52	16	14	22	64	79
Blades' cup record:	12	3	4	5	16	18
TOTAL:	**116**	**42**	**37**	**37**	**161**	**151**

FACT FILE

- **Robert Hill was the Blades' first league goalscorer against their big city rivals.**
- **United currently lead the series of league matches 39-32. United have led the series since September 1951. Neither side has ever led the series by more than seven.**
- **The sides have won three ties each in the FA Cup, but Wednesday have won both League Cup ties.**
- **Wednesday have not won at Bramall Lane since 1967.**
- **United have achieved nine league doubles, most recently in 1991-92.**
- **Wednesday have achieved five league doubles, most recently in 1913-14.**
- **In 1933-34, United had an appalling season and finished bottom of the division. Their one away win of the season came at Hillsborough.**

Blades' top scorers vs Wednesday

Alan Birchenall, Jimmy Dunne, Derek Pace,
Fred Priest, Fred Tunstall 6
Harold Brook, Arthur Brown, Harry Johnson,
Alf Ringstead 5
Derek Hawksworth 4

Blades hat-tricks vs Wednesday

22 Feb 1928 Harry Johnson (cup)
 3 Mar 1934 Willie Boyd

Played for both clubs

Billy Mellor	Blades 1892-93	Wednesday 1893-94
Ollie Tummon	Wednesday 1905-10	Blades 1919-20
Charles Taylor	Wednesday 1919-20	Blades 1923-24
Bernard Oxley	Blades 1928-34	Wednesday 1933-35
Walter Rickett	Blades 1946-48	Wednesday 1949-53
Joe Cockroft	Wednesday 1946-49	Blades 1948-49
Bernard Shaw	Blades 1962-69	Wednesday 1973-76
David Ford	Wednesday 1965-70	Blades 1970-73
Alan Warboys	Wednesday 1968-71	Blades 1972-73
Simon Stainrod	Blades 1975-79	Wednesday 1984-86
Imre Varadi	Blades 1978-79	Wednesday 1983-85/88-90
Neil Ramsbottom	Wednesday 1975-76	Blades 1979-80
Jeff King	Wednesday 1979-82	Blades 1981-83
Terry Curran	Wednesday 1978-82	Blades 1982-83
Wilf Rostron	Wednesday 1988-89	Blades 1989-91
Carl Bradshaw	Wednesday 1986-89	Blades 1989-94
Brian Marwood	Wednesday 1984-88	Blades 1990-92
Franz Carr	Wednesday 1989-90	Blades 1992-94
Earl Barrett	Blades 1997-98	Wednesday 1997-99
Owen Morrison	Wednesday 1998-2003	Blades 2002-03
Dean Windass	Wednesday 2001-02	Blades 2002-03
Carl Robinson	Wednesday 2002-03	Blades 2003-04

Paul Peschisolido.

v. Shrewsbury Town

Season	League	Date	Result	Home Blades	Shrewsb'y	Date	Result	Away Blades	Shrewsb'y	Final Positions Blades	Shrewsb'y
1984-85	Division 2	27 April	Lost	0	1	24 November	Drew	3	3	18th	8th
1985-86	Division 2	31 August	Drew	1	1	18 January	Lost	1	3	7th	17th
1986-87	Division 2	23 August	Drew	1	1	24 January	Lost	0	1	9th	18th
1987-88	Division 2	13 February	Lost	0	1	17 November	Lost	0	2	21stR	18th

League Cup

Season	Round	Date	Result	Blades	Shrewsb'y	Date	Result	Blades	Shrewsb'y	Division Blades	Shrewsb'y
1983-84	Round 2	25 October	Drew	2	2	4 October	Lost	1	2	Div 3	Div 2
1999-00	Round 1	10 August	Won	3	0	24 August	Won	3	0	Div 1	Div 3

Summary

	P	W	D	L	F	A
Blades' home league record:	4	0	2	2	2	4
Blades' away league record:	4	0	1	3	4	9
Blades' cup record:	4	2	1	1	9	4
TOTAL:	**12**	**2**	**4**	**6**	**15**	**17**

FACT FILE

- **Shrewsbury have played the Blades eight times without defeat in the league. No other side comes close to matching this record against United.**
- **Shrewsbury were undefeated in their first 10 matches in the series in all competitions.**

Blades' top scorers vs Shrewsbury
Andy Smith 3
Marcelo, Colin Morris, Paul Stancliffe 2

Played for both clubs
Ted Hemsley	Shrewsbury 1960-69	Blades 1968-77
John Moore	Blades 1988-89	Shrewsbury 1990-91
Brian Gayle	Blades 1991-96	Shrewsbury 1997-99
Ross Davidson	Blades 1994-96	Shrewsbury 1999-2001
Jonathan Cullen	Blades 1997-99	Shrewsbury 1999-2000
Carl Robinson	Shrewsbury 1995-96	Blades 2003-04

v. Southampton

Season	League	Date	Result	Blades	So'ton	Date	Result	Blades	So'ton	Blades	So'ton
			Home				**Away**			*Final Positions*	
1934-35	Division 2	16 February	Won	6	1	6 October	Drew	1	1	11th	19th
1935-36	Division 2	21 September	Won	2	1	5 February	Won	1	0	3rd	17th
1936-37	Division 2	11 February	Drew	0	0	26 September	Lost	0	4	7th	19th
1937-38	Division 2	18 December	Won	5	0	30 April	Lost	1	2	3rd	15th
1938-39	Division 2	26 December	Won	5	1	27 December	Drew	2	2	2ndP	18th
1949-50	Division 2	11 February	Lost	0	1	10 April	Lost	0	1	3rd	4th
1950-51	Division 2	23 December	Lost	1	2	26 August	Lost	0	1	8th	12th
1951-52	Division 2	8 December	Drew	2	2	26 April	Won	1	0	11th	13th
1952-53	Division 2	8 November	Won	5	3	28 March	Drew	4	4	1stP	21stR
1960-61	Division 2	15 April	Won	2	1	12 November	Won	1	0	2ndP	8th
1966-67	Division 1	25 February	Won	2	0	8 October	Won	3	2	10th	19th
1967-68	Division 1	30 December	Won	4	1	26 December	Drew	3	3	21stR	16th
1971-72	Division 1	14 August	Won	3	1	16 October	Lost	2	3	10th	19th
1972-73	Division 1	2 September	Won	3	1	20 January	Drew	1	1	14th	13th
1973-74	Division 1	22 December	Won	4	2	29 September	Lost	0	3	13th	20thR
1976-77	Division 2	12 February	Drew	2	2	4 September	Drew	1	1	11th	9th
1977-78	Division 2	1 October	Won	3	2	25 February	Lost	1	2	12th	2ndP
1990-91	Division 1	2 February	Won	4	1	15 September	Lost	0	2	13th	14th
1991-92	Division 1	24 August	Lost	0	2	11 January	Won	4	2	9th	16th
1992-93	Premiership	3 October	Won	2	0	27 February	Lost	2	3	14th	18th
1993-94	Premiership	26 March	Drew	0	0	2 October	Drew	3	3	20thR	18th

FA Cup

						Result		Blades	So'ton	Division	
1901-02	Final	19 April		Crystal Palace		Drew		1	1	Div 1	Non L
		28 April		Crystal Palace (replay)		Won		2	1		
1924-25	Semi-Final	28 March		Stamford Bridge		Won		2	0	Div 1	Div 2
1962-63	Round 5			16 March		Lost		0	1	Div 1	Div 2
2000-01	Round 3			6 January		Lost		0	1	Div 1	Prem

Summary

	P	W	D	L	F	A
Blades' home league record:	21	14	4	3	55	24
Blades' away league record:	21	5	7	9	31	40
Blades' cup record:	5	2	1	2	5	4
TOTAL:	**47**	**21**	**12**	**14**	**91**	**68**

Blades' top scorers vs Southampton
Alan Woodward 10
Jock Dodds 9
Harold Barton 5
Billy Dearden, Jimmy Hagan 4
Harold Brook, Alf Ringstead 3

Blades hat-tricks vs Southampton
16 Feb 1935 Jock Dodds (4)
8 Nov 1952 Jimmy Hagan
22 Dec 1973 Alan Woodward

- The 1902 FA Cup Final was the last to feature a non-league side. It was United's second successive final against non-league opposition. In those days, however, the Southern League was very strong, although few of their members got elected to the Football League until a third division was added in 1920.
- From 1952 to 1973, United enjoyed seven successive home wins over the Saints.
- United were undefeated in eleven league games between 1951 and 1971, although the Saints pulled off a surprise FA Cup win in 1963.
- United have won one of their last 11 matches in Southampton.

Played for both clubs

Jimmy Dunne	Blades 1926-34	Southampton 1936-37
Wallie Boyd	Blades 1933-35	Southampton 1936-37
Charlie Wilkinson	Blades 1933-38	Southampton 1938-39
Steve Neville	Southampton 1977-78	Blades 1980-82
Terry Curran	Southampton 1978-79	Blades 1982-83
Glenn Cockerill	Blades 1983-86	Southampton 1985-94
John Burridge	Blades 1984-87	Southampton 1987-89
Chris Marsden	Blades 1987-88	Southampton 1998-2004
Phil Kite	Southampton 1984-86	Blades 1990-92
Scott Marshall	Blades 1994-95	Southampton 1998-99

v. Southend United

Season	League	Date	Result	Home Blades	Southend	Date	Result	Away Blades	Southend	Final Positions Blades	Southend
1979-80	Division 3	21 December	Won	2	0	4 April	Lost	1	2	12th	22ndR
1982-83	Division 3	13 November	Lost	0	1	26 March	Lost	1	3	11th	15th
1983-84	Division 3	26 November	Won	5	0	28 April	Won	1	0	3rdP	22ndR
1988-89	Division 3	17 December	Lost	1	2	31 March	Lost	1	2	2ndP	21stR
1994-95	Division 1	26 November	Won	2	0	18 February	Won	3	1	8th	13th
1995-96	Division 1	2 April	Won	3	0	14 October	Lost	1	2	9th	14th
1996-97	Division 1	18 January	Won	3	0	1 October	Lost	2	3	5th	24thR

FA Cup

										Division	
1919-20	Round 1	10 January	Won	3	0					Div 1	Non L
1934-35	Round 3					12 January	Won	4	0	Div 2	Div 3S
1951-52	Round 5					23 February	Won	2	1	Div 2	Div 3S

Summary

	P	W	D	L	F	A
Blades' home league record:	7	5	0	2	16	3
Blades' away league record:	7	2	0	5	10	13
Blades' cup record:	3	3	0	0	9	1
TOTAL:	**17**	**10**	**0**	**7**	**35**	**17**

FACT FILE

- There has never been a draw in 17 clashes between the Uniteds of Sheffield and Southend.
- United have kept six clean sheets in their eight home games in the series.
- United have failed to score only once in the 17 matches.

Terry Nicholl played for Sheffield and Southend United in the mid-1970s.

Blades' top scorers vs Southend
Andy Walker 4
Keith Edwards 3

Blades hat-tricks vs Southend
26 Nov 1983 Keith Edwards

Played for both clubs

Walter Brayshaw	Blades 1919-20	Southend 1926-27
Percy Beaumont	Blades 1919-21	Southend 1926-27
Jimmy Shankly	Blades 1926-28	Southend 1928-33
Fred Cheesemur	Blades 1930-34	Southend 1934-36
Bert Oswald	Blades 1930-34	Southend 1934-39
Don Bird	Blades 1935-37	Southend 1936-37
Dennis Thompson	Blades 1946-51	Southend 1951-54
Gordon Loukes	Blades 1950-51	Southend 1951-52
Pat Laverty	Blades 1956-60	Southend 1960-61
Bill Punton	Southend 1958-59	Blades 1966-68
Michael Harmston	Blades 1968-69	Southend 1970-71
Ian MacKenzie	Blades 1969-75	Southend 1974-75
Terry Nicholl	Blades 1973-75	Southend 1975-77
Chris Guthrie	Southend 1972-75	Blades 1975-77
Chico Hamilton	Southend 1968-69	Blades 1976-78
Ian Benjamin	Blades 1978-80	Southend 1989-93
Colin Morris	Southend 1976-80	Blades 1981-88
John Burridge	Southend 1977-78	Blades 1984-87
Richard Cadette	Southend 1985-87	Blades 1987-88
Tony Battersby	Southend 1994-95	Blades 1995-96
Brett Angell	Southend 1990-94	Blades 1995-96
Mark Beard	Blades 1995-98	Southend 1997-2003
Mark Patterson	Blades 1995-98	Southend 1996-97/98-99
Jonathan Hunt	Southend 1993-95	Blades 1998-2000
Tommy Mooney	Southend 1993-94	Blades 2002-03

v. Stockport County

Season	League	Date	Result	Home Blades	Stockport	Date	Result	Away Blades	Stockport	Final Positions Blades	Stockport
1937-38	Division 2	25 September	Won	2	0	5 February	Drew	1	1	3rd	22ndR
1981-82	Division 4	9 February	Won	4	0	21 September	Lost	0	1	1stP	18th
1997-98	Division 1	21 October	Won	5	1	3 May	Lost	0	1	6th	8th
1998-99	Division 1	20 October	Drew	1	1	10 April	Lost	0	1	8th	16th
1999-00	Division 1	18 March	Won	1	0	20 November	Drew	1	1	16th	17th
2000-01	Division 1	24 October	Won	1	0	2 December	Won	2	0	10th	19th
2001-02	Division 1	2 March	Won	3	0	18 September	Won	2	1	13th	24thR

FA Cup

Season	Round	Date	Result	Blades	Stockport	Date	Result	Blades	Stockport	Division	
1925-26	Round 3	9 January	Won	2	0					Div 1	Div 2
1980-81	Round 1	25 November	Won*	3	2	22 November	Drew	0	0	Div 3	Div 4

League Cup

Season	Round	Date	Result	Blades	Stockport	Date	Result	Blades	Stockport	Division	
1994-95	Round 2	27 September	Won	5	1	20 September	Won	1	0	Div 1	Div 2
1996-97	Round 2	24 September	Lost	2	5	17 September	Lost	1	2	Div 1	Div 2

Summary

	P	W	D	L	F	A
Blades' home league record:	7	6	1	0	17	2
Blades' away league record:	7	2	2	3	6	6
Blades' cup record:	7	4	1	2	14	10
TOTAL:	**21**	**12**	**4**	**5**	**37**	**18**

Action from United v Stockport in March 2002.

FACT FILE

- United have lost only once in their 11 home games – an embarrassing 5-2 reverse in the 1996-97 League Cup.
- Ten meetings in Stockport have produced only 16 goals.
- United have five wins and a draw from the last six meetings.

Blades' top scorers vs Stockport
Dane Whitehouse 4
Jan Aage Fjortoft 3

Blades hat-tricks vs Stockport
20 Sep 1994 Dane Whitehouse (cup)
21 Oct 1997 Jan Aage Fjortoft

Played for both clubs

Arthur Wharton	Blades 1894-95	Stockport 1901-02
Joe Davies	Blades 1894-96	Stockport 1901-02
Walter Davies	Stockport 1912-13	Blades 1913-15
Bert Pearson	Blades 1912-14	Stockport 1925-29
Bernard Oxley	Blades 1928-34	Stockport 1936-37
George Farrow	Stockport 1931-32	Blades 1947-48
John Nibloe	Blades 1958-61	Stockport 1964-65
Len Allchurch	Blades 1960-65	Stockport 1965-69
Barry Hartle	Blades 1960-66	Stockport 1967-70
Steve Cammack	Blades 1971-76	Stockport 1985-86
Steve Faulkner	Blades 1972-77	Stockport 1977-78
Keith Edwards	Blades 1975-78/81-86	Stockport 1989-90
John Ryan	Blades 1980-82	Stockport 1983-84
Paul Smith	Blades 1982-86	Stockport 1985-86
Jeff Eckhardt	Blades 1984-88	Stockport 1994-96
David Frain	Blades 1985-88	Stockport 1989-95
Chris Marsden	Blades 1987-88	Stockport 1995-98
Paul Williams	Blades 1987-89	Stockport 1990-91/92-93
Peter Duffield	Blades 1987-92	Stockport 1992-93
Chris Downes	Blades 1988-89	Stockport 1989-90
Phil Kite	Blades 1990-92	Stockport 1992-93
Alan Kelly	Blades 1992-99	Stockport 2000-01
Brett Angell	Stockport 1988-90/96-2000	Blades 1995-96
Carl Muggleton	Stockport 1989-90	Blades 1995-96
Gordon Cowans	Blades 1995-96	Stockport 1996-97
Lee Sandford	Blades 1996-2002	Stockport 2001-02
Laurent D'Jaffo	Stockport 1999-2000	Blades 1999-2002
Shane Nicholson	Stockport 1999-2001	Blades 2001-02
Owen Morrison	Blades 2002-03	Stockport 2003-04

v. Stoke City

Season	League	Date	Result	Home Blades	Stoke	Date	Result	Away Blades	Stoke	Final Positions Blades	Stoke
1893-94	Division 1	3 February	Drew	3	3	16 December	Lost	0	5	10th	11th
1894-95	Division 1	9 February	Won	3	0	22 September	Won	3	1	6th	14th
1895-96	Division 1	28 September	Won	1	0	2 November	Lost	0	4	12th	6th
1896-97	Division 1	27 March	Won	1	0	15 April	Lost	0	2	2th	13th
1897-98	Division 1	11 September	Drew	4	3	11 December	Lost	1	2	1st	16th
1898-99	Division 1	17 September	Drew	1	1	14 January	Lost	1	4	16th	12th
1899-00	Division 1	9 December	Won	1	0	14 April	Drew	1	1	2nd	9th
1900-01	Division 1	19 January	Lost	0	4	22 September	Won	1	0	14th	16th
1901-02	Division 1	28 September	Drew	1	1	26 December	Lost	2	3	10th	16th
1902-03	Division 1	24 January	Lost	1	3	27 September	Won	1	0	4th	6th
1903-04	Division 1	16 January	Drew	1	1	19 September	Won	4	3	7th	16th
1904-05	Division 1	26 December	Won	5	2	8 October	Lost	1	2	6th	12th
1905-06	Division 1	25 December	Drew	1	1	16 April	Lost	1	2	13th	10th
1906-07	Division 1	26 January	Won	2	0	22 September	Drew	1	1	4th	20thR
1922-23	Division 1	21 October	Won	2	0	28 October	Lost	0	4	10th	21stR
1933-34	Division 1	7 October	Lost	1	2	22 February	Lost	0	3	22ndR	12th
1946-47	Division 1	14 June	Won	2	1	5 October	Lost	0	3	6th	4th
1947-48	Division 1	14 February	Won	3	0	27 September	Drew	1	1	12th	15th
1948-49	Division 1	23 October	Drew	2	2	16 April	Won	1	0	22ndR	11th
1956-57	Division 2	2 March	Drew	1	1	20 October	Drew	3	3	7th	5th
1957-58	Division 2	22 March	Won	3	0	9 November	Won	3	2	6th	11th
1958-59	Division 2	22 November	Won	2	1	11 April	Won	2	1	3rd	5th
1959-60	Division 2	5 December	Lost	0	1	23 April	Won	2	1	4th	17th
1960-61	Division 2	21 January	Won	4	1	10 September	Lost	0	2	2ndP	18th
1963-64	Division 1	11 September	Won	4	1	18 September	Won	2	0	12th	17th
1964-65	Division 1	26 August	Lost	0	1	2 September	Won	1	0	19th	11th
1965-66	Division 1	16 October	Won	3	2	25 March	Lost	0	2	9th	10th
1966-67	Division 1	21 January	Won	2	1	17 September	Lost	0	3	10th	12th
1967-68	Division 1	29 August	Won	1	0	23 August	Drew	1	1	21stR	18th
1971-72	Division 1	9 October	Lost	2	3	11 March	Drew	2	2	10th	17th
1972-73	Division 1	4 November	Drew	0	0	23 August	Drew	2	2	14th	15th
1973-74	Division 1	16 February	Drew	0	0	13 October	Won	2	1	13th	5th
1974-75	Division 1	12 April	Won	2	0	5 October	Lost	2	3	6th	5th
1975-76	Division 1	18 October	Lost	0	2	22 November	Lost	1	2	22ndR	12th
1977-78	Division 2	14 March	Lost	1	2	10 September	Lost	0	4	12th	7th
1978-79	Division 2	10 March	Drew	0	0	28 October	Lost	1	2	20thR	3rdP
1985-86	Division 2	14 December	Lost	1	2	17 August	Won	3	1	7th	10th
1986-87	Division 2	15 November	Won	3	1	27 December	Lost	2	5	9th	8th
1987-88	Division 2	5 September	Drew	0	0	6 February	Lost	0	1	21stR	11th
1989-90	Division 2	21 October	Won	2	1	31 March	Won	1	0	2ndP	24thR
1994-95	Division 1	11 February	Drew	1	1	2 November	Drew	1	1	8th	11th
1995-96	Division 1	9 March	Drew	0	0	23 December	Drew	2	2	9th	4th
1996-97	Division 1	25 April	Won	1	0	19 October	Won	4	0	5th	12th
1997-98	Division 1	2 December	Won	3	2	26 December	Drew	2	2	6th	23rdR

Season	League	Date	Result	Blades	Stoke	Date	Result	Blades	Stoke	Blades	Stoke
				Home				**Away**		*Final Positions*	
2002-03	Division 1	23 October	Won	2	1	15 March	Drew	0	0	3rd	21st
2003-04	Division 1	17 April	Lost	0	1	1 November	Drew	2	2	8th	11th

FA Cup

Season	Round	Date	Result	Blades	Stoke	Date	Result	Blades	Stoke	Division	
1945-46	Round 4	28 January	Won	3	2	26 January	Lost	0	2	Div 1	Div 1
1946-47	Round 5					8 February	Won	1	0	Div 1	Div 1
1982-83	Round 3	8 January	Drew	0	0	12 January	Lost	2	3	Div 3	Div 1

Summary	P	W	D	L	F	A
Blades' home league record:	46	23	13	10	73	49
Blades' away league record:	46	14	12	20	60	86
Blades' cup record:	5	2	1	2	6	7
TOTAL:	**97**	**39**	**26**	**32**	**139**	**142**

FACT FILE

- **United were unbeaten in 12 matches against Stoke from 1989 to 2003.**
- **The two-legged nature of the 1946 FA Cup meant that United exited the competition with a win.**
- **In 1947, United played their latest-ever league game, on 14 June, and beat Stoke 2-1.**
- **From 1975 to 1978, Stoke won five in a row against United.**

Now with Tottenham Hotspur, Michael Brown is seen here in a game against Stoke City.

Blades' top scorers vs Stoke
Arthur Brown, Colin Collindridge 6
Colin Morris, Derek Pace, Fred Priest 5
Derek Hawksworth, Mick Jones, Gil Reece,
Alan Woodward 4

Blades hat-tricks vs Stoke
26 Dec 1904 Arthur Brown
28 Jan 1946 Colin Collindridge (cup)

Played for both clubs

Billy Hendry	Stoke 1888-90	Blades 1892-95
George Brown	Stoke 1904-05	Blades 1908-09
Albert Sturgess	Stoke 1902-08	Blades 1908-23
George Gallimore	Stoke 1903-08	Blades 1908-10
Jack Evans	Blades 1923-24	Stoke 1924-25
John Roxburgh	Stoke 1923-24	Blades 1925-27
Roy John	Stoke 1931-34	Blades 1934-36
Bobby Howitt	Blades 1955-58	Stoke 1958-63
John Nibloe	Blades 1958-61	Stoke 1961-63
Geoff Salmons	Blades 1967-74/77-78	Stoke 1974-78
John Tudor	Blades 1968-71	Stoke 1976-77
Simon Stainrod	Blades 1975-79	Stoke 1987-89
Viv Busby	Stoke 1977-80	Blades 1979-80
Paul Richardson	Stoke 1977-81	Blades 1981-83
Steve Foley	Blades 1985-87	Stoke 1991-94
Peter Beagrie	Blades 1986-88	Stoke 1988-90
Hans Segers	Stoke 1986-87	Blades 1987-88
Billy Whitehurst	Blades 1989-91	Stoke 1990-91
Tom Cowan	Blades 1991-94	Stoke 1993-94
Chris Kamara	Stoke 1988-90	Blades 1992-94
Adrian Heath	Stoke 1978-82/91-92	Blades 1995-96
Carl Muggleton	Stoke 1993-2001	Blades 1995-96
Christian Short	Blades 1995-98	Stoke 1998-2000
Lee Sandford	Stoke 1989-96	Blades 1996-2002
Carl Asaba	Blades 2000-03	Stoke 2003-04
Paul Peschisolido	Stoke 1994-96	Blades 2000-04
Tommy Mooney	Blades 2002-03	Stoke 2002-03

v. Sunderland

		Home					**Away**			*Final Positions*	
Season	*League*	*Date*	*Result*	Blades	Sun'land	*Date*	*Result*	Blades	Sun'land	Blades	Sun'land
1893-94	Division 1	7 October	Won	1	0	20 January	Lost	1	4	10th	2nd
1894-95	Division 1	9 March	Won	4	0	23 February	Lost	0	2	6th	1st
1895-96	Division 1	7 October	Lost	1	2	11 January	Drew	1	1	12th	5th
1896-97	Division 1	19 September	Won	3	0	27 February	Won	1	0	2nd	15th
1897-98	Division 1	2 April	Won	1	0	5 March	Lost	1	3	1st	2nd
1898-99	Division 1	17 December	Won	2	0	29 April	Lost	0	1	16th	7th
1899-00	Division 1	2 October	Drew	2	2	16 December	Drew	1	1	2nd	3rd
1900-01	Division 1	13 October	Won	2	0	16 February	Lost	0	3	14th	2nd
1901-02	Division 1	12 October	Lost	0	1	2 September	Lost	1	3	10th	1st
1902-03	Division 1	20 September	Won	1	0	17 January	Drew	0	0	4th	3rd
1903-04	Division 1	16 April	Lost	1	2	19 December	Lost	1	2	7th	6th
1904-05	Division 1	17 December	Won	1	0	24 April	Lost	1	2	6th	5th
1905-06	Division 1	23 September	Won	4	1	27 January	Lost	0	2	13th	14th
1906-07	Division 1	9 February	Won	3	2	6 October	Won	2	1	4th	10th
1907-08	Division 1	26 October	Won	5	3	22 February	Lost	1	4	17th	16th
1908-09	Division 1	29 January	Lost	0	2	12 September	Lost	1	3	12th	3rd
1909-10	Division 1	9 October	Won	3	0	16 March	Lost	0	1	6th	8th
1910-11	Division 1	3 September	Lost	1	2	31 December	Won	2	0	9th	3rd
1911-12	Division 1	21 October	Lost	1	2	28 February	Drew	0	0	14th	8th
1912-13	Division 1	24 March	Lost	1	3	21 March	Lost	0	1	15th	1st
1913-14	Division 1	7 February	Won	1	0	4 October	Won	2	1	10th	7th
1914-15	Division 1	5 April	Drew	1	1	2 September	Lost	2	3	6th	8th
1919-20	Division 1	28 February	Won	3	0	17 March	Lost	2	3	14th	5th
1920-21	Division 1	28 August	Drew	1	1	4 September	Lost	1	3	20th	12th
1921-22	Division 1	29 April	Won	4	1	4 March	Lost	0	1	11th	12th
1922-23	Division 1	3 March	Won	3	1	11 April	Won	5	2	10th	2nd
1923-24	Division 1	26 January	Drew	1	1	19 January	Drew	2	2	5th	3rd
1924-25	Division 1	26 December	Won	2	1	25 December	Won	1	0	14th	7th
1925-26	Division 1	23 January	Won	4	1	12 September	Lost	1	6	5th	3rd
1926-27	Division 1	16 April	Won	2	0	27 November	Lost	0	3	8th	3rd
1927-28	Division 1	16 April	Won	5	1	8 October	Won	1	0	13th	15th
1928-29	Division 1	4 May	Won	4	0	22 December	Drew	4	4	11th	4th
1929-30	Division 1	26 October	Won	4	2	1 March	Lost	2	3	20th	9th
1930-31	Division 1	3 September	Drew	3	3	2 May	Lost	1	2	15th	11th
1931-32	Division 1	26 September	Drew	1	1	6 February	Lost	0	1	7th	13th
1932-33	Division 1	25 March	Won	3	0	12 November	Drew	2	2	10th	12th
1933-34	Division 1	29 January	Won	2	0	16 September	Lost	0	5	22ndR	6th
1946-47	Division 1	23 November	Won	4	2	29 March	Lost	1	2	6th	9th
1947-48	Division 1	11 October	Won	3	2	28 February	Drew	1	1	12th	20th
1948-49	Division 1	6 September	Lost	2	5	15 September	Lost	0	2	22ndR	8th
1953-54	Division 1	19 April	Lost	1	3	16 April	Drew	2	2	20th	18th
1954-55	Division 1	14 March	Won	1	0	23 October	Drew	2	2	13th	4th
1955-56	Division 1	21 April	Lost	2	3	10 December	Lost	2	3	22ndR	9th
1958-59	Division 2	18 April	Won	3	1	29 November	Lost	1	4	3rd	15th

		Home					Away			Final Positions	
Season	League	Date	Result	Blades	Sun'land	Date	Result	Blades	Sun'land	Blades	Sun'land
1959-60	Division 2	7 September	Lost	1	2	16 September	Lost	1	5	4th	16th
1960-61	Division 2	10 December	Lost	0	1	26 December	Drew	1	1	2ndP	6th
1964-65	Division 1	21 November	Won	3	0	3 April	Lost	1	3	19th	15th
1965-66	Division 1	5 February	Drew	2	2	28 August	Lost	1	4	9th	19th
1966-67	Division 1	15 October	Won	2	0	5 November	Lost	1	4	10th	17th
1967-68	Division 1	16 March	Lost	1	2	25 October	Lost	1	2	21stR	15th
1970-71	Division 2	20 February	Won	1	0	21 November	Drew	0	0	2ndP	13th
1977-78	Division 2	3 September	Drew	1	1	21 January	Lost	1	5	12th	6th
1978-79	Division 2	7 October	Won	3	2	25 April	Lost	2	6	20thR	4th
1985-86	Division 2	31 March	Won	1	0	26 December	Lost	1	2	7th	18th
1986-87	Division 2	1 November	Won	2	1	11 April	Won	2	1	9th	20thR
1989-90	Division 2	3 April	Lost	1	3	30 September	Drew	1	1	2ndP	6thP
1990-91	Division 1	24 November	Lost	0	2	9 March	Won	1	0	13th	19thR
1994-95	Division 1	13 September	Drew	0	0	1 April	Lost	0	1	8th	20th
1995-96	Division 1	13 April	Drew	0	0	18 November	Lost	0	2	9th	1stP
1997-98	Division 1	10 August	Won	2	0	10 January	Lost	2	4	6th	3rd
1998-99	Division 1	28 November	Lost	0	4	24 April	Drew	0	0	8th	1stP
2003-04	Division 1	4 October	Lost	0	1	9 April	Lost	0	3	8th	3rd

Division 1 Play-offs

										Final positions	
1997-98	Semi-Final	10 May	Won	2	1	13 May	Lost	0	2	6th	3rd

FA Cup

										Division	
1892-93	Round 2	4 February	Lost	1	3					Div 2	Div 1
1900-01	Round 1					9 February	Won	2	1	Div 1	Div 1
1908-09	Round 1	16 January	Lost	2	3					Div 1	Div 1
1925-26	Round 4	30 January	Lost	1	2					Div 1	Div 1
1930-31	Round 5					14 February	Lost	1	2	Div 1	Div 1
1955-56	Round 5	18 February	Drew	0	0	22 February	Lost	0	1	Div 1	Div 1
2003-04	Q'ter Final					7 March	Lost	0	1	Div 1	Div 1

League Cup

1965-66	Round 2					22 September	Lost	1	2	Div 1	Div 1
1966-67	Round 2	20 September	Won*	1	0	14 September	Drew	1	1	Div 1	Div 1
2002-03	Round 4	3 December	Won	2	0					Div 1	Prem

League Cup action from December 2002 with Carl Asaba in the thick of things during the Blades 2-0 win.

Summary	P	W	D	L	F	A
Blades' home league record:	62	35	10	17	117	74
Blades' away league record:	62	9	14	39	65	136
Blades' cup record:	14	4	2	8	14	19
TOTAL:	**138**	**48**	**26**	**64**	**196**	**229**

FACT FILE

- **Sheffield United have lost more matches to Sunderland than to any other club.**
- **From 1914 to 1947, United were unbeaten in 19 league games at home, although they lost the only FA Cup meeting at Bramall Lane in this period (as holders, in 1926).**
- **United have won two of their last 36 matches in Sunderland.**

Blades' top scorers vs Sunderland

Harry Johnson 19
Jack Pickering 8
Arthur Brown, Jimmy Hagan, Fred Tunstall 6
Jimmy Dunne, Ernest Needham 5
Billy Gillespie, Fred Priest 4

Blades hat-tricks vs Sunderland

26 Oct 1907 Arthur Brown (4)
11 Apr 1923 Harry Johnson

Played for both clubs

Peter Boyle	Sunderland 1896-99	Blades 1898-1904
Alf Common	Sunderland 1900-02/04-05	Blades 1901-04
Archie Annan	Sunderland 1902-03	Blades 1903-05
James Raine	Blades 1904-05	Sunderland 1906-08
Arthur Brown	Blades 1902-08	Sunderland 1908-10
Joe McGhie	Sunderland 1906-08	Blades 1908-09
Jock Gibson	Sunderland 1920-22	Blades 1928-33
Clifford Whitelum	Sunderland 1938-48	Blades 1947-49
Bill Wood	Sunderland 1949-50	Blades 1952-53
Colin Grainger	Blades 1953-57	Sunderland 1956-60
Sam Kemp	Sunderland 1952-57	Blades 1956-58
Dennis Longhorn	Sunderland 1973-77	Blades 1976-78
John MacPhail	Blades 1978-83	Sunderland 1987-91
Terry Curran	Blades 1982-83	Sunderland 1986-87
Mick Henderson	Sunderland 1975-79	Blades 1982-85
Kevin Arnott	Sunderland 1976-82	Blades 1982-87
Joe Bolton	Sunderland 1971-81	Blades 1983-86
Peter Beagrie	Blades 1986-88	Sunderland 1991-92
John Moore	Sunderland 1984-88	Blades 1988-89
Wilf Rostron	Sunderland 1977-80	Blades 1989-91
Billy Whitehurst	Sunderland 1988-89	Blades 1989-91
Brett Angell	Sunderland 1994-96	Blades 1995-96
Don Hutchison	Blades 1995-98	Sunderland 2000-02
Martin Smith	Sunderland 1993-99	Blades 1999-2000
Jody Craddock	Sunderland 1997-2003	Blades 1999-2000
David Kelly	Sunderland 1995-97	Blades 2000-01
Carl Robinson	Sunderland 2003-04	Blades 2003-04

v. Swansea City

Season	League	Home Date	Result	Blades	Swansea	Away Date	Result	Blades	Swansea	Final Positions Blades	Swansea
1934-35	Division 2	19 January	Drew	1	1	8 September	Drew	0	0	11th	17th
1935-36	Division 2	26 December	Won	4	1	25 December	Won	3	1	3rd	13th
1936-37	Division 2	17 October	Won	1	0	25 February	Lost	1	2	7th	16th
1937-38	Division 2	28 March	Drew	1	1	13 November	Won	5	3	3rd	18th
1938-39	Division 2	11 March	Lost	1	2	5 November	Won	2	1	2ndP	19th
1949-50	Division 2	22 August	Drew	1	1	1 September	Lost	0	1	3rd	8th
1950-51	Division 2	28 August	Won	6	1	24 August	Won	2	1	8th	18th
1951-52	Division 2	29 September	Won	5	0	9 February	Lost	1	3	11th	19th
1952-53	Division 2	20 December	Won	7	1	23 August	Won	2	1	1stP	11th
1956-57	Division 2	1 January	Drew	2	2	13 September	Lost	1	4	7th	10th
1957-58	Division 2	21 September	Drew	2	2	1 February	Won	2	0	6th	19th
1958-59	Division 2	4 April	Won	2	0	15 November	Won	2	0	3rd	11th
1959-60	Division 2	21 November	Drew	3	3	9 April	Lost	1	2	4th	12th
1960-61	Division 2	17 September	Won	3	0	4 February	Lost	0	3	2ndP	7th
1988-89	Division 3	6 May	Won	5	1	3 December	Drew	2	2	2ndP	12th

FA Cup

										Division	
1932-33	Round 3					14 January	Won	3	2	Div 1	Div 2
1963-64	Round 4	25 January	Drew	1	1	28 January	Lost	0	4	Div 1	Div 2

Summary

	P	W	D	L	F	A
Blades' home league record:	15	8	6	1	44	16
Blades' away league record:	15	7	2	6	24	24
Blades' cup record:	3	1	1	1	4	7
TOTAL:	**33**	**16**	**9**	**8**	**72**	**47**

Terry Phelan served both clubs.

FACT FILE

- United have lost only one of their 16 home games, and have scored in all of them.
- Between 1950 and 1952, United scored 18 goals in just three home games.
- Every single season where United and Swansea have been in the same division has seen United finish the higher of the two.

Blades' top scorers vs Swansea
Jock Dodds 9
Alf Ringstead 6
Harold Brook 5
Tony Agana 4
Bill Hodgson, Derek Pace 3

Blades hat-tricks vs Swansea
25 Dec 1935 Jock Dodds
13 Nov 1937 Jock Dodds
28 Aug 1950 Harold Brook
6 May 1989 Tony Agana

Played for both clubs

Bill Sampy	Blades 1924-27	Swansea 1926-30
Jack Pears	Blades 1934-35	Swansea 1935-36
Roy John	Blades 1934-36	Swansea 1937-39
George Henson	Swansea 1936-37	Blades 1938-40
Len Allchurch	Swansea 1951-61/69-71	Blades 1960-65
Gil Reece	Blades 1965-73	Swansea 1976-77
Paul Richardson	Blades 1981-83	Swansea 1984-85
Ray McHale	Blades 1982-85	Swansea 1984-86
Charlie Hartfield	Blades 1991-97	Swansea 1997-98
Dean Saunders	Swansea 1983-85	Blades 1997-99
James Thomas	Blades 2000-01	Swansea 2002-04
Terry Phelan	Swansea 1986-87	Blades 2001-02

Jock (Ephraim) Dodds, top scorer against Swansea and a hat-trick hero in 1935.

Gil Reece.

v. Swindon Town

Season	League	Date	Result	Blades	Swindon	Date	Result	Blades	Swindon	Blades	Swindon
			Home						**Away**	*Final Positions*	
1969-70	Division 2	9 February	Lost	1	2	11 October	Lost	1	2	6th	5th
1970-71	Division 2	22 August	Won	2	1	19 December	Lost	0	3	2ndP	12th
1979-80	Division 3	18 August	Won	2	1	3 November	Lost	2	3	12th	10th
1980-81	Division 3	6 September	Won	3	0	14 February	Lost	2	5	21stR	17th
1987-88	Division 2	20 December	Won	1	0	22 August	Lost	0	2	21stR	12th
1989-90	Division 2	12 September	Won	2	0	10 December	Won	2	0	2ndP	4th
1993-94	Premiership	14 August	Won	3	1	4 December	Drew	0	0	20thR	22ndR
1994-95	Division 1	15 April	Drew	2	2	27 December	Won	3	1	8th	21stR
1996-97	Division 1	26 November	Won	2	0	1 February	Lost	1	2	5th	19th
1997-98	Division 1	13 December	Won	2	1	13 April	Drew	1	1	6th	18th
1998-99	Division 1	8 August	Won	2	1	9 January	Drew	2	2	8th	17th
1999-00	Division 1	7 May	Drew	2	2	23 October	Drew	2	2	16th	24thR

FA Cup

Season	League	Date	Result	Blades	Swindon	Date	Result	Blades	Swindon	Division	
1907-08	Round 1	16 January	Lost*	2	3	11 January	Drew	0	0	Div 1	Non L
1920-21	Round 1					8 January	Lost	0	1	Div 1	Div 3

Summary	P	W	D	L	F	A
Blades' home league record:	12	9	2	1	24	11
Blades' away league record:	12	2	4	6	16	23
Blades' cup record:	3	0	1	2	2	4
TOTAL:	**27**	**11**	**7**	**9**	**42**	**38**

FACT FILE

- United lost their first two home games against Swindon, but have not lost in the 11 home games since.
- United lost six games in a row at Swindon between 1921 and 1987.
- United are unbeaten in their last six games with Swindon.

Blades' top scorers vs Swindon
David Holdsworth 3
Tony Kenworthy, Paul Rogers, Andy Smith,
Graham Stuart, Alan Woodward 2

Played for both clubs

Billy Batty	Blades 1907-10	Swindon 1920-22
Fred Hawley	Blades 1912-15	Swindon 1920-23
Sam Furniss	Blades 1920-21	Swindon 1924-27
Tom Phillipson	Swindon 1921-24	Blades 1927-30
Bernie Harris	Blades 1924-27	Swindon 1933-34
Jack Fountain	Blades 1950-56	Swindon 1956-60
Brian Richardson	Blades 1955-65	Swindon 1965-66
David Munks	Blades 1965-69	Swindon 1973-75
Tom McAlister	Blades 1971-76	Swindon 1980-81
Chris Guthrie	Blades 1975-77	Swindon 1977-79
Peter Dornan	Blades 1976-77	Swindon 1978-79
Paul Richardson	Blades 1981-83	Swindon 1983-84
Ray McHale	Swindon 1976-80	Blades 1982-85
Glenn Cockerill	Swindon 1979-81	Blades 1983-86
Steve Foley	Blades 1985-87	Swindon 1987-92
Mark Dempsey	Swindon 1984-85	Blades 1986-88
Brian Marwood	Blades 1990-92	Swindon 1992-93
Chris Kamara	Swindon 1977-81/85-88	Blades 1992-94
Graham Anthony	Blades 1994-97	Swindon 1996-97
Jan Aage Fjortoft	Swindon 1993-95	Blades 1996-98
Carl Tiler	Swindon 1994-95	Blades 1996-98
Frank Talia	Swindon 1995-2000	Blades 2000-01
Darren Bullock	Swindon 1996-99	Blades 2000-01
Grant Smith	Blades 2001-03	Swindon 2003-04
Iffy Onoura	Swindon 1997-2000	Blades 2002-03
Tommy Mooney	Blades 2002-03	Swindon 2003-04
Wayne Allison	Swindon 1995-98	Blades 2002-04

Iffy Onoura played for Swindon and later joined the Blades.

v. Torquay United

			Home					**Away**		*Final Positions*	
Season	*League*	*Date*	*Result*	Blades	Torquay	*Date*	*Result*	Blades	Torquay	Blades	Torquay
1981-82	Division 4	3 April	Won	4	1	14 November	Drew	1	1	1stP	15th

Summary	P	W	D	L	F	A
Blades' home league record:	1	1	0	0	4	1
Blades' away league record:	1	0	1	0	1	1
TOTAL:	2	1	1	0	5	2

Blades' top scorers vs Torquay
Keith Edwards 2

Played for both clubs
Harold Gough	Blades 1913-24	Torquay 1928-30
Dave Mercer	Blades 1920-28	Torquay 1929-30
Wally Webster	Blades 1925-30	Torquay 1931-33
Don Bird	Torquay 1932-34	Blades 1935-37
Colin Rawson	Blades 1953-56	Torquay 1959-62
Tony Currie	Blades 1967-76	Torquay 1983-85
John Connaughton	Torquay 1971-72	Blades 1973-74
Bruce Rioch	Blades 1978-79	Torquay 1980-84
John Matthews	Blades 1978-82	Torquay 1989-90
Paul Hall	Torquay 1989-93	Blades 1999-2000
Keith Curle	Torquay 1983-84	Blades 2000-02
Dean Sturridge	Torquay 1994-95	Blades 2003-04

Keith Curle had a short spell with Torquay early in his career and a longer one at United in the twilight of his playing days.

v. Tottenham Hotspur

Season	League	Date	Result	Home Blades	Home Spurs	Date	Result	Away Blades	Away Spurs	Final Positions Blades	Final Positions Spurs
1909-10	Division 1	9 April	Drew	1	1	27 November	Lost	1	2	9th	15th
1910-11	Division 1	12 November	Won	3	0	18 March	Lost	1	2	14th	12th
1911-12	Division 1	2 December	Lost	1	2	6 April	Drew	1	1	20th	6th
1912-13	Division 1	16 November	Won	4	0	22 February	Lost	0	1	5th	15th
1913-14	Division 1	1 September	Lost	1	4	8 September	Lost	1	2	3rd	5th
1914-15	Division 1	17 October	Drew	1	1	17 April	Drew	1	1	7th	10th
1920-21	Division 1	11 December	Drew	1	1	4 December	Lost	1	4	2ndP	8th
1921-22	Division 1	10 December	Won	1	0	3 December	Lost	1	2	10th	6th
1922-23	Division 1	26 December	Won	2	0	25 December	Lost	1	2	13th	11th
1923-24	Division 1	8 March	Won	6	2	1 March	Won	2	1	6th	19th
1924-25	Division 1	4 April	Won	2	0	29 November	Lost	1	4	22ndR	9th
1925-26	Division 1	31 August	Lost	2	3	7 September	Lost	2	3	9th	15th
1926-27	Division 1	5 March	Drew	3	3	16 October	Lost	1	3	15th	17th
1927-28	Division 1	31 March	Won	3	1	19 November	Drew	2	2	10th	17th
1933-34	Division 1	26 August	Drew	0	0	30 December	Lost	1	4	6th	20thR
1935-36	Division 2	14 September	Drew	1	1	18 January	Drew	1	1	10th	12th
1936-37	Division 2	6 February	Won	3	2	3 October	Drew	2	2	5th	15th
1937-38	Division 2	18 April	Won	1	0	15 April	Won	2	1	8th	13th
1938-39	Division 2	6 May	Won	6	1	12 September	Drew	2	2	3rd	1stP
1949-50	Division 2	15 April	Won	2	1	12 November	Lost	0	7	20th	16th
1953-54	Division 1	28 November	Won	5	2	17 April	Lost	1	2	13th	16th
1954-55	Division 1	30 October	Won	4	1	19 March	Lost	0	5	5th	3rd
1955-56	Division 1	5 September	Won	2	0	28 April	Lost	1	3	21stR	7th
1961-62	Division 1	4 September	Drew	1	1	9 April	Drew	3	3	14th	8th
1962-63	Division 1	22 September	Won	3	1	4 May	Lost	2	4	6th	15th
1963-64	Division 1	5 October	Drew	3	3	15 February	Drew	0	0	11th	2nd
1964-65	Division 1	12 December	Drew	3	3	22 August	Lost	0	2	14th	12th
1965-66	Division 1	28 December	Lost	1	3	27 December	Lost	0	1	13th	21stR
1966-67	Division 1	6 September	Won	2	1	13 May	Lost	0	2	22ndR	3rd
1967-68	Division 1	26 February	Won	3	2	7 October	Drew	1	1	3rd	5th
1971-72	Division 1	11 September	Drew	2	2	25 March	Lost	0	2	22ndR	18th
1972-73	Division 1	2 May	Won	3	2	23 December	Lost	0	2	10th	2nd
1973-74	Division 1	12 January	Drew	2	2	15 September	Won	2	1	12th	4th
1974-75	Division 1	30 November	Lost	0	1	18 January	Won	3	1	19th	6th
1975-76	Division 1	6 December	Lost	1	2	27 March	Lost	0	5	9th	8th
1977-78	Division 2	2 January	Drew	2	2	20 August	Lost	2	4	10th	3rd
1990-91	Division 1	20 April	Drew	2	2	20 October	Lost	0	4	12th	3rdP
1991-92	Division 1	14 April	Won	2	0	23 November	Won	1	0	13th	10th
1992-93	Premiership	2 March	Won	6	0	2 September	Lost	0	2	14th	8th
1993-94	Premiership	11 September	Drew	2	2	5 March	Drew	2	2	20thR	15th

FA Cup

Season		Date		Result	Blades	Spurs	Division
1900-01	Final	20 April	Crystal Palace	Drew	2	2	Div 1 Non L
		27 April	Burnden Park, Bolton (replay)	Lost	1	3	

FA Cup cont.	Date	Result	Home Blades	Home Spurs	Date	Result	Away Blades	Away Spurs	Division Blades	Division Spurs
1935-36 Q'ter Final	29 February	Won	3	1					Div 2	Div 2
1957-58 Round 4					25 January	Won	3	0	Div 2	Div 1

League Cup

	Date	Result	Home Blades	Home Spurs	Date	Result	Away Blades	Away Spurs	Division Blades	Division Spurs
1970-71 Round 3					7 October	Lost	1	2	Div 2	Div 1
1990-91 Round 4	27 November	Lost	0	2					Div 1	Div 1

Summary	P	W	D	L	F	A
Blades' home league record:	40	20	14	6	93	55
Blades' away league record:	40	5	10	25	42	93
Blades' cup record:	6	2	1	3	10	10
TOTAL:	**86**	**27**	**25**	**34**	**145**	**158**

FACT FILE

- **The Blades were unbeaten in 16 home matches between 1927 and 1964.**
- **Spurs were unbeaten in 14 home league matches between 1938 and 1972.**
- **Twenty successive games were played without an away win in this period.**
- **In 1993, United beat Spurs 6-0 – United's biggest Premiership win.**
- **The Blades have failed to score only once in their last 25 home league games.**

Blades' top scorers vs Spurs
Billy Gillespie 9
Harry Johnson, Fred Tunstall 7
Jock Dodds, Bert Menlove, Alf Ringstead 5
Brian Deane, Colin Grainger, Jimmy Hagan 4

Blades hat-tricks vs Spurs
16 Nov 1912 Billy Gillespie
8 Mar 1924 Bert Menlove
6 May 1939 Jimmy Hagan
28 Nov 1953 Alf Ringstead

Played for both clubs

Joe Walton	Spurs 1908-09	Blades 1909-11
John Blair	Spurs 1926-28	Blades 1927-29
Jack Chisholm	Spurs 1947-48	Blades 1948-50
George Hutchinson	Blades 1954-58	Spurs 1957-59
Jim Iley	Blades 1954-58	Spurs 1957-59
Andy Keeley	Spurs 1976-77	Blades 1977-81
Martin Peters	Spurs 1969-75	Blades 1980-81
Hans Segers	Blades 1987-88	Spurs 1998-99
Simon Webster	Spurs 1982-84	Blades 1987-90
David Tuttle	Spurs 1990-93	Blades 1993-96
Roger Nilsen	Blades 1993-99	Spurs 1998-99
Michael Brown	Blades 1999-2004	Spurs 2003-04

v. Tranmere Rovers

Season	League	Date	Result	Home Blades	Home Tranmere	Date	Result	Away Blades	Away Tranmere	Final Positions Blades	Final Positions Tranmere
1938-39	Division 2	25 March	Won	2	0	19 November	Won	2	0	2ndP	22ndR
1981-82	Division 4	7 November	Won	2	0	27 March	Drew	2	2	1stP	11th
1994-95	Division 1	7 March	Won	2	0	3 September	Lost	1	2	8th	5th
1995-96	Division 1	19 August	Lost	0	2	13 January	Drew	1	1	9th	13th
1996-97	Division 1	12 October	Drew	0	0	19 April	Drew	1	1	5th	11th
1997-98	Division 1	1 November	Won	2	1	28 April	Drew	3	3	6th	14th
1998-99	Division 1	7 November	Drew	2	2	13 March	Won	3	2	8th	15th
1999-00	Division 1	5 February	Won	3	1	30 August	Won	3	1	16th	13th
2000-01	Division 1	26 August	Won	2	0	1 January	Lost	0	1	10th	24thR

Summary	P	W	D	L	F	A
Blades' home league record:	9	6	2	1	15	6
Blades' away league record:	9	3	4	2	16	13
TOTAL:	**18**	**9**	**6**	**3**	**31**	**19**

FACT FILE

- **United's defeat in January 2001 ended a run of 10 games unbeaten in the series.**

Blades' top scorers vs Tranmere
Paul Devlin 4
Marcus Bent 3

Played for both clubs

Vince Matthews	Tranmere 1925-27	Blades 1927-31
Martin Pike	Blades 1986-90	Tranmere 1989-90
Nick Henry	Blades 1996-99	Tranmere 1999-2002
Des Hamilton	Blades 1998-99	Tranmere 2000-01
Paul Hall	Blades 1999-2000	Tranmere 2003-04
David Kelly	Tranmere 1997-2000	Blades 2000-01
George Santos	Tranmere 1998-2000	Blades 2000-02
Shane Nicholson	Blades 2001-02	Tranmere 2002-04
Steve Yates	Tranmere 1999-2002	Blades 2002-03
Iffy Onoura	Blades 2002-03	Tranmere 2003-04
Wayne Allison	Tranmere 1999-2002	Blades 2002-04
Andy Parkinson	Tranmere 1997-2003	Blades 2003-04

v. Walsall

Season	League	Date	Result	Home Blades	Walsall	Date	Result	Away Blades	Walsall	Final Positions Blades	Walsall
1892-93	Division 2	7 January	Won	3	0	15 April	Drew	1	1	2ndP	12th
1980-81	Division 3	2 May	Lost	0	1	29 November	Drew	4	4	21stR	20th
1982-83	Division 3	19 February	Won	3	1	9 October	Drew	0	0	11th	10th
1983-84	Division 3	31 March	Won	2	0	6 September	Won	2	1	3rdP	6th
1999-00	Division 1	14 August	Drew	1	1	15 January	Lost	1	2	16th	22ndR
2001-02	Division 1	13 April	Lost	0	1	24 November	Won	2	1	13th	18th
2002-03	Division 1	17 August	Drew	1	1	26 December	Won	1	0	3rd	17th
2003-04	Division 1	9 December	Won	2	0	24 April	Won	1	0	8th	22ndR

FA Cup										Division	
2002-03	Round 5	15 February	Won	2	0					Div 1	Div 1

League Cup											
1966-67	Round 4	26 October	Won	2	1					Div 1	Div 3
1997-98	Round 3					14 October	Lost	1	2	Div 1	Div 2

Summary	P	W	D	L	F	A
Blades' home league record:	8	4	2	2	12	5
Blades' away league record:	8	4	3	1	12	9
Blades' cup record:	3	2	0	1	5	3
TOTAL:	19	10	5	4	29	17

FACT FILE

- United's first defeat to Walsall did not come for 87 years after their first meeting, though this is admittedly a somewhat misleading statistic!
- Sadly for United, this defeat was perhaps the blackest day in the club's proud history. United needed only a draw to avoid relegation and send Walsall down instead. Three minutes from time, a Don Givens penalty was saved, and this sealed United's fate. They were relegated to Division Four for the first time, although a year later they were back, and were a top-flight team once more less than a decade later.

Blades' top scorers vs Walsall
Michael Brown, Harry Hammond, Bob Hatton,
Mike Trusson, Alan Woodward 2

Played for both clubs

Jack Evans	Walsall 1921-22	Blades 1923-24
Wally Webster	Walsall 1921-25	Blades 1925-30
Tom Phillipson	Blades 1927-30	Walsall 1931-32
Roy John	Walsall 1928-32	Blades 1934-36
Gerry Summers	Blades 1957-64	Walsall 1965-67
Derek Pace	Blades 1957-65	Walsall 1966-67
Jeff King	Walsall 1977-79	Blades 1981-83
Gary West	Blades 1982-85	Walsall 1992-93
Chris Wilder	Blades 1986-92/97-99	Walsall 1989-90
Adrian Littlejohn	Walsall 1989-91	Blades 1991-95/2001-02
Brett Angell	Blades 1995-96	Walsall 2000-02
Paul Simpson	Blades 1996-97	Walsall 1998-99
Nick Henry	Blades 1996-99	Walsall 1998-99
David Holdsworth	Blades 1996-99	Walsall 2001-02
Marcelo	Blades 1997-2000	Walsall 2001-02
Paul Hall	Blades 1999-2000	Walsall 1999-2001
David Kelly	Walsall 1983-88	Blades 2000-01
Gus Uhlenbeek	Blades 2000-02	Walsall 2001-02
Carl Robinson	Walsall 2002-03	Blades 2003-04

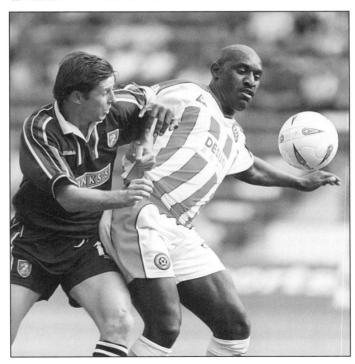

Wayne Allison, now with Chesterfield, in action against relegated Walsall in December 2004.

Season	League	Date	Result	Blades	Watford	Date	Result	Blades	Watford	Blades	Watford
		Home						**Away**		*Final Positions*	
1969-70	Division 2	27 December	Drew	1	1	30 August	Won	2	1	6th	19th
1970-71	Division 2	1 May	Won	3	0	26 September	Drew	0	0	2ndP	18th
1989-90	Division 2	10 April	Won	4	1	28 October	Won	3	1	2ndP	15th
1994-95	Division 1	13 August	Won	3	0	17 December	Drew	0	0	8th	7th
1995-96	Division 1	20 January	Drew	1	1	12 August	Lost	1	2	9th	23rdR
1998-99	Division 1	6 March	Won	3	0	29 September	Drew	1	1	8th	5thP
2000-01	Division 1	13 January	Lost	0	1	28 August	Lost	1	4	10th	9th
2001-02	Division 1	30 October	Lost	0	2	6 April	Won	3	0	13th	14th
2002-03	Division 1	28 September	Lost	1	2	4 May	Lost	0	2	3rd	13th
2003-04	Division 1	13 December	Drew	2	2	13 March	Won	2	0	8th	16th

FA Cup

Season	Round	Date	Result	Blades	Watford	Date	Result	Blades	Watford	Division	
1959-60	Round 5	20 February	Won	3	2					Div 2	Div 4
1967-68	Round 3					27 January	Won	1	0	Div 1	Div 3
1972-73	Round 3					13 January	Won	1	0	Div 1	Div 3
1984-85	Round 3					5 January	Lost	0	5	Div 2	Div 1
1989-90	Round 4	27 January	Drew	1	1	30 January	Won	2	1	Div 2	Div 2

League Cup

Season	Round	Date	Result	Blades	Watford	Date	Result	Blades	Watford	Division	
1997-98	Round 2	23 September	Won	4	0	16 September	Drew	1	1	Div 1	Div 2

Summary	P	W	D	L	F	A
Blades' home league record:	10	4	3	3	18	10
Blades' away league record:	10	4	3	3	13	11
Blades' cup record:	8	5	2	1	13	10
TOTAL:	**28**	**13**	**8**	**7**	**44**	**31**

Watford came away with all three points when they visited Bramall Lane in October 2001. However, United gained revenge later that season with a 3-0 victory at Vicarage Road in May 2002.

- Watford waited nine matches for a win at Bramall Lane, and then three came along in successive seasons.
- United were unbeaten in their first 11 meetings.

Blades' top scorers vs Watford

Brian Deane 4
Derek Pace 3
John Francis, Phil Jagielka, Jack Lester, Gil Reece,
Mitch Ward, Dane Whitehouse 2

Blades hat-tricks vs Watford

20 Feb 1960 Derek Pace (cup)

Played for both clubs

Bob Barnshaw	Blades 1913-14	Watford 1920-21
Ted Hufton	Blades 1912-15	Watford 1932-33
Harry Savage	Blades 1920-21	Watford 1921-22
Barry Hartle	Watford 1958-60	Blades 1960-66
Tony Currie	Watford 1967-68	Blades 1967-76
Stewart Scullion	Watford 1965-71/73-76	Blades 1971-74
Keith Eddy	Watford 1966-72	Blades 1972-76
Terry Garbett	Watford 1966-72	Blades 1973-76
Colin Franks	Watford 1969-73	Blades 1973-79
Keith Waugh	Blades 1981-85	Watford 1991-93
Mick Henderson	Watford 1979-82	Blades 1982-85
Andy Kennedy	Blades 1986-87	Watford 1990-92
Martin Kuhl	Blades 1986-88	Watford 1987-88
Peter Hetherston	Watford 1987-88	Blades 1987-88
Tony Agana	Watford 1987-88	Blades 1987-92
Mark Morris	Watford 1987-89	Blades 1989-91
Wilf Rostron	Watford 1979-89	Blades 1989-91
David Barnes	Blades 1989-94	Watford 1993-96
Glyn Hodges	Watford 1987-90	Blades 1990-96
Mel Rees	Watford 1987-88	Blades 1991-92
Willie Falconer	Watford 1988-91	Blades 1993-94
David Holdsworth	Watford 1988-96	Blades 1996-99
Paul Devlin	Blades 1997-2002	Watford 2003-04
Paul Furlong	Watford 1992-94	Blades 2001-02
Robert Page	Watford 1993-2001	Blades 2001-04
Tommy Mooney	Watford 1993-2001	Blades 2002-03
Wayne Allison	Watford 1989-90	Blades 2002-04

v. West Bromwich Albion

Season	League	Date	Result	Home Blades	WBA	Date	Result	Away Blades	WBA	Final Positions Blades	WBA
1893-94	Division 1	28 October	Lost	0	2	26 December	Lost	1	3	10th	8th
1894-95	Division 1	1 September	Won	2	1	3 November	Lost	0	1	6th	13th
1895-96	Division 1	4 January	Won	2	0	22 February	Lost	0	1	12th	16th
1896-97	Division 1	5 December	Lost	0	1	14 November	Won	1	0	2nd	12th
1897-98	Division 1	11 April	Won	2	0	26 March	Lost	0	2	1st	7th
1898-99	Division 1	25 March	Won	5	0	26 November	Lost	0	3	16th	14th
1899-00	Division 1	23 December	Drew	1	1	6 November	Won	2	1	2nd	13th
1900-01	Division 1	29 September	Drew	1	1	30 April	Won	2	0	14th	18thR
1902-03	Division 1	18 October	Lost	1	2	14 February	Drew	3	3	4th	7th
1903-04	Division 1	26 December	Won	4	0	23 April	Drew	2	2	7th	18thR
1911-12	Division 1	17 February	Drew	1	1	14 October	Won	1	0	14th	9th
1912-13	Division 1	15 February	Won	1	0	12 October	Lost	1	3	15th	10th
1913-14	Division 1	19 March	Drew	1	1	18 October	Lost	1	2	10th	5th
1914-15	Division 1	16 January	Won	2	0	12 September	Drew	1	1	6th	10th
1919-20	Division 1	14 February	Won	1	0	7 February	Won	2	0	14th	1st
1920-21	Division 1	30 April	Lost	0	2	23 April	Drew	1	1	20th	14th
1921-22	Division 1	18 March	Drew	0	0	25 March	Lost	0	3	111th	13th
1922-23	Division 1	7 April	Won	3	1	31 March	Lost	0	4	10th	7th
1923-24	Division 1	26 April	Won	2	0	3 May	Lost	1	3	5th	16th
1924-25	Division 1	22 November	Won	2	0	30 March	Lost	1	2	14th	2nd
1925-26	Division 1	20 February	Won	3	2	10 October	Lost	0	2	5th	13th
1926-27	Division 1	4 December	Won	2	1	23 April	Lost	0	1	8th	22ndR
1931-32	Division 1	12 September	Won	1	0	25 January	Won	1	0	7th	6th
1932-33	Division 1	8 April	Drew	1	1	26 November	Won	1	0	10th	4th
1933-34	Division 1	14 April	Lost	0	1	2 December	Lost	0	3	22ndR	7th
1938-39	Division 2	14 January	Drew	1	1	10 September	Won	4	3	2ndP	10th
1953-54	Division 1	17 October	Lost	1	2	6 March	Drew	2	2	20th	2nd
1954-55	Division 1	4 September	Lost	1	2	12 March	Drew	3	3	13th	17th
1955-56	Division 1	31 December	Drew	2	2	3 September	Lost	1	2	22ndR	13th
1961-62	Division 1	7 April	Drew	1	1	18 November	Lost	1	3	5th	9th
1962-63	Division 1	17 November	Won	1	0	6 April	Won	2	1	10th	14th
1963-64	Division 1	18 April	Won	2	1	7 December	Lost	0	2	12th	10th
1964-65	Division 1	3 October	Drew	1	1	13 February	Won	1	0	19th	14th
1965-66	Division 1	30 April	Lost	0	2	4 December	Drew	1	1	9th	6th
1966-67	Division 1	1 October	Won	4	3	11 February	Won	2	1	10th	13th
1967-68	Division 1	10 February	Drew	1	1	30 September	Lost	1	4	21stR	8th
1971-72	Division 1	28 August	Drew	0	0	8 January	Drew	2	2	10th	16th
1972-73	Division 1	6 January	Won	3	0	26 August	Won	2	0	14th	22ndR
1986-87	Division 2	3 January	Drew	1	1	25 August	Lost	0	1	9th	15th
1987-88	Division 2	23 April	Drew	0	0	4 November	Lost	0	4	21stR	20th
1989-90	Division 2	2 December	Won	3	1	19 August	Won	3	0	2ndP	20th
1994-95	Division 1	10 December	Won	2	0	18 October	Lost	0	1	8th	19th
1995-96	Division 1	20 February	Lost	1	2	2 September	Lost	1	3	9th	11th
1996-97	Division 1	5 April	Lost	1	2	13 November	Won	2	1	5th	16th

			Home				Away			Final Positions	
Season	League	Date	Result	Blades	WBA	Date	Result	Blades	WBA	Blades	WBA
1997-98	Division 1	25 April	Lost	2	4	25 October	Lost	0	2	6th	10th
1998-99	Division 1	6 February	Won	3	0	15 August	Lost	1	4	8th	12th
1999-00	Division 1	19 February	Won	6	0	27 November	Drew	2	2	16th	21st
2000-01	Division 1	26 December	Won	2	0	20 January	Lost	1	2	10th	6th
2001-02	Division 1	16 March	Lost	0	3	8 December	Won	1	0	13th	2ndP
2003-04	Division 1	21 February	Lost	1	2	14 October	Won	2	0	8th	2ndP

FA Cup

										Division	
1894-95	Round 2	16 February	Drew	1	1	20 February	Lost	1	2	Div 1	Div 1
1924-25	Q'ter Final	7 March	Won	2	0					Div 1	Div 1
1934-35	Round 4					26 January	Lost	1	7	Div 2	Div 1
1957-58	Round 5	15 February	Drew	1	1	19 February	Lost	1	4	Div 2	Div 1

League Cup

1973-74	Round 2					8 October	Lost	1	2	Div 1	Div 2

Summary

	P	W	D	L	F	A
Blades' home league record:	50	23	14	13	78	49
Blades' away league record:	50	16	9	25	57	85
Blades' cup record:	7	1	2	4	8	17
TOTAL:	**107**	**40**	**25**	**42**	**143**	**151**

Ashley Ward in action for the Blades against Albion in 2003/04.

FACT FILE

- **Unprecedented scenes took place at Bramall Lane on 16 March 2002. With just under 10 minutes remaining, United were reduced to six players after three red cards and two injuries. Under the laws of the game, the referee had no option but to abandon the match, and the scoreline (3-0 to West Brom) stood as a result. Incidentally, that one day saw a record 16 red cards in Premiership and Football League matches.**
- **Thirteen home wins in a row were recorded in the series between 1922 and 1931.**
- **United were undefeated at home for eight matches between 1966 and 1994.**

Blades' top scorers vs West Brom
Harry Johnson 6
Billy Gillespie, Alan Woodward 5
George Hedley, Fred Priest, Fred Tunstall 4

Blades hat-tricks vs West Brom
19 Feb 2000 Marcus Bent

Played for both clubs

Billy Hendry	West Brom 1888-89	Blades 1892-95
Dickie Bourne	Blades 1900-02	West Brom 1906-08
Teddy Sandford	West Brom 1930-39	Blades 1938-39
Gerry Summers	West Brom 1955-57	Blades 1957-64
Eddie Colquhoun	West Brom 1966-69	Blades 1968-78
Imre Varadi	Blades 1978-79	West Brom 1985-86
Ian Benjamin	Blades 1978-80	West Brom 1980-81
Ken McNaught	West Brom 1983-84	Blades 1985-86
Paul Williams	Blades 1987-89	West Brom 1990-92
Martin Dickinson	West Brom 1985-88	Blades 1988-89
Paul Beesley	Blades 1990-95	West Brom 1997-98
Mel Rees	West Brom 1990-91	Blades 1991-92
Franz Carr	Blades 1992-94	West Brom 1997-98
Brett Angell	Blades 1995-96	West Brom 1995-96
Ian Hamilton	West Brom 1992-98	Blades 1997-2000
Paul Hall	Blades 1999-2000	West Brom 1999-2000
Shaun Murphy	West Brom 1996-99	Blades 1999-2003
James Thomas	West Brom 1997-98	Blades 2000-01
George Santos	West Brom 1999-2000	Blades 2000-02
Paul Peschisolido	West Brom 1996-98	Blades 2000-04
Shane Nicholson	West Brom 1995-98	Blades 2001-02
Alan Fettis	West Brom 1995-96	Blades 2003-04

v. West Ham United

		Home				Away				Final Positions	
Season	League	Date	Result	Blades	WHU	Date	Result	Blades	WHU	Blades	WHU
1923-24	Division 1	1 January	Lost	0	2	21 April	Drew	2	2	5th	13th
1924-25	Division 1	22 September	Drew	1	1	14 April	Lost	2	6	14th	13th
1925-26	Division 1	27 February	Drew	1	1	17 October	Won	3	1	5th	18th
1926-27	Division 1	23 October	Lost	0	2	12 March	Lost	0	3	8th	6th
1927-28	Division 1	26 December	Won	6	2	27 December	Drew	1	1	13th	17th
1928-29	Division 1	29 December	Drew	3	3	25 August	Lost	0	4	11th	17th
1929-30	Division 1	1 January	Won	4	2	18 April	Lost	0	1	20th	7th
1930-31	Division 1	7 March	Lost	1	2	1 November	Lost	1	4	15th	18th
1931-32	Division 1	7 September	Won	6	0	21 September	Won	2	1	7th	22ndR
1934-35	Division 2	30 March	Lost	1	2	17 November	Lost	0	2	11th	3rd
1935-36	Division 2	2 May	Won	4	2	16 September	Lost	2	3	3rd	4th
1936-37	Division 2	14 September	Won	2	0	1 May	Lost	0	1	7th	6th
1937-38	Division 2	23 April	Won	3	1	11 December	Won	2	0	3rd	9th
1938-39	Division 2	26 November	Won	3	1	1 April	Drew	0	0	2ndP	11th
1949-50	Division 2	10 September	Drew	0	0	14 January	Drew	0	0	3rd	19th
1950-51	Division 2	17 February	Drew	1	1	30 September	Won	5	3	8th	13th
1951-52	Division 2	15 September	Won	6	1	19 January	Lost	1	5	11th	12th
1952-53	Division 2	18 April	Won	3	1	29 November	Drew	1	1	1stP	14th
1956-57	Division 2	29 September	Won	1	0	9 February	Lost	2	3	7th	8th
1957-58	Division 2	16 September	Won	2	1	9 September	Won	3	0	6th	1stP
1961-62	Division 1	23 September	Lost	1	4	10 February	Won	2	1	5th	8th
1962-63	Division 1	16 February	Lost	0	2	29 September	Drew	1	1	10th	12th
1963-64	Division 1	11 January	Won	2	1	7 September	Won	3	2	12th	14th
1964-65	Division 1	6 February	Won	2	1	26 September	Lost	1	3	19th	9th
1965-66	Division 1	4 September	Won	5	3	19 February	Lost	0	4	9th	12th
1966-67	Division 1	29 October	Won	3	1	4 April	Won	2	0	10th	16th
1967-68	Division 1	27 April	Lost	1	2	2 December	Lost	0	3	21stR	12th
1971-72	Division 1	29 February	Won	3	0	6 November	Won	2	1	10th	14th
1972-73	Division 1	10 March	Drew	0	0	14 October	Lost	1	3	14th	6th
1973-74	Division 1	23 March	Won	1	0	10 November	Drew	2	2	13th	18th
1974-75	Division 1	22 March	Won	3	2	7 September	Won	2	1	6th	13th
1975-76	Division 1	10 April	Won	3	2	20 September	Lost	0	2	22ndR	18th
1978-79	Division 2	2 April	Won	3	0	23 September	Lost	0	2	20thR	5th
1989-90	Division 2	14 October	Lost	0	2	21 March	Lost	0	5	2ndP	7th
1991-92	Division 1	20 August	Drew	1	1	21 December	Drew	1	1	9th	22ndR
1993-94	Premiership	28 March	Won	3	2	3 January	Drew	0	0	20thR	13th
2003-04	Division 1	17 January	Drew	3	3	16 August	Derw	0	0	8th	4th

FA Cup

										Division	
1951-52	Round 4	6 February	Won	4	2	2 February	Drew	0	0	Div 2	Div 2
1967-68	Round 5					9 March	Won	2	1	Div 1	Div 1
1986-87	Round 4					9 February	Lost	0	4	Div 2	Div 1

League Cup		Date	Result	Blades	WHU	Date	Result	Blades	WHU	Division Blades	WHU
			Home				**Away**			*Division*	
1971-72	Q'ter Final					17 November	Lost	0	5	Div 1	Div 1
1991-92	Round 3	29 October	Lost	0	2					Div 1	Div 1

Summary	P	W	D	L	F	A
Blades' home league record:	37	21	8	8	82	51
Blades' away league record:	37	10	10	17	44	72
Blades' cup record:	6	2	1	3	6	14
TOTAL:	80	33	19	28	132	137

FACT FILE

- **From 1936 to 1957, United were undefeated for 11 games at home.**
- **West Ham have won the last three cup matches with an 11-0 aggregate.**

Blades' top scorers vs West Ham

Bobby Barclay, Harry Johnson 8
Jimmy Dunne, Derek Hawksworth, Fred Tunstall, Alan Woodward 6
Billy Dearden, Jock Dodds, Mick Jones, Derek Pace, Jack Pickering 4

Blades hat-tricks vs West Ham

26 Dec 1927 Harry Johnson (5)
1 Jan 1930 Jimmy Dunne (4)
7 Sep 1931 Bobby Barclay
2 May 1936 Bobby Barclay
15 Sep 1951 Derek Hawksworth
9 Sep 1957 Tommy Hoyland
29 Feb 1972 Billy Dearden

Played for both clubs

Dicky Leafe	Blades 1911-13	West Ham 1919-22
Ted Hufton	Blades 1912-15	West Ham 1919-32
Jim Simmons	Blades 1908-20	West Ham 1920-22
Jack Ball	Blades 1919-21	West Ham 1929-30
Percy Thorpe	Blades 1930-33	West Ham 1933-34
Jim Holmes	Blades 1931-36	West Ham 1936-37
Joe Cockroft	West Ham 1932-39	Blades 1948-49
Tom McAlister	Blades 1971-76	West Ham 1981-89
Martin Peters	West Ham 1961-70	Blades 1980-81
Simon Webster	Blades 1987-90	West Ham 1994-95
Brian Deane	Blades 1988-93/97-98	West Ham 2003-04
Mervyn Day	West Ham 1973-79	Blades 1991-92
Franz Carr	West Ham 1990-91	Blades 1992-94
Don Hutchison	West Ham 1994-96/2001-04	Blades 1995-98
Wayne Quinn	Blades 1997-2001/02-03	West Ham 2003-04
David Kelly	West Ham 1988-90	Blades 2000-01
Jon Harley	Blades 2002-04	West Ham 2003-04

Alan Woodward, scorer of six goals against West Ham United during his career with the Blades.

v. Wigan Athletic

Season	League	Date	Result	Home Blades	Wigan	Date	Result	Away Blades	Wigan	Final Positions Blades	Wigan
1981-82	Division 4	23 March	Won	1	0	5 September	Won	1	0	1stP	3rdP
1982-83	Division 3	9 April	Won	2	0	4 December	Lost	2	3	11th	18th
1983-84	Division 3	24 September	Drew	2	2	11 February	Lost	0	3	3rdP	15th
1988-89	Division 3	22 October	Won	2	1	4 March	Won	2	1	2ndP	17th
2003-04	Division 1	28 December	Drew	1	1	21 October	Drew	1	1	8th	7th

League Cup

										Division	
1991-92	Round 2	8 October	Won	1	0	24 September	Drew	2	2	Div 1	Div 3

Summary

	P	W	D	L	F	A
Blades' home league record:	5	3	2	0	8	4
Blades' away league record:	5	2	1	2	6	8
Blades' cup record:	2	1	1	0	3	2
TOTAL:	**12**	**6**	**4**	**2**	**17**	**14**

FACT FILE

● **Wigan have never won at Bramall Lane.**

Blades' top scorers vs Wigan
Brian Deane 5
Keith Edwards, Tony Kenworthy, Jack Lester, Mike Trusson 2

Played for both clubs
Bobby Campbell	Blades 1977-78	Wigan 1986-88
Ian Benjamin	Blades 1978-80	Wigan 1994-96
Peter Beagrie	Blades 1986-88	Wigan 2000-01
Carl Bradshaw	Blades 1989-94	Wigan 1997-2001
Paul Beesley	Wigan 1984-90	Blades 1990-95
Paul Rogers	Blades 1991-96	Wigan 1996-99

Brian Deane, top scorer against
Wigan for the Blades.

v. Wimbledon

Season	League	Date	Result		Blades Wimb'don	Date	Result		Blades Wimb'don	Blades	Wimb'don
				Home				**Away**		*Final Positions*	
1979-80	Division 3	26 April	Won	2	1	8 December	Drew	1	1	12th	24thR
1983-84	Division 3	5 May	Lost	1	2	2 January	Lost	1	3	3rdP	2ndP
1984-85	Division 2	27 October	Won	3	0	2 March	Lost	0	5	18th	12th
1985-86	Division 2	24 August	Won	4	0	21 December	Lost	0	5	7th	3rdP
1990-91	Division 1	6 October	Lost	1	2	23 March	Drew	1	1	13th	7th
1991-92	Division 1	28 September	Drew	0	0	2 May	Lost	0	3	9th	13th
1992-93	Premiership	25 August	Drew	2	2	20 February	Lost	0	2	14th	12th
1993-94	Premiership	24 August	Won	2	1	18 December	Lost	0	2	20thR	6th
2000-01	Division 1	17 April	Lost	0	1	28 October	Drew	0	0	10th	8th
2001-02	Division 1	1 April	Lost	0	1	9 November	Drew	1	1	13th	9th
2002-03	Division 1	26 October	Drew	1	1	7 April	Lost	0	1	3rd	10th
2003-04	Division 1	12 April	Won	2	1	30 September	Won	2	1	8th	24thR

Summary	P	W	D	L	F	A
Blades' home league record:	12	5	3	4	18	12
Blades' away league record:	12	1	4	7	6	25
TOTAL:	**24**	**6**	**7**	**11**	**24**	**37**

Neil Shipperley and Michael Tonge battle for possession in the 1-1 draw at Bramall Lane in October 2002.

FACT FILE

- United won an away match in the series for the first time in 2003, at their 12th attempt.
- United had not won in their last 12 matches with Wimbledon prior to the 2003-04 season.

Blades' top scorers vs Wimbledon
Colin Morris 3
Keith Edwards, Andy Gray 2

Played for both clubs

Ray Lewington	Wimbledon 1979-80	Blades 1985-86
Wally Downes	Wimbledon 1978-87	Blades 1987-88
Hans Segers	Blades 1987-88	Wimbledon 1988-96
Simon Tracey	Wimbledon 1988-89/95-96	Blades 1988-2002
Francis Joseph	Wimbledon 1980-82/86-87	Blades 1988-89
Vaughan Ryan	Wimbledon 1986-92	Blades 1988-89
John Gannon	Wimbledon 1985-88	Blades 1988-96
Mark Morris	Wimbledon 1981-87	Blades 1989-91
Andy Sayer	Wimbledon 1983-88	Blades 1990-91
Vinnie Jones	Wimbledon 1986-89/92-98	Blades 1990-92
Glyn Hodges	Wimbledon 1980-87	Blades 1990-96
Alan Cork	Wimbledon 1978-92	Blades 1991-94
Kevin Gage	Wimbledon 1980-87	Blades 1991-96
Brian Gayle	Wimbledon 1984-88	Blades 1991-96
Alan McLeary	Blades 1992-93	Wimbledon 1992-93
Scott Fitzgerald	Wimbledon 1989-96	Blades 1995-96
Jonathan Hunt	Blades 1998-2000	Wimbledon 2000-01
Keith Curle	Wimbledon 1988-91	Blades 2000-02
Terry Phelan	Wimbledon 1987-92	Blades 2001-02
Jon Harley	Wimbledon 2000-01	Blades 2002-04

Season	League	Date	Result	Blades	Wolves	Date	Result	Blades	Wolves	Blades	Wolves
				Home				**Away**		*Final Positions*	
1893-94	Division 1	13 January	Won	3	2	30 September	Won	4	3	10th	9th
1894-95	Division 1	19 January	Won	1	0	3 September	Won	3	0	6th	11th
1895-96	Division 1	8 February	Won	2	1	19 October	Lost	1	4	12th	14th
1896-97	Division 1	23 January	Lost	1	3	6 March	Drew	1	1	2nd	10th
1897-98	Division 1	22 January	Won	2	1	2 October	Drew	1	1	1st	3rd
1898-99	Division 1	12 September	Won	1	0	24 December	Lost	1	4	16th	8th
1899-00	Division 1	14 October	Won	5	2	17 April	Won	2	1	2nd	4th
1900-01	Division 1	25 March	Drew	1	1	17 November	Lost	0	3	14th	13th
1901-02	Division 1	29 March	Drew	0	0	30 November	Drew	1	1	10th	14th
1902-03	Division 1	21 March	Won	3	0	22 November	Won	3	1	4th	11th
1903-04	Division 1	17 October	Won	7	2	13 February	Lost	0	1	7th	8th
1904-05	Division 1	5 November	Won	4	2	5 September	Lost	2	4	6th	14th
1905-06	Division 1	19 March	Won	4	1	23 December	Drew	1	1	13th	20thR
1932-33	Division 1	11 February	Drew	0	0	1 October	Lost	1	5	10th	20th
1933-34	Division 1	24 February	Won	3	1	14 October	Lost	2	3	22ndR	15th
1946-47	Division 1	22 March	Won	2	0	16 November	Lost	1	3	6th	3rd
1947-48	Division 1	25 October	Drew	2	2	13 March	Drew	1	1	12th	5th
1948-49	Division 1	18 April	Drew	1	1	19 April	Lost	0	6	22ndR	6th
1953-54	Division 1	3 October	Drew	3	3	20 February	Lost	1	6	20th	1st
1954-55	Division 1	23 April	Lost	1	2	20 November	Lost	1	4	13th	2nd
1955-56	Division 1	2 May	Drew	3	3	15 October	Lost	2	3	22ndR	3rd
1961-62	Division 1	19 August	Won	2	1	16 December	Won	1	0	5th	18th
1962-63	Division 1	8 September	Lost	1	2	19 January	Drew	0	0	10th	5th
1963-64	Division 1	31 March	Won	4	3	30 March	Drew	1	1	12th	16th
1964-65	Division 1	10 April	Lost	0	2	28 November	Lost	0	1	19th	21stR
1967-68	Division 1	28 October	Drew	1	1	23 March	Won	3	1	21stR	17th
1971-72	Division 1	11 December	Drew	2	2	28 April	Won	2	1	10th	9th
1972-73	Division 1	25 November	Lost	1	2	31 March	Drew	1	1	14th	5th
1973-74	Division 1	5 February	Won	1	0	28 August	Lost	0	2	13th	12th
1974-75	Division 1	8 March	Won	1	0	24 September	Drew	1	1	6th	12th
1975-76	Division 1	13 March	Lost	1	4	11 October	Lost	1	5	22ndR	20thR
1976-77	Division 2	24 August	Drew	2	2	9 February	Lost	1	2	11th	1stP
1984-85	Division 2	26 January	Drew	2	2	25 August	Drew	2	2	18th	22ndR
1988-89	Division 3	8 October	Won	2	0	9 May	Drew	2	2	2ndP	1stP
1989-90	Division 2	17 March	Won	3	0	7 October	Won	2	1	2ndP	10th
1994-95	Division 1	22 April	Drew	3	3	2 January	Drew	2	2	8th	4th
1995-96	Division 1	6 April	Won	2	1	28 October	Lost	0	1	9th	20th
1996-97	Division 1	24 January	Lost	2	3	21 September	Won	2	1	5th	3rd
1997-98	Division 1	17 January	Won	1	0	16 August	Drew	0	0	6th	9th
1998-99	Division 1	5 April	Drew	1	1	10 November	Lost	1	2	8th	7th
1999-00	Division 1	25 September	Won	3	0	26 October	Lost	0	1	16th	7th
2000-01	Division 1	20 February	Won	1	0	12 September	Drew	0	0	10th	12th
2001-02	Division 1	27 August	Drew	2	2	29 December	Lost	0	1	13th	3rd
2002-03	Division 1	26 April	Drew	3	3	5 October	Won	3	1	3rd	5thP

Division 1 Play-offs	Date	Result	Home Blades	Wolves	Date	Result	Away Blades	Wolves	Final Positions Blades	Wolves
2002-03 Final	26 May	Millennium Stadium				Lost	0	3	3rd	5thP

FA Cup

			Home				Away		Division	
		Date	Result	Blades	Wolves	Date	Result	Blades	Wolves	Blades	Wolves
1891-92	Round 2					30 January	Lost	1	3	Non L	Div 1
1900-01	Q'ter Final					23 March	Won	4	0	Div 1	Div 1
1927-28	Round 4	28 January	Won	3	1					Div 1	Div 2
1936-37	Round 4	4 February	Lost	1	2	30 January	Drew	2	2	Div 2	Div 1
1946-47	Round 4	29 January	Won	2	0	25 January	Drew	0	0	Div 1	Div 1
1948-49	Round 4	29 January	Lost	0	3					Div 1	Div 1
1949-50	Round 4	31 January	Lost	3	4	28 January	Drew	0	0	Div 2	Div 1
1965-66	Round 4					12 February	Lost	0	3	Div 1	Div 2

Summary	P	W	D	L	F	A
Blades' home league record:	44	22	15	7	90	61
Blades' away league record:	44	10	14	20	54	85
Blades' cup record:	12	3	3	6	16	21
TOTAL:	**100**	**35**	**32**	**33**	**160**	**167**

Paul Peschisolido lets fly against the Wolves.

FACT FILE

- The Blades enjoyed an exciting season in 2002-03. They reached the semi-finals of both cups and finished third in Division One. Sadly, it all ended in disappointment with a 3-0 defeat to Wolves in Cardiff.
- The Blades were unbeaten in 15 home league games from 1898 to 1953.

Blades' top scorers vs Wolves

Fred Priest 9

Derek Pace 6

Billy Beer, Harold Brook, Arthur Brown,
Jimmy Donnelly, Alf Ringstead, Peter Withe,
Alan Woodward 4

Blades hat-tricks vs Wolves

14 Oct 1899 Billy Beer

1 Feb 1950 Harold Brook (cup)

Played for both clubs

Charlie Henderson	Wolves 1895-96	Blades 1896-97
George Hedley	Blades 1897-1903	Wolves 1906-13
Archie Needham	Blades 1902-04	Wolves 1910-11
Stan Fazackerley	Blades 1912-21	Wolves 1922-25
Tom Phillipson	Wolves 1923-28	Blades 1927-30
Martin Johnson	Blades 1927-28	Wolves 1928-29
George Henson	Wolves 1935-36	Blades 1938-40
George Farrow	Wolves 1932-33	Blades 1947-48
Bernard Shaw	Blades 1962-69	Wolves 1969-73
Pat Buckley	Wolves 1964-68	Blades 1967-71
Bob Hatton	Wolves 1966-67	Blades 1980-83
John McAlle	Wolves 1967-81	Blades 1981-82
Tony Towner	Blades 1982-83	Wolves 1983-84
Paul Stancliffe	Blades 1983-91	Wolves 1990-91
Mel Eves	Wolves 1977-84	Blades 1984-86
John Burridge	Wolves 1982-84	Blades 1984-87
Peter Withe	Wolves 1973-75	Blades 1985-88
Chris Marsden	Blades 1987-88	Wolves 1993-94
Hans Segers	Blades 1987-88	Wolves 1997-98
Roger Hansbury	Blades 1987-88	Wolves 1988-89
Mark Todd	Blades 1987-91	Wolves 1990-91
David Barnes	Wolves 1984-88	Blades 1989-94
Nathan Blake	Blades 1993-96	Wolves 2001-04
Gordon Cowans	Wolves 1994-96	Blades 1995-96
Paul Simpson	Blades 1996-97	Wolves 1997-2000
Jody Craddock	Blades 1999-2000	Wolves 2003-04
Manuel Thetis	Blades 2000-01	Wolves 2000-01
David Kelly	Wolves 1993-96	Blades 2000-01
Keith Curle	Wolves 1996-2000	Blades 2000-02
Mark Rankine	Wolves 1991-96	Blades 2002-04
Carl Robinson	Wolves 1996-2002	Blades 2003-04
Dean Sturridge	Wolves 2001-04	Blades 2003-04

v. Worcester City

FA Cup				Date	Result	Away Blades	Worcester	Division Blades	Worcester
1958-59 Round 4				24 January	Won	2	0	Div 2	Non L

Summary	P	W	D	L	F	A
Blades' cup record:	1	1	0	0	2	0
TOTAL:	**1**	**1**	**0**	**0**	**2**	**0**

FACT FILE

- Nine days earlier, Worcester had caused a big shock by eliminating Liverpool. Goals from Lewis and Simpson ensured lightning did not strike twice.

v. Workington

League Cup				Date		Result	Away Blades	Work'ton	Division Blades	Work'ton
1972-73 Round 2				6 September		Won	**1**	**0**	Div 1	Div 4

Summary	P	W	D	L	F	A
Blades' cup record:	1	1	0	0	1	0
TOTAL:	**1**	**1**	**0**	**0**	**1**	**0**

FACT FILE

- **Billy Dearden scored the goal.**

Played for both clubs

John Flynn	Workington 1966-69	Blades 1969-78
David Irving	Workington 1970-73	Blades 1975-76
John Burridge	Workington 1968-71	Blades 1984-87

John Flynn joined the Blades from his home-town club, Workington, then a Football League outfit, in July 1969.

v. Wrexham

			Home						**Away**		*Final Positions*	
Season	*League*	*Date*	*Result*	Blades	Wrexham	*Date*	*Result*	Blades	Wrexham	Blades	Wrexham
1978-79	Division 2	17 April	Drew	1	1	28 February	Lost	0	4	20thR	15th
1982-83	Division 3	16 October	Won	2	0	26 February	Lost	1	4	11th	22ndR

FA Cup *Division*

1983-84	Round 1					19 November	Won	5	1	Div 3	Div 4

League Cup

1997-98	Round 1	26 August	Won	3	1	12 August	Drew	1	1	Div 1	Div 2

Summary	*P*	*W*	*D*	*L*	*F*	*A*
Blades' home league record:	2	1	1	0	3	1
Blades' away league record:	2	0	0	2	1	8
Blades' cup record:	3	2	1	0	9	3
TOTAL:	**7**	**3**	**2**	**2**	**13**	**12**

FACT FILE

- **Both sides have failed to score only once each in the seven games.**

Blades' top scorers vs Wrexham
Keith Edwards 5

Blades hat-tricks vs Wrexham
19 Nov 1983 Keith Edwards (4) (cup)

Played for both clubs

Colin Grainger	Wrexham 1950-53	Blades 1953-57
David Powell	Wrexham 1962-69	Blades 1968-71
Steve Charles	Blades 1979-85	Wrexham 1984-87
Mike Lake	Blades 1989-93	Wrexham 1992-95
Ian Rush	Blades 1997-98	Wrexham 1998-99
Ashley Ward	Wrexham 1990-91	Blades 2003-04

v. Wycombe Wanderers

League Cup		Date	Result	**Home** Blades Wycombe							Division Blades Wycombe
2002-03	Round 2	1 October	Won	**4**	**1**						Div 1 Div 2

Summary	P	W	D	L	F	A
Blades' cup record:	1	1	0	0	4	1
TOTAL:	**1**	**1**	**0**	**0**	**4**	**1**

Blades' top scorers vs Wycombe
Michael Brown 2

Played for both clubs

David Tuttle	Blades 1993-96	Wycombe 2001-02
Mark Foran	Blades 1994-96	Wycombe 1995-96
Scott Marshall	Blades 1994-95	Wycombe 2003-04
Gary Ablett	Blades 1995-96	Wycombe 1999-2000
Frank Talia	Blades 2000-01	Wycombe 2002-04
Iffy Onoura	Blades 2002-03	Wycombe 2003-04

Peter Ndlovu in action againt Wycombe, when they met in the League Cup, October 2002.

v. York City

					Home					Away			Final Positions	
Season	League	Date	Result	Blades	York	Date	Result	Blades	York	Blades	York
1981-82	Division 4	13 February	Won	4	0	3 October	Won	4	3	1stP	17th

FA Cup

											Division	
1930-31	Round 3	10 January	Drew	1	1	14 January	Won	2	0	Div 1	Div 3N

League Cup

1971-72	Round 3	5 October	Won	3	2					Div 1	Div 3
1981-82	Round 1	1 September	Won	1	0	15 September	Drew	1	1	Div 4	Div 4
2002-03	Round 1	10 September	Won	1	0					Div 1	Div 3

Summary	P	W	D	L	F	A
Blades' home league record:	1	1	0	0	4	0
Blades' away league record:	1	1	0	0	4	3
Blades' cup record:	6	4	2	0	9	4
TOTAL:	8	6	2	0	17	7

FACT FILE

- **Only Northampton have played United more times without at least one victory.**

These two pictures are from the hard-fought 1-0 victory when York were the visitors in September 2002.

Blades' top scorers vs York
Bob Hatton, Mike Trusson 3

Played for both clubs

Norman Wharton	Blades 1928-30	York 1936-39
Reg Baines	York 1931-33/37-38	Blades 1933-34
Peter Spooner	York 1931-33/35-39	Blades 1933-35
Jim Coop	Blades 1947-49	York 1949-51
Arthur Bottom	Blades 1948-54	York 1954-58
Jack Fountain	Blades 1950-56	York 1960-64
Howard Johnson	Blades 1950-57	York 1957-58
Sam McNab	Blades 1952-54	York 1954-55
Peter Wragg	Blades 1952-56	York 1956-63
Des Thompson	York 1950-53	Blades 1955-64
Bill Hodgson	Blades 1957-64	York 1967-70
Wally Gould	Blades 1958-59	York 1960-64
Bob Widdowson	Blades 1961-68	York 1968-70
Colin Addison	York 1957-61	Blades 1967-71
Graeme Crawford	Blades 1969-71	York 1971-77/79-80
Ian Holmes	Blades 1971-73	York 1973-78
Alan Ogden	Blades 1971-74	York 1974-75
Steve Faulkner	Blades 1972-77	York 1978-81
Cliff Calvert	York 1972-76	Blades 1975-79
John McPhail	Blades 1978-83	York 1982-86
Viv Busby	Blades 1979-80	York 1982-84
Paul Stancliffe	Blades 1983-91	York 1991-95
Andy Leaning	York 1985-87	Blades 1987-88
Peter Duffield	Blades 1987-92	York 2000-03
Mitch Ward	Blades 1990-98	York 2003-04
Tom Cowan	Blades 1991-94	York 2002-03
Jon Newby	Blades 2000-01	York 2003-04
Alan Fettis	York 1999-2003	Blades 2003-04

Roll of Honour

Geoff Allen
Chris Almgill
Paul Mark Anderson
Greg Atherton
Chris Bailey
Sarah Barber
David Barnsley
Darren Beecham
Phillip Beighton
Jarrod Billard
Richard Bird
J L Bishton
S V Bishton
Kevin John Booth
Dave Bowden
Oliver Bradbury
Stephen Paul Bradley
Michael RicharBradley
Scott Andrew Bradley
David Breen
Richard Brewin
Josh Briggs
Andre Brown
Ian Bunting
Jim Burke
David Burkinshaw
John Burton
Oliver Ian Byne
John Cadman
Andrew Calow
John Calvert
Matt Casbolt

Christopher Clark
Ian Clarke
Trevor Coleman
Robert Coleman
Brian Cooper
Stephen Neil Copley
Steve Cryan
Clive Deighton
Keith Dobson
Pat Draper
Mick Draper
Patrick Duggan
David Elliott
The Korkin Family
Roy Fisher
Stuart Fisher
Daniel Martin Fletcher
Arthur Foreman
Richard Gilson
Lee Glave
Derek Goodison
D Goodison
Leonard Green
Dominic Green
Mark Groves
David T Guyler
Adam D Guyler
David Hague
Mark Hallatt
Andrew Hallatt
Matt Hamilton
Julie Hartshorn
Eric Hilton
Marie Hirons

William Hitchmough
Andrew C Hooper
David Howden
Stuart Howden
Alan Hughes
Howard Humphries
Alan Hunt
Alan T Ibbotson
Suzanne Ibbotson
John Illingworth
Sean Jackson
Rose Jeffery
Melvyn Jeffery
Paul Jeffries
Brian Jessop
Samantha JayneJessop
Trevor Jones
Danny Jones
Susan Jordan
Jimi Kelly
Martin Kershaw
Phil Leonard
Andrew Lockwood
Bill Loftus
Paul William Ludlam
S Maccagnan
John Marsh
William Mason
S.T. Mattock
Simon Mazengarb
Megan McClure
David Mottishaw
Peter O'Driscoll
Marc O'Driscoll

Gerald Oliver
Sue Oliver
Michelle Oliver
Katie Oliver
Garry P Martin
Andrew Palfreyman
Louise Palmer
Bob Payne
Ian Perrett
Debs Perry
Steve Pickering
Daniel Martin Pigott
George Pinder
Keith Plowman
Brett Price
Thomas Price
Simon Quance
Ian Rainford
James Rayner
Ken Redfern
John George Revill
Anthony. W. Rider
Lewis James Riley
Lee Roberts
Jordan Robinson
Liam E Robinson
Bob Rodgers
Dan Rodgers
Malcolm Roper
Alec Ross
Peter Schofield
David Sharp
Ian Shepherd
Hanae Shimada

Ian Siddall
James M Slack
Steve Speczyk
John Barry Staniland
Karen Stewart
Robert Stockley
Ben Stubbs
Graham Robert Thomas
R Tingle
Andrew Treherne
David A Turner
David Turner
Peter Turney
Nicholas John Udall
Tony Urbano
Janis Walker
Kit Walker-Grice
Andrew Walton
Stephen Ward
Trevor Webster
Alex Welch
Jonty Welch
John Welch
Damien Wheeler
James Whitworth
Matthew Wilton
Carl Witham
Adam Wragg
David Wright
Timothy Yates